Contents

To Anne and Laura who have shared in two voyages
and to the crew of InterSpray

'Grab a chance and you won't be sorry for a might-have-been.'
Commander Ted Walker in *We Didn't Mean to Go to
Sea* by Arthur Ransome

Photograph credits
Pickthall Picture Library (Mark Pepper, Paul Buchanan and Barry Pickthall): pages 22,
31 (top left), 42 (bottom), 64 (bottom), 77 (top), 80, 100-101, 104, 105, 108, 109, 116,
139, 149, 156 (top), 157, 161, 165, 168, 176 (top), 184 (top), 188 (left). Patrick Roach
Picture Agency: pages 19, 27, 42 (top), 43, 47. Paul Buchanan and crew: pages 30, 31,
34, 35, 53, 77 (bottom), 97, 112, 113, 128, 130, 131, 134, 135, 142-143, 145, 148, 153,
156 (bottom), 169, 172, 177, 184 (bottom). Paul Gelder: pages 30, 34, 46, 49, 52, 56,
57, 60, 61 (top), 64 (top), 65, 69, 121, 124, 160, 176 (bottom), 180-181, 185, 189.
Yachting Monthly: pages 38-39. John Davies: page 61 (bottom). (Jeff Plummer: pages
35 (top left), 152. Julian Wells: page 72. Gail Turner, *Shropshire Star*: page188 (right).
Cedric Roberts (PPL): page 161

BUCKINGHAM PALACE

Those of us who have long relished the
excitement and the rigors of yachting will understand and perhaps
even feel a twinge of envy on reading of the joys and the
deprivations experienced by the crews of the British Steel
Challenge yachts as they circumnavigated the globe. As patron of
the Challenge and president of its official charity, The Save the
Children Fund, I followed their progress with great interest from
the start.

What has impressed everyone associated
with this bold adventure is the degree of dedication and sacrifice
which imbued the 140 volunteer crew members: all are amateurs and
many had never before sailed when accepted by Chay Blyth to
participate in the race.

I feel certain that all the competitors
will in some way have found their lives to have been changed as a
result of the opportunity to take part in this unique endeavour
and hopefully their achievements will serve as an inspiration to
others to rise to similar challenges in the future.

Acknowledgements

The British Steel Challenge was an epic event in which every competitor taking part had a book inside him waiting to be written. My good fortune was to combine the tales of 16 adventurers for this account of *InterSpray's Race Around the World*. It could not have been written without the wholehearted enthusiasm and assistance of the yacht's crew.

Having gained their trust and friendship on the first leg of the race to Rio de Janeiro, I sometimes felt like their father confessor, agony aunt, undercover mole and interrogator during our subsequent close encounters around the world. The skipper, Paul Jeffes, allowed me to eavesdrop on his innermost thoughts as he confided in his 'black box' (mini-tape recorder) on dark nights at the bottom of the globe. When he arrived in port at the end of each leg he submitted graciously to the third degree. He read the manuscript for accuracy from his own inside knowledge of events. Senior Watch-leader Julian Wells was an invaluable source of information with his steady flow of vivid telexes home. His wife Trisha, who ran *InterSpray's* Supporters' Club, provided me with transcripts of Julian's own taped diaries. Watchleader John Davis also allowed me to use extracts from his personal log, kept for his wife, Jocelyn. Paul Buchanan has the eyes and ears of a reporter and displayed a dry sense of humour in the dampest parts of the Southern Ocean. His off-the-wall, on-the-ball personal observations were an essential ingredient of this book, as were his many photographs. Others who allowed me to read and quote from their personal journals were Alison Smith and fellow one-leggers Barry Ford and Roger Peek.

I am grateful to Jeff Plummer and Carol Preston for dragging me away from my word processor to show me the parts of Hobart and Cape Town which I would surely have otherwise missed.

In Hobart, John Roberts, a member of the Royal Yacht Club of Tasmania, was the perfect host, offering me solitude, tranquillity and inspiration, with a spectacular vista over the River Derwent from his home high up in the hills. I am indebted to him for his generosity.

In Cape Town, Luke Werth and Bernie Probert, from the local International Paint office, assisted me and took me out to meet *InterSpray* on a memorable evening as she ghosted out of the darkness after 36 days in the Southern Ocean.

Back home in Southampton the team at International Paint were very supportive. I would specially thank David Hodgson, General Manager European Yacht Operations, for his enthusiastic help, Melony Lethbridge (who relayed the telexes). Gay McNab, Roy Spacey and Peter Sims, Regional Manager Northern Europe Coastal Marine.

Others who offered me encouragement at the start of this enterprise are Charles Lewis, Director of Corporate Communications at British Steel plc, skippers Pete Goss and Ian MacGillivray, Challenge Project Director Andrew Roberts, and Greg Bertram. Steve Walker of IBM computers generously loaned me a laptop computer, so I could write my way around the world.

Others who contributed to making my task easier are Maxine Kilburn, Peter Nielsen, who read the proofs, Sarah Beavers and Danielle Pearson, in the Challenge Press Office, and Peta Stuart Hunt and Tina Mansell, at Willoughby Stewart Associates Public Relations.

I would like to thank photographers Barry Pickthall, Mark Pepper, Patrick and Karen Roach and Rick Tomlinson for making their pictures available, as well as *InterSpray's* crew. Tony Garrett, drew the charts of each leg, and Mike Peyton, allowed me to use his cartoon.

I am also grateful to Andrew Bray, former Editor of *Yachting Monthly*, for his initial encouragement in covering the British Steel Challenge and to his successor Geoff Pack for his continued support while I followed the fleet and wrote this book.

Finally, my special thanks must go to Chay Blyth, who provided me with a berth on *InterSpray's* first leg to Rio, as well as the adventure of a lifetime shared with 178 other crew volunteers.

Paul Gelder

6

Foreword

by Robin Knox-Johnston CBE

A circumnavigation by way of Cape Horn and the Cape of Good Hope is the ultimate voyage for any sailor. Apart from the distance, some 27,000 miles or the equivalent of nine times across the Atlantic, nearly half the passage is through the Roaring Forties of the Southern Ocean. This is the real Everest of the sea where waves roll unimpeded around the world and can reach heights of 120 feet, the height of a 12-storey building. Even if equipment has improved, the weather conditions have not changed in a hundred years, since the great age of sail when heavy clippers forced their way through these seas. The waves are still as large, wet and powerful and just as capable of smashing a boat to smithereens as they ever were.

The crew of *Interspray* were not hardened shellbacks with years of experience, they were largely amateurs, drawn together for the experience of a lifetime. For most of them, although the voyage would have romance to compensate for the hardship, the real work came with the decision to go in the first place. Next came the problem of finding the money to pay for it. Modern society still sees a voyage like this as an aberration from the norm, a dangerous departure from the predictable, sober and pensionable path of life so beloved by the unadventurous. It is seldom seen for what it really is, a test of management ability under stress and the opportunity to stretch and strengthen a character. As a result, there are usually sacrifices to be made in career prospects by those who think life should offer a little more than a daily commute to an office.

Racing a large boat is a team job. The better the crew pull together, the safer and happier the voyage. Everything and everyone is interdependent on a boat from the moment the crew first walk aboard. Living together for prolonged periods in a wet, bouncing and confined space, and working unsociable hours with only short bursts of sleep, calls for a high degree of selflessness if the crew are not to get on each other's nerves. This story is as much about how the crew forged themselves into a happy team as it is about sailing around the world.

The ten identical British Steel Challenge yachts set off together in a race. In these circumstances there is a tendency for a team to sacrifice everything to win and those with talent for a particular task find themselves confined exclusively to that work. *Interspray's* skipper decided that the Challenge was an adventure in which all aboard should share equally in the experience. They came second on the first leg, which is an indication of the high standard and commitment aboard. They finished sixth overall at the end, after a number of mishaps, a good average position.

This racing position was secondary, however, to the real prize for all who sailed aboard during the voyage. At the end of such an adventure everyone finishes a winner.

The toughest yacht race is born

The 'toughest yacht race ever' was born out of Chay Blyth's frustration with the yachting establishment. His achievements and the titles of his books – *A Fighting Chance, Innocent Aboard* and *The Impossible Voyage* – are a testament to triumph over taboo and inexperience. His conviction that enthusiasm and determination mattered more than years of seafaring experience earned him a degree of unpopularity among ocean racing cliques. But his own frequent brushes with death subtracted nothing from his daring.

While believing that sailing was something of a closed world he went on to carve a marathon wake across the world's oceans, making waves in the yachting establishment as he went, stripping away elitism and breaking records.

The creation of The British Steel Challenge – Chay's ultimate global yachting adventure – was sparked when he was approached by a company interested in entering a yacht in the 1989 Whitbread Round the World Race. Blyth warned them that it took years and millions to get an entry together. They offered to charter a yacht. He said he thought it would be too late, but obligingly telephoned the Royal Naval Sailing Association to request a set of race rules.

'Send £200,' he was told.

'I don't want to enter the race, I just want a set of rules!' explained Blyth, who had entered and sailed three Whitbread races.

The fee was still £200.

So infuriated was he, thinking he'd already done his bit for the Whitbread, that he slammed down the phone and thought: 'Damn it, I'll run my own race!'

Thus Blyth, the maverick lone adventurer of the sixties and seventies and one of Britain's biggest yachting heroes, became yachting's biggest entrepreneur.

Having decided to launch his own race to rival the Whitbread, the next step was to design a yacht to attract sponsors. Andrew Roberts, a close associate who became a key figure in the Challenge – 'probably more important than me,' says Blyth – became Challenge Project Manager. Between them there was no shortage of experience when they sat down in 1987 to draw the blueprint of a boat for the longest one-design race in the world.

THE TOUGHEST YACHT RACE IS BORN

By the time Blyth and Roberts approached designer David Thomas, they had a strong idea of what they wanted... built in wood, it was a 65ft strip-planked hull. The length was subsequently extended to 67ft for accommodation.

A few months later, when British Steel became involved as sponsors, wood naturally gave way to the strength of steel. It also became apparent that the orthodox downwind route around the world would have to be reversed. An uphill battle against prevailing winds and currents would mark the 21st anniversary of Blyth's first epic 292-day solo circumnavigation in *British Steel*.

Chay went live on News at Ten in January 1989 to announce his dream of a once-in-a lifetime adventure – a 28,000 mile race for 120 men and women who would pay £14,850 to race 10 identical yachts round the world westabout under professional skippers. The stopovers would be Rio de Janeiro, Hobart and Mauritius (later amended to Cape Town). To discourage time wasters, there was a non-returnable registration fee of £75 for the privilege of sending an application form. A 14th berth on each yacht was reserved for one-leggers, journalists and sponsors' employees. British Steel had the right to cancel the event if less than 35 people had signed up 10 months after the launch.

As a result of the TV news bulletin and press reports, there were 300 serious inquiries, with deposits paid, and interviewing began next day at the 1989 London Boat Show. Chay himself hand-picked the crews.

The occupations of the crew volunteers, half of whom had never sailed before, including some 23 women, varied from butcher, baker and undertaker, to dentist, doctor, vet, carpenter, and 17 company directors. There were students, grandmothers and grandfathers. But by the time the race started at least 20 would become RYA Ocean Yachtmasters and most would have sailed an average of 3,000 sea miles.

Their motivations for signing up were as varied as their backgrounds. Some had dreamt of running away to sea since childhood. For others the Challenge promised 'to totally change my life', or offered escape from mid-life crisis.

Some 500 applicants lined up for 120 places over the coming months and there was to be a waiting list numbering 176, all eager to step into the deck shoes of any faint-hearts who changed their minds along the way.

Crews would not be assigned to sponsors' yachts for another 20 months. But among the volunteers who would later be assigned to Courtaulds' *InterSpray* was Dominic Mathews, who ran his own business as an independent financial advisor,

Dominic arranged to meet Chay at a London hotel. The receptionist had never heard of The British Steel Challenge or Chay Blyth.

'I thought I'd come to the wrong hotel or got my dates mixed up, but there in the vestibule, behind the rubber plants was Chay fast asleep. . .'

It is not recorded whether Dominic told Chay at this delicate stage of negotiations of his ambition to morris dance round the Horn.

Alison Cave, who was also to join *InterSpray*, met Chay in a Midlands hotel. 'I'd never heard of him before, I thought he was an opera singer or maybe an MP,' she recalled.

For Julian Wells, the only veterinary surgeon in the fleet, soon to become *InterSpray*'s doctor, Monday nights were taken up by a night school Yachtmaster course. Julian reflected that 'as Mrs. Jones Rottweiler opens its jaws for the next attempt at removing my left arm and Mrs. Smith's hamster bites out a triangular piece of flesh from my thumb, the excesses of the Southern Oceans beckon appealingly.'

Just fifteen months after the announcement of the race, more than 100 crew volunteers watched Her Royal Highness the Princess Royal unveil the first of the fleet of Challenge yachts at builders DML, in Devonport Dockyard, Plymouth, on April 5, 1990. The Princess gave a signal which raised a high security fence to reveal the fleet's flagship and training yacht *British Steel Challenge* 'floating' in a sea of dry ice. There was a spontaneous burst of applause.

Over the next two years greenhorn crew members attended as many four-day training sessions aboard the *British Steel Challenge* as they could. For some at this stage of the enterprise it was still the thought of a £14,850 bank overdraft that caused anxieties, not the Southern Ocean storms. Some volunteers sold houses, cars and even businesses to participate.

Crews sailed in winter into Force 10 winds in the English Channel with a -30°C wind chill factor and ice-covered decks. The level of training left no room for cosy illusions.

The carefully planned two-year sailing 'assault course' to knock the neophytes into shape was led by former Royal Marine and Green Beret Pete Goss, later to become skipper of *Hofbrau Lager.* 'Can't be done' was not an acceptable phrase in Goss's book. Like Blyth he had proved wrong too many critics who might have poured cold water on his 'foolhardy' ventures, including a solo transatlantic crossing in a tiny catamaran.

Goss was a marvel of quietly-spoken modesty and patience who inspired confidence in all who sailed with him. It was a rare gift and he used it to tap into the hidden resources of many volunteers.

The average distance covered by sail training sessions was 350 miles. It was intensive and relentless and the learning curve for most was steep – sometimes sailing around the Eddystone Lighthouse for three days with never more than half an hour going by without a sail or course

change. Goss would lead crew members, two at a time, on to the foredeck in blinding icy spray, just to prove that it was possible to work there in the worst conditions. There was no luxury of roller reefing headsails. Many fears were faced and vanquished during these training sessions.

'If they packed us off without this sort of training, there'd be a 15 per cent drop out rate by the time we got to Rio,' one recruit speculated.

Seasickness was prevalent among some crew volunteers. But most found their sealegs, somehow – copper bracelets, acupressure, acupuncture, high-tech patches behind the ears, or old-fashioned tablets. Some self-confessed ex-couch potatos couldn't wait to sail around the world backwards.

Thirteen strangers would join the training yacht on a Friday night and by Wednesday morning solid friendships had been forged. The camaraderie was extraordinary to witness. There were personality clashes, too, of course, but this had been taken into consideration by the Challenge. When crew selections were made there was an opportunity to name in confidence the people you would least like to sail with.

Some professional yachties poured scorn on the Challenge project. The yachts were referred to as bullet-proof steel clunkers. The crews were amateurs facing what *The Daily Mail* called 'the mid-life crisis challenge'

But critics missed the vital element that captured people's imagination – the spirit of human endeavour. The ethos of Chay's Challenge was to give ordinary people a taste of the extraordinary. A chance to conquer the odds, whether rounding Cape Horn, battling with the Roaring Forties or achieving a more personal goal. It was impossible for anyone with a spirit of adventure to be cynical in the face of crews' unbounded enthusiasm.

Ian MacGillivray, who helped to train

crews with Goss, said: 'When I first heard about the Challenge I thought they were a bunch of suicidal madmen. But I didn't understand the training and organisation that was going into the project.'

Skip Novak, organiser of several Whitbread projects, felt 'humbled and somewhat inadequate' when he realised the full depth of Peter Goss's accomplishment in training crews from scratch.

John Chittenden had another perspective, likening the amateur crews to battery hens being set free from conventional lives: 'If you let them out, you'll have a hell of a job getting them back,' he warned.

During the months of training that followed a selection process was going on for potential watchleaders and compatible crew members for the ten yachts.

By the end of 1991 crew members who had declared special interests were being sent on maintenance courses to learn more about their chosen fields: budding sailmakers went to Hoods; riggers to Proctors; engineers to Mermaid; and others to Lewmar, to strip winches and deck gear. There was a troubleshooting course for most things. McDougalls even ran courses for galley slaves on how to cope with hot pans at heel angles of 25 degrees and avoid stabbing crew mates with kitchen knives.

The one-design philosophy meant that the winning yacht would be sailed by the crew that pushed the yacht hardest, but not beyond the point where they paid the penalty for gear failure.

The sails provided were expected to last the whole race. The penalty for having any new sail would be a short extra course to be sailed after the leg start. This was in stark contrast to the 1990 Whitbread Race winner *Steinlager 2*, which ordered 110 sails for her campaign – a sizeable chunk of the budget.

While The British Steel Challenge, like the Whitbread, would have its rich, corporate sponsors, it was a race that would be a test of seamanship, not a measurement of the thickness of a sponsor's wallet. Perhaps this was just as well, since Blyth was launching his multi-million pound fleet and seeking out ten sponsors in the depths of Britain's worst recession for 20 years.

Race rules forbid sponsors spending an extra penny on the yachts, beyond the £225,000 sponsorship package. The only difference would be the yachts' names and the colours of their hulls. As rule 5.11 stipulated: 'Identical yachts with identical sails, fittings and equipment will be handed over to skippers and no modifications will be allowed.'

The sponsorship package bought the yacht's livery, plus the opportunity to entertain clients and staff aboard a £5m fleet of ocean racing yachts. On the strength of this Chay managed a series of spectacular sponsorship coups. But the fleet remained the property of The Challenge Business Ltd.

Courtaulds' International Paint company had been on board the Challenge from its early days. They had painted Chay's original 59ft *British Steel* cutter, in which he undertook his solo circumnavigation in 1971. Indeed, all his subsequent yachts had been protected by International Paint products and The *British Steel Challenge* fleet was no exception. As sole supplier of paint above and below the waterline on all ten competing yachts the arduous voyage would provide an ideal test bed for their products. Already half the Whitbread Round the World Race fleet used International paints.

With more than a year to the race start, sponsorship for the Challenge already came from a wide range of companies. Apart from British Steel, there were two insurance companies, The Heath Group and Commercial Union Assurance; Hofbrau Lager, a German beer distributed in the UK by Hall & Woodhouse; Rhone-Poulenc, the French-based chemical company; Group 4 Securitas, the security organisation and Nuclear Electric.

INTERSPRAY'S RACE AROUND THE WORLD

When Courtaulds signed up to become the eighth sponsor, through their International Paint division, they not only put the top coat on a long relationship with Chay, but they became the first marine industry company to sponsor a yacht in the race. Courtaulds already sponsored the successful McLaren Formula One motor racing team.

The deal was announced at a reception at the Royal Southampton Yacht Club in June 1991 by Sipko Huismans, then Courtaulds' Managing Director and soon to become Chief Executive, and Chay Blyth. It was also the occasion for the first unveiling by a sponsor of its yacht's colours for the round the world race. Trafford Corke's eye-catching design for the yacht, *InterSpray*, showed a navy blue hull with a rainbow coloured wave sweeping down the sides, together with the familiar International Paint propeller logo. The 3,780sq ft spinnaker was the company's largest ever advertisement.

'There is no truth in the rumour,' joked Chay with assembled guests, 'that Courtaulds has developed two types of anti-fouling for the race – Barnacle Attraction and International Superfast.'

While Courtaulds were negotiating their sponsorship deal, unknown to them they already had one of their employees onboard the Challenge. Ricky Scott, employed by Courtaulds Fibres at the Courtelle division in Grimsby and a keen sailor for many years, had already signed up and was busy training for the race. He was the first obvious recruit for *InterSpray* and found himself whisked down to Southampton for the reception at a day's notice, meeting Courtaulds' and International Paint's top management.

Sipko Huismans told his audience: 'The people I see winning in business, sport or any endeavour are the ones who are truly motivated and committed and prepared for much sacrifice.'

Soon after the announcement of Courtaulds' sponsorship, trials were starting for the 23 sailors Chay had shortlisted to skipper his yachts.

Paul Jeffes, who trained as a Naval Architect and is a keen racing yachtsman with many successes in keelboats, first heard about the Challenge through his girlfriend, Carolyn Elder. He became one of 167 yachtsmen, including 12 women, who applied to skipper the Challenge yachts. Blyth whittled the applications of the men and women who would make life and death decisions down to 42 or so.

Jeffes, Managing Director of Silvers Marine Ltd, a leading Scottish boat-building yard on the Clyde, was interviewed by Chay at the Royal Ocean Racing Club in St James, London, early in 1991. Present in the room was yachting journalist Bob Fisher, who was writing a story for *The Guardian* to be headlined 'Round the world with a boatload of trouble'.

Jeffes may have had cause to wonder later, when he eventually met his motley crew, if the headline was prophetic?

Fisher thought that the responsibility of skippering a big yacht round the world with an amateur crew who had first learned to sail a year ago would deter all but the strongest candidates.

Blyth's interrogation began: 'Do you believe you have leadership qualities?'

Jeffes explained that Silvers shipyard, which had employed just a boy in 1983, now had 30 people on the payroll. Blyth answered his own question: 'I guess you do.'

Shortlisted, Jeffes' next test was a trial sail with Peter Goss and some crew volunteers on the Bristol to Swansea leg of the *British Steel Challenge* around Britain promotion tour. He was one of 26 skippers to get through to the sailing trials. He later joined Goss for the 900-mile delivery trip of *British Steel Challenge* to Spain where she was the flagship at the British Pavilion at Seville's Expo '92. The trip served as Jeffes' practical for his Yachtmaster Ocean ticket.

THE TOUGHEST YACHT RACE IS BORN

By October Jeffes was accepted and had signed his contract and started fitness training with a daily 10-mile bike ride. But a month later he was still trying to find a replacement to cover for his absence at work for nearly a year. For a time he faced an impossible decision: abandon the race or give up his job. In the midst of this his father 'phoned to break the news that Jeffes' grandmother had died. 'I drove up to the snow-covered hills overlooking Gareloch. Everything was grey, cold, wintry and depressing. I thought about my grandmother and the job and I made my mind up that I was going to have to go and do Chay's expedition. Life is a finite thing if you don't go and do what you've got to do, you spend the rest of your life wondering if you should have done it.'

A month later, with the nine other skippers Chay had selected, Jeffes found himself aboard a Thames barge in St Katharine Yacht Haven, London, facing the press and TV cameras. Each skipper had been asked to wear work clothes. Hence there was Mike Golding in his fireman's uniform and Alec Honey, Chay's First Mate on *Great Britain II* in the 1973 Whitbread, in an AA uniform. Jeffes wore a hardhat. Training skippers Pete Goss and Ian MacGillivray had both been selected. Completing Chay's Top Ten were the only woman skipper, Vivien Cherry, ex-1989 Whitbread skipper John Chittenden, Welsh sailmaker Richard Tudor, Adrian Donovan and Will Sutherland. The ninth yacht sponsor, *Coopers & Lybrand*, had also been signed up.

It didn't take much convincing for Jeffes to become the skipper of *InterSpray*, since his Scottish boatyard happened to be the newest Interspray paint centre.

But it wasn't until January 1992, nine months before setting off around the world the wrong way, that Jeffes and the other skippers met their crews for the first time at the Earls Court Boat Show.

Jeffes, like other skippers, 'inherited' a crew picked by Blyth and the Challenge business. *InterSpray*'s crew came from a wide variety of backgrounds. It included a vet, an HGV driver, an oil field technician, a corporate account manager, an independent financial advisor, an engineer, and two young North Country women, Alison Smith (23) from Yorkshire and Alison Cave (21) from Sunderland,

Ali Smith was soon christened 'Bob' to distinguish her from her namesake.

Absent was the only Australian crew volunteer who had signed up for the Challenge, John Davis, Managing Director of a petroleum distributors, assigned to *InterSpray*.

There was some trepidation among crew members on discovering that Julian Wells, the veterinary surgeon, was to be the ship's doctor. Julian was quick to re-assure his new shipmates that since he was used to treating dumb animals diagnosing vocal sailors' ailments would be a snip, so to speak. He was also having a crash course in human dentistry and traumatic injuries: bangs on the head, scalds in the galley, explosions on board, shock and that sort of thing. It included emergency appendectomies.

By a strange coincidence John Davis, who heard none of this, decided to have his perfectly healthy appendix removed before he left Australia. 'You should have had a couple of fingers amputated to save getting them trapped in a winch,' joked one of the crew when he told them.

The finishing touches to the Challenge fleet were being added early in 1992. Some 70,000sq ft of steel had to be coated by International Paint. At builders DML the legend 'Peak panic period' was writ large on wall charts monitoring delivery of everything from spars and keels to bunk leecloths and hose clips. It was a massive logistical exercise.

During March the yachts were launched at the Plymouth yard at the rate of two a day. The day after John Major was elected Prime Minister was the first chance for skippers and crew volunteers to meet aboard their yachts at Brixham, where final fitting out and sea trials were performed.

'No other British seaman in history has made such a widespread reputation without the use of gunfire,' one commentator observed of Chay Blyth more than a decade ago.

If Nelson's finest hour was at Trafalgar, Blyth, self-appointed 'Admiral' of a fleet of ten newly launched steel cutters, counted the days to his latest conquest in five months' time, on September 26.

One evening at a lively party to celebrate the milestone, the 'Admiral' was crowned when Chay was presented by crew with a modern Navy Admiral's cap, complete with scrambled egg on the peak.

During Easter weekend in April the Challenge fleet set sail from Brixham, emerging from the mist into brilliant sunshine as they came past the Needles and up Southampton Water to Ocean Village, the base for the yachts until the race started. By now Chay had clinched the long-awaited deal to announce the elusive sponsor for the tenth yacht, the Teesside Development Corporation.

Her Royal Highness the Princess Royal, now patron of The British Steel Challenge, was guest of honour at a dinner at the Botley Park Hotel and Country Club at the end of that week to officially 'launch the fleet'. All the skippers and sponsors were present.

Chay raised a knowing laugh when he described himself as 'an amateur businessman among professional negotiators.'

He said that since the Challenge had been announced three and a half years ago it had been overbooked by 22 per cent – 'just like the airlines – in case we get any cancellations.'

Since the training yacht had been launched 98 per cent of the original crew volunteers were still aboard the project; most had sailed 3,000 miles and 14 had

qualified for their Ocean Yachtmaster theory exam.

The Princess praised the 'exceptional feat of management and organisation' behind the Challenge and congratulated Chay on his unique venture. Having just bought her own 36ft sailing yacht, she added: 'There is something about sailing – as my mother-in-law said about riding "it's character building". One day it will pay off, but nobody has told me when yet!'

Chay joked: 'We've still got one berth unoccupied. . . we need one more volunteer ma'am!'

Next day, on a damp blustery morning in Ocean Village, the fleet was unveiled to the media and the Princess smashed a champagne bottle over the bows of the newly sponsored *Pride of Teesside*. Up until then the yacht, skippered by Ian MacGillivray, had simply been named, in discreet small black letters on the transom, *Ian's Boat*.

Sod's law of the sea, ignoring royal protocol, meant that five minutes after the Princess boarded Ian's boat for a day's sail it developed propshaft trouble and started to leak. Luckily for Ian he somehow managed to manoeuvre the yacht back to a pontoon berth without the engine. Unluckily for him, the Princess had to be transferred to another yacht for her sail. *Coopers & Lybrand*, skippered by Vivien Cherry, was the lucky substitute.

With the Princess Royal's divorce from Captain Mark Phillips having been announced the previous day, a posse of waterbound paparazzi pursued the yacht. Out in Southampton Water there was 30 knots of wind across the deck and some of Fleet Street's finest were looking decidedly green.

On the last day of April, Courtaulds' *Interspray* was berthed alongside the Royal Southampton Yacht Club for her official naming ceremony by former Prime Minister and yachtsman Sir Edward Heath.

THE TOUGHEST YACHT RACE IS BORN

John Davis, our Australian crew volunteer, was the one crewman none of us had met. John flew 12,000 miles from his home near Sydney, in Orange, New South Wales, specially to attend the launch party and meet the rest of the 14-man, three-women crew.

Three years before he had seen a news story on Australian television about the Challenge launch. Later he found more details in a copy of *Yachting Monthly* magazine. His wife Jocelyn, recognising the signs of latent adventurism, thought that perhaps he should get sailing out of his system. He applied for a place but was told that all the positions had been taken up. He went on the reserve list and kept on hoping. In 1990 he was told he'd got a place, subject to an interview with Chay. Could he come to London? Fortunately, Chay was coming to Australia to check out details for the Hobart stopover, so in June John met Chay *en-route* to Tasmania over a cup of coffee in Sydney. Chay's selection process was fairly informal and mostly intuitive. 'I know within a couple of seconds if a guy is right,' he says. 'First impressions count for a lot.'

John was accepted.

InterSpray, the Rainbow warrior

As the crew gathered aboard the yacht on the morning of *InterSpray*'s launch there were photocalls and introductions to the local dignitaries. Things went with an unscheduled bang when Sir Edward cracked the champagne bottle over the bows to the accompaniment of cannon fire from the balcony of the Royal Southampton Yacht Club in Ocean Village. The champagne splattered the Deputy Mayor and the cannon fire shattered one of the balcony's glass screens which showered into the marina, to the amusement of the 150 guests.

Twenty-one years before, in August 1971, Sir Edward, together with members of the Royal family, had welcomed Chay Blyth back from his non-stop circumnavigation. During a speech later in the RSYC he joked: 'I regret I cannot afford a yacht anymore. . . not under this Government!'

Sir Edward, who skippered his own yacht, *Morning Cloud*, for many years, winning the classic Sydney-Hobart race in 1969-70, and later captained Britain's winning Admiral's Cup team, told the audience of Courtaulds staff and guests: 'There is a special value in a yacht being backed by a sponsor with a direct interest in sailing.'

Sipko Huismans, now Courtaulds' Chief Executive, and himself a keen yachtsman with his own 12-metre motorsailer, spoke of Chay's British bulldog attitude and bloody-mindedness that got things done. He presented Sir Edward with a print of *InterSpray* signed by all the crew members.

Skipper Paul Jeffes got the crew to line up on board the yacht for official photographs with Sipko and Sir Edward. Irrepressible Barry Ford, a British Steel worker who would be sailing the toughest and longest leg of the race around Cape Horn, was threatening to do some gurning through a toilet seat – a North Country 'sport' which involved pulling ugly faces. As the Ford grin widened, you could tell that some of the crew were wondering what they would be in for during the 9,800 miles from Rio to Hobart.

John Davis moved aboard *InterSpray* for the next two weeks before returning to Australia to tie up loose ends and rejoin the yacht for the race. He hadn't been sailing on *InterSpray* before and found himself thrown in the deep end, crewing for Jeffes when Courtaulds' directors were taken sailing. 'You get to know how everything works very quickly doing half a dozen jobs simultaneously,' he said. 'I even suggested to Sipko that he might let me have a little steer since it was my first time on the yacht.'

The weekend after the launch was the first of several crew training sessions that went on throughout the summer to build up teamwork. By mid-summer the adrenalin was flowing and there was no mistaking the intense rivalry between old friends now assigned as crew on different, competing, yachts.

Those who once exchanged confidences now found themselves on their guard against revealing the secrets of their own yacht's training methods. Blyth's big, happy family, with ages ranging from 20 to 60, found itself split into opposing teams, each with their own intensive training programmes.

Some skippers were going back to basics in sailing dinghies, others, like French-sponsored *Rhone-Poulenc*, skippered by Alec Honey, hired Frenchman Lionel Péan, the 1985 Whitbread skipper of *L'Esprit d'Equipe*, to drill his crew in the finer points of sail trim and tactics.

Honey, who had served in the same Parachute Brigade as Chay Blyth and John Ridgeway, put his crew through a similiar 'Exercise Dry Sail' programme that Blyth had devised for his first Whitbread race crew. Honey took his crew to live in one room in his French cottage for a week to gauge their reaction to the prospect of living on top of one another for eight months. 'I believe the most compatible crew will be the one that wins,' he said.

Paul Jeffes applied team management techniques to *InterSpray*'s crew, among other ploys. *Group 4* reportedly used psychometric tests. Getting total strangers to work as a team was the name of the game.

With some four months to the start of the Challenge there were crew members on all yachts showing early signs of mettle fatigue. Fears and uncertainties were being exposed as crew asked themselves,

'Am I up to it?'

Fear is a natural response to danger. Like adrenalin, it sharpens the senses and improves anticipation. It helps to avoid trouble. Sailing round the world may have been a dream in the making for 120 amateur sailors, but enjoying the dream also meant enduring the nightmare – anything from man overboard, to losing the rig, or the anxiety of a sail change on a wave-swept foredeck.

John Chittenden, skipper of *Nuclear Electric*, and the only skipper to have raced round the world before, gave voice to the feelings of many when he observed: 'People still don't know what they've got themselves into.' Chittenden had lost a crewman in the Southern Ocean when skippering *Creighton's Naturally* in the 1989-90 Whitbread. Another crewman had been revived after an act of great heroism. Chittenden knew the rigours that lay ahead in the Roaring Forties and Furious Fifties.

InterSpray was not immune to these uncertainties as up to 17 strangers at any one time were fused into a single competitive unit. Any personality clashes had to be put aside with 14 people crammed into the confined space of a 67ft yacht.

With a few weeks to go before the start of the race, the killer instinct often emerged undisguised, even during corporate day sailing events with sponsor's guests aboard.

For two days in June, the City of London based insurance brokers, Heath Group, sponsor of *Heath Insured*, had the fleet at their disposal for 'corporate day sails' – a phrase redolent of Hooray Henrys and Henriettas sporting blazers and clutching gin and tonics or bucks fizz.

Corporate day sailing aboard the Challenge Fleet, however, given the right conditions, offered raw excitement more intoxicating than mere alcohol. There was sometimes a 'Fun Race' round the Solent to Gilkicker.

With sponsor's guests aboard, there

THE TOUGHEST YACHT RACE IS BORN

was frequently only room left for three or four regular crew. Perhaps it was another of Chay's methods for ensuring that the Challenge race crew got short-handed experience.

For Heath Group's fleet outing, the regular crew aboard Interspray, were Skipper Jeffes, Alison 'Bob' Smith, Barry Ford, his girlfriend, Kerry, and me. Some of the guests were dressed for action in full oilskins. One or two had sailed on friends' yachts. Another had his own yacht. But they had never been on board an ocean racer. The excitement was palpable. So was the learning curve, once we hoisted the sails in Southampton Water.

In the stiff Solent breeze there were riding turns on winches, fingers perilously close to being trapped, sheets let go at inauspicious moments, or winched in at grinding-to-a-halt speed.

'Bob' looked at me on the winch, gasping for breath, my heart thumping and ears ringing. It was a look that said she'd got a chimpanzee instead of a winch gorilla. And that was just the secondary winch. I promised myself then and there that I'd start my fitness regime when I got home. Then I went back to winding in the film in my 35mm camera.

Two months after the yachts had sailed to Southampton there were still one or two skippers who were concerned about stretching their brand new sails. Sails that would, after all, have to last them round the world, with penalties applied for any replacements required. We weren't taking any chances either. With one reef in the main and the yankee and staysail sheets winched bar taut, Courtaulds' Interspray, gracefully heeled as we hardened up in a Force 5 wind. For a bunch of insurance folk, the guest crew seemed blissfully unaware of our high-risk activities.

Racing the yacht, entertaining the guests and training his depleted crew – all with the calm authority that help earn him a place as a Challenge skipper – Jeffes seemed imperturbable.

He didn't blanch when someone let the foresail sheet slip off the primary winch, losing us precious seconds and two places. He was too diplomatic to comment when the guest helmsman lost the course. But then it *was* only a 'Fun Race'.

Heath's Mavis Chapman looked petrified when handed the helm. Expressing admiration for the crew's resolution in the face of their forthcoming ordeal, she confessed 'Oh! I couldn't do this for days on end for the life of me. The noise when that boom crashes over is terrifying. . .'

As *InterSpray*'s forty-four tons of steel thundered towards the southern end of the finish line, between a yellow racing buoy and Gilkicker Point, the log registered 9.2 knots. Jeffes sighted down the line and looked across to our nearest rival.

'I'm sorry lunch is delayed,' he intoned smoothly to the guests (like a mâitre d'hotel with a minor hiccup in the kitchens), as we pounded through the Solent chop towards the line. Jeffes invited the dinner guests to sit on the weather rail

Rhone-Poulenc, under skipper Alec Honey, was also tearing towards the line, at right angles to us. As the yachts converged at ramming speed, it was anyone's guess who would be in the lead. Nerves of steel and split-second timing were critical.

In an act of daring opportunism, Jeffes bought into play an old tactic which had once been used against him when racing International One Designs in America – an inside overlap around the buoy marking the end of the line.

We were racing parallel to the line on port tack. At the buoy we would tack in front of *Rhone-Poulenc*, now rapidly coming up on our right flank on starboard tack. Thus we would thrust our bow across the line and gain a place.

As the bearing between the two boats remained the same, there seemed a terrible inevitability about the plan. The corporate guest on the helm willingly surrendered the wheel to Jeffes.

Rhone-Poulenc was only yards away, heading for us broadside on.

'Tacking now!' bellowed Jeffes. There was a frenzied clatter of winches. The rudder bit the water. The two yachts closed. Jaws dropped and eyes widened.

For a few seconds frozen in time, *Rhone-Poulenc* surged alongside us, the plume of her bow wave exploding against our hull. I waited for the shattering sound of 88 tons of steel colliding at a combined 18 knots. I could have leaned across and shaken hands with the winchman in their cockpit. Except everyone looked as though they were frozen in a tableau. There was a moment of stunned silence. *Rhone-Poulenc* slid away from our starboard quarter in slow motion, turning into the wind, sails flapping. Someone cried ecstatically: 'We beat them!'

'For a moment I thought that was one boat that wouldn't be going around the world in September,' said one of our guests.

'Two!' said another.

If Alec Honey had been smoking a cigar it would probably have dropped out of his mouth. Instead, Jeffes lit up his own last cigar and wiped away mock beads of sweat in relief.

It was the sort of daring that marked out the unique spirit of The British Steel Challenge.

'Chay would have my guts for garters if he saw this,' Jeffes confided as we turned for home and 14 plates of beef stroganoff were served up. 'I needed another 10ft,' he explained. 'I knew I'd pushed my luck. In the protest room Alec would have won because he had to alter course to avoid me. But you've got to very aggressive in tight boat handling situations.'

Back in Ocean Village later, Alec Honey recollected nonchalantly: 'We were as close, if not closer, with another boat yesterday . . .'

If this was corporate day sailing, it would be something to behold when the gloves came off at the start line on September 26 with £4,000 prize money for the winning crews first through two start gates.

'The crews will be knackered before they've passed the Needles,' speculated one commentator.

Meanwhile, Jeffes announced that *Interspray's* next corporate day sail would begin at 0700 hours.

'I can't work that early on a Sunday, I'm a methodist!' protested Alison.

'And I'm an atheist,' countered Barry, 'I can't work at all!'

During June the fleet crossed to Scheveningen in Holland for another fleet gathering, but the next real test of *InterSpray's* mettle was to be the Challenge Ushant-Fastnet Training Race, an 850-mile qualifying race around that renowned rock off the Irish coast on July 8.

The race incorporated crisis management practise; dress rehearsals for emergency procedures, like man or woman overboard, a sinking yacht, an engine room fire and a dismasting. It was a test of crews' competence, as well as communications between the fleet and its Petersfield Race HQ. Yachts sailed with sealed envelopes containing instructions to be opened at specified times.

The course took the fleet to Ushant, on the north-west corner of France, across to the Fastnet Rock, and back to Southampton. But because it was the first time the yachts had raced together the event assumed an importance out of all proportion to its significance. It was billed as a training exercise. In reality it turned into a full-blown, no-holds-barred contest.

The early morning start was inauspicious, with hardly a breath of wind and current to ghost the yachts over the start line at Gilkicker. In search of breeze some yachts went aground off Cowes.

Later *Rhone-Poulenc* and *Coopers & Lybrand* sailed against the traffic flow in the Casquets separation lane and *British Steel II* reportedly clipped the corner of

Sir Edward Heath and Sipko Huismans with the crew at InterSpray's christening

the purple 'no-go' area. The French authorities tracking them on radar were after someone's blood. Chittenden, a Master Mariner with 100,000 sea miles to his credit, told a skippers' meeting he would have lost his ticket for sailing against traffic lanes.

InterSpray, first around the Fastnet Rock, lost something else – a £6,000 spinnaker emblazoned with the sponsor's logo and blown to pieces in 40 knots of wind.

Crewman Jeff Plummer was slammed into the primary winch in the cockpit by the mainsheet during an accidental gybe and suffered cracked ribs and a badly bruised back. Jeff's agonised shriek (described as 'a stuck pig') was to echo down the annals of *InterSpray* history for months to come. But it never sounded quite the same as it did on that black night in the Irish Sea. He needed £260 worth of physiotherapy on his back during the next few weeks. Julian also found a chance to

practise his new-found human dentistry skills on Alison Smith.

Shredding the most expensive kite in the fleet did nothing to shake the confidence of Jeffes. *InterSpray* finished second in the race behind *British Steel II* when *Rhone-Poulenc* was given a time penalty for carrying their professional race trainer Lionel Pean on board. The skipper of *British Steel II*, Richard Tudor, had helmed his yacht for 10 hours to win the race. Jeffes' philosophy was more democratic. He liked everyone to take a turn if conditions allowed.

'The conditions proved the yacht is every bit as tough as we wanted it to be,' said Jeffes afterwards. 'It goes like a train up-wind. But we must be careful with the spinnaker. We cannot afford to repeat that mistake.'

Jeffes was not alone in counting the cost of sail damage as crews sailed in with their first real battlescars. *Rhone-Poulenc* damaged two spinnakers and her mainsail; *Heath Insured* sailed home with a badly damaged pulpit, wrenched loose when a sail tied to it was washed by a wave. The accident exposed a potentially lethal weakness in all ten pulpit fittings – which subsequently had to be removed and rewelded. If the fault had been discovered 10,000 miles later in the Southern Ocean the consequences could have been disastrous.

Meanwhile, Michael Calvin, on board *Hofbrau*, reported in *The Daily Telegraph* a 'flagrant disregard of rules' by *Rhone-Poulenc* when they illegally swapped sails and carried Whitbread veteran Lionel Pean as a professional race trainer. It was, said Calvin, 'an ominous warning about unchecked ambition.'

Alec Honey, *Rhone-Poulenc's* skipper, was less than popular with some of his colleagues in the fleet.

The Corinthian spirit of the Challenge was in danger of being hijacked by the competitive spirit. Sponsors wanted success and while some were paying for professional trainers, others were paying expensive hotel bills. The boats may have been one-design with a ban on any go-faster add-ons, but the sponsors were not restrained on what they chose to spend on crew training.

Chittenden observed dispassionately: 'People are much more competitive than I thought. Some are losing sight of the fact that getting round in one piece would be one hell of an achievement.'

As a result of the Fastnet race, Chay was moved to write to his crews of the 'open and frank exchange which took place' afterwards when all skippers 'gave an assurance that they would abide by the rules of the Challenge in letter and in spirit.'

He reminded crews that their signature on race declaration forms was the strongest lever to ensure that rules were adhered to regarding the conduct of a race. He also reminded crews of the ethos behind the Challenge: to reduce the escalating costs to sponsors of round the world yacht racing. The lynchpin in his scheme was skill and seamanship which would help control maintenance and repair costs which can run riot during such races.

'I wanted to break the mould of the throw-away mentality that is so prevalent in this day and age – an example is sails automatically replaced for new ones when they become "used". I also wanted to go back to the time when seamanship and style were part and parcel of racing. This ethos means that by damaging your sails, you are in effect penalising your own yacht.'

Chay confided: 'We are all on a learning curve. As we get nearer to the start tension and pressure will build up. Try and take this in your stride. I suggest that you should be laid back about it and enjoy the whole lead up to the event and even the event itself.'

It took the sting out of some of the criticism, but nothing, it seemed, could arrest people's desire to see their yacht win. Having offered people who had never even set foot on a yacht before the adventure of a lifetime, Chay must have wondered on occasions if he had created some sort of Frankenstein monster.

For some the Fastnet race had been their first experience of competitive upwind sailing in gale-force conditions. Alison Cave had reluctantly come to terms with the realisation that it wasn't for her. Her crewmates admired her courage in confronting the disappointment after months of commitment to the Challenge, but when Alison stepped off the yacht in Ocean Village it would be her last time aboard.

After the Fastnet, Jeffes announced his selection of watch leaders. Julian, for whom the training race had been his practical qualifying passage for Ocean Yachtmaster, was named Senior Watch leader. John Davis, and Carlton Dodd, were the other watch leaders.

Later, through a combination of family and business commitments, another *InterSpray* crew member, Kevin Mackness, was forced to drop out of the race. By the start 27 volunteers had dropped out of the Challenge – the figure was lower than expected. Chay's standby list came into play and replacements for Alison Cave and Kevin were found.

Juliet Connell, an air stewardess with extensive Tall Ships experience, and Duggie Gillespie, a Scotsman who had applied for Chay's 1996 Round the World Race, joined the intensive round of training in August.

John Davis, who had flown back to Sydney earlier in the summer to sort out his business affairs, stepped off the plane at Heathrow and a few hours later found himself helming *InterSpray* in a match race with *Hofbrau* down Southampton Water one August evening.

Ocean greyhounds and dog otters

Right up to the start of the round the world race, Jeffes and *Hofbrau*'s skipper Pete Goss had a deliberate policy of sharing information. The two yachts frequently sailed alongside one another in the Solent, experimenting with rig tuning under identical sail combinations to get optimum speed.

They found that by locking the prop shaft when one blade of the self-feathering prop was in line with the skeg they got a significant improvement in speed.

John Davis, meanwhile, who had built his own ultra-light displacement yacht, *State of the Ark*, out of a duracore and had done JOG racing around Sydney Harbour, was given the job of Rigger, with Duggie assisting. He spent many hours tuning *InterSpray*'s rig to get the best mast rake and pre-bend.

John's sailing friend and fellow Australian Paul Coles, in Britain on an extended holiday, lived aboard the yacht for a time and contributed a lot to race preparations.

Alison (now no longer 'Bob') Smith, our fitness fanatic, provided an exercise regime with a new body language of press ups, squat thrusts, stomach crunches, and triceps dips which translated into one word – pain. The price of a Mars bar on training sails ascended to 40 press ups.

Alison carried out a lot of research on the crew's behalf on cold weather gear for the Southern Ocean and arranged for marine company reps to come and talk about their clothing.

Some of the crew regretted missing an evening underwear fashion show/striptease in thermal silk by a girl aboard *Rhone-Poulenc* (a guest, we were assured), but we did witness *InterSpray*'s 14-stone crew member Paul Buchanan rehearsing for the Southern Ocean, parading around the saloon in a thick pink pile Polartec romper suit. The tears of laughter would have melted an iceberg.

What to wear around the world became a popular topic of saloon talk.

Chemically treated thermal underwear that wouldn't smell and wicked litres of moisture from bodies. Even edible underwear. 'That could spice up the dried food,' said Jeff Plummer, by now elected Ship's Entertainments Officer. The most common ailments on the race were expected to be dermatological. Skin needing protection against sunburn and rope burns. Sunglasses for the tropics and glare on water. Goggles for the ice spray of the Southern Ocean. Those who wore specs were told to consider extended-wear contact lenses. 'But remember, they can freeze to your eyeballs in the Southern Ocean,' cautioned Julian.

He also stressed the importance of preventive medicine. Routine cleanliness

Ricky Scott (centre) with his boss, Sipko Huismans (left), and Chay Blyth

and personal hygiene was a hot topic. The prospect of living for weeks on end with 13 strangers in an area the size of your bedroom concentrated the mind wonderfully, not to mention the nostrils.

'Body and feet odours are bad for morale. Yeasts and fungi thrive in warm, damp conditions and fungal skin problems will occur,' we were warned.

Alcohol baby wipes were recommended for nether regions. 'Feet should be dusted twice a day with anti-foot rot powder and sailing shoes and trainers should have odour-eating insoles.' Under arm deodorant was compulsory on *InterSpray*. A man-made chamois leather, instead of a damp, smelly towel, was recommended.

'At this rate, we'll be the cleanest, freshest smelling *and* fastest yacht in the fleet,' announced our optimistic skipper.

Barry was more of a pragmatist: 'Whatever happens, you're bound to end up smelling like a dog otter,' he asserted.

Barry was from Yorkshire, home of the dog otter. His perceptive and accurate assumption became an historic quote that was to be typeset and pinned to the saloon bulkhead for the next 28,000 miles.

Later, a Henri-Lloyd one-piece SISSTEMAIR survival suit, on loan to *InterSpray*, and the Musto Ocean Drysuits, purchased by crew for the more extreme conditions, were rechristened 'dog otter suits'. Once they had been worn a few times the malodorous, trapped air developed an unmistakable dog otterish aroma.

By Cape Town the yacht had inherited a new stowaway mascot – a soft toy dog otter, berthed, naturally, in the doghouse.

Apocryphal stories developed among the fleet about the effects of the dehydrated food that was being taken. They varied from constipation and kidney failure (if you didn't drink enough liquids) to the apparent wind and velocity made good aboard a 44-ton steel yacht.

THE TOUGHEST YACHT RACE IS BORN

Bowel function was another topic at crew training sessions. 'Constipation, a common complaint at sea, can be quite distressing. . . bowels will give some problems,' admitted Julian. 'So will sea-sickness. I will bring stocks of medical aids for both ends of the spectrum,' he reassured us.

The estimable Dr Campbell Mackenzie, Fleet Doctor and medic/crew member on *Plonkers*, as *Rhone-Poulenc* was affectionately known, recommended crew carry a 'small self-care pack in their baggage', including favourite occasional medicines. . . 'aspirins, vitamins, suppositories, pessaries etc. Start the voyage with your ears empty of wax. Get your doctor to syringe them,' he counselled. He forgot those of us who had bought wax earplugs to turn a deaf ear to the snorers.

With our on-board vet facing eight months before the mast with a crew of dog otters, hygiene was uniquely dealt with on *InterSpray*. We sailed around the world with disposable paper towel holders and antiseptic soap dispensers in heads and galleys. Unlike other yachts that suffered plagues of boils and illness, *InterSpray* was a model of health and efficiency. . . most of the time.

Early in September the fleet sailed from Southampton to London and St Katharine Haven, by Tower Bridge, for Press conferences, sponsors' and family open days. *En route* up the River Thames *InterSpray* performed a couple of 360 degree turns outside International Paint's riverside factory at Silvertown. A rousing three cheers and a few blasts on the yacht's fog horn from the crew brought surprised staff waving from their windows.

For many of the crew who made the trip to London it was a chance to meet the first man to sail non-stop round the world singlehanded, Robin Knox-Johnston, Managing Director at St Katharine Haven. *Suhaili*, his legendary 32ft 5in teak ketch was berthed across from the fleet. Robin was then hatching his own plans to sail non-stop around the world in 80 days. The crew would meet him seven months later under different circumstances in Cape Town.

It was in London that Chay ended weeks of rumour by announcing the resignation of Alec Honey. The reason given for Honey's withdrawal was his wife's serious illness. Chay introduced *Rhone-Poulenc*'s new skipper, John O'Driscoll (49), a lieutenant-commander in the Royal Navy with 42,000 miles' racing experience. O'Driscoll had reportedly confirmed his acceptance only after meeting the crew of *Rhone-Poulenc* and sailing with them on the trip up to London.

Bookmakers William Hill had opened a book on the Challenge race and on the strength of the Fastnet race were announcing odds. 'It's a bit like watching Lindford Christie in a sprint and then pricing him up for a marathon,' said Chay.

Radio and television personality Cliff Michelmore announced he was putting £5 on *InterSpray*.

Tower Bridge was raised for a parade of sail by the fleet in the Pool of London on Sunday September 13, before the yachts sailed back to Southampton for the end of the boat show and final preparations for the race.

Suddenly the countdown had dissolved from years, months and weeks into days. If the gruelling training schedule and build up to the race had demanded much commitment and sacrifice, the final frantic hours of getting the yacht ready to cross the start line was a race of its own – against time. In two words it was frustration and mayhem.

All 17 *InterSpray* crew members toiled during the last six days in Ocean Village to whittle down a job list of essentials that was pages long. Food and spares equipment for the first leg had to be moved from the warehouse and carefully packed and stowed aboard. If tins were square rather than round it would be easier for sailors to stow them. But McDougalls' vacuum-packed dehydrated food was even easier to stow. Normally supplied to hospitals, schools, and the Armed Services the menu provided a nutritionally balanced diet. Each yacht was offered the same quantities of McDougalls (with a choice of menu) which skippers supplemented with tins and fresh food at their own discretion. Stores for the following three legs also had to be divided into weeks and packed for shipping containers sent ahead of the fleet to stopover ports.

The last five days

Delivery vans, couriers, and consignments of all sorts queued up to be loaded onto yachts. Every time you turned your back the chart table was piled high with more boxes – personal EPIRBS, a compass specially calibrated for the Southern Ocean, man overboard lights, cameras (still and video), rigging spares, spare light bulbs, a JVC music centre for the saloon, replacement fire extinguishers, and a crate of suntan creams and sunblockers from our support sponsor Bergasol. Next morning things appeared which had been delivered during the night. It was like Christmas. The one piece Musto Ocean drysuits arrived, but the lifejackets all had to be sent back for modifications. Everyone's personal space allocation was discussed. Julian's and Carlton's sextants and Duggie's bagpipes were regarded as ship's equipment.

The steering wheel had to be removed so that extra strengthening fillets could be welded on. Remember the buckled wheel on *Maiden* in the 1989-90 Whitbread, after a wave hurled a crew member against it? Every winch was stripped and serviced. Anti-chafe measures were taken on the stays and spreaders. And all this had to be fitted around a timetable of receptions and parties thrown by the city's mayor and sponsors, as well as dragon boat racing, photocalls, press, radio and TV interviews and crew briefings on everything from weather to the Ocean Vigil dolphin watch. There was a compulsory safety demonstration in the local swimming pool, to practise righting a capsized liferaft, and Chay's briefing in a local cinema with crews and the Race Committee, including Captain Spencer Drummond and RORC Director of Racing Alan Green.

Crew were also disappearing to see doctors for stopover injections. Rio topped the list for jabs. You name it, we were vaccinated against it (twice, if you counted booster jabs): yellow fever, cholera, hepatitis, typhoid, tetanus, polio. Malaria pills were optional. We swarmed with antibodies, our right arms containing as much culture as Sydney Opera House.

Getting private lives in order and things put in cold storeage became a sudden priority for those who hadn't planned ahead. Pressures mounted from all directions; sponsors, skippers, wives, husbands, children, employers. Nerves got edgy.

InterSpray was lucky and unlucky in being berthed well away from the rest of the fleet, on the end of a pontoon. We were cut-off, except by water, and we didn't have a dinghy. But we were also inaccessible to the hordes of sightseers who were flocking to Ocean Village. It was almost worth the long trek backwards and forwards to the Challenge offices to pick up equipment and use 'phones.

What proved a convenient bonus was having the extra support and facilities of our sponsor's local offices and warehouse, around the corner in Canute Road. International Paint's offices in Southampton had been an annexe for the crew ever since the fleet berthed in Ocean Village. Now it became our unofficial 'headquarters'. Trisha Wells, Julian's wife, who ran

THE TOUGHEST YACHT RACE IS BORN

InterSpray's Supporters' Club, helped with the mass of paperwork that week, assisted by Carol Preston, Jeff's girlfriend. David Hodgson and all his staff, who were trying to run a busy office with an endless stream of *InterSpray* crew tramping in and out, using 'phones, faxes, and photocopiers, were not only patient but understanding and helpful.

The planned week of Ocean Village festivities, with funfair, steam rally and marching bands, lived up to its name in more ways than intended. Chay Blyth was thrown into the dock after a photocall with all the women crew members; three days later he gave the push to *The Independent*'s Sailing Correspondent Stuart Alexander (was it something he wrote?). This prompted a concerned leading article in *Yachts and Yachting* magazine on buoyancy aids for journalists and a reprimand for Chay, who later apologised to Alexander and his editor.

Then there was Chay's final rallying call – a briefing for all crews in the Hofbrau beer tent. It's easy to be impressed by the exploits of a man who rowed the Atlantic in a 20ft open dory and challenged the Forties to Roar *against* him as he sailed solo the wrong way round the rim of the world. Easier sometimes to admire Blyth's down-to-earth normality. 'I'm just a little fat man of 50, who's done a few things in the past. . .' is a quote he's given more than one reporter. It also sums up the way the Challenge crews see him.

Blyth in the midst of his hand-picked amateur yachtsmen, who are cast in his own mould, is Blyth in his element. He came into yachting overnight himself, his self-proclaimed credentials for the 1968 *Sunday Times* Golden Globe race 'two arms, two legs and a sense of humour!' He retired from the race in Cape Town boasting 'I learned sailing by getting into a boat and disappearing over the horizon. . .' A typical Blyth quote, designed to confound sceptics and experts and incite the dreams and aspirations of adventurers. kBlyth had been in the business of making dreams come true before. He loaned Naomi James his 53ft yacht, renamed *Express Crusader*, so that she would become the first woman to sail solo round the world, via the Great Capes. The card he sent to her at the start of her voyage said: 'Only three turns left, then one right and home sweet home!'. Dame Naomi said: 'He was so matter-of-fact it was easy to get things done when Chay was around.'

This time he was no less matter-of-fact.

Loved ones, he advised, should be told to ignore newspaper reports making a drama out of the race, which had attracted its share of critics – some likening the event to sending a bunch of ramblers up Everest, others calling it 'an extended flotilla cruise for wide-eyed beginners to play the role of intrepid Cape Horners'.

Whitbread Round the World Yacht Race director Ian Bailey-Willmot was reported to have said that a get-rich-quick formula would be to set up a travel agency in Hobart selling one-way air tickets home to Challenge crews who made it that far.

Chay's advice on the perils of racing to windward was that it was tougher, maybe, but safer than the Whitbread route. 'When you're running downwind and surfing at great speed if someone falls overboard he's either lost immediately, or, when you turn back into the wind, you're carrying too much canvas. Going to windward, the yacht is heeled over and the crew are always looking for their next handhold. That's a safety factor in itself. If the true wind is 20 knots, you're carrying canvas for 30 knots. If you have to turn downwind you've less of a problem.'

Chay's golden rule, which he would elaborate on and repeatedly underline over the following months at every stopover port around the world, came down to ten life and death words:

'Remember – one hand for yourself and one for the boat.'

'Watch out and listen to your skipper. He knows best,' he added. 'You've got something quite unique here, but make sure you all come back safely.'

Crews emerged from the tent as if they'd been at a religious revival meeting.

Safety aspects of the race exceeded the requirements of statutory bodies. But to cap it all the official race scrutineer from the RORC decided that the entire fleet needed some last-minute re-welding to the stanchions – there was a span between the pushpit and first stanchion of more than 7ft. With less than 24 hours to go we still had not complied with or found a means of securing the mast heel to its step.

On top of these last-minute modifications, the weatherfax laptop computers were delivered the night before the race start and had to be installed. Nobody had had a chance to try them out but skippers had been on a two-hour crash course. It was to become a contentious point by the time we reached Rio.

With the antifouling given a final scrub by divers we were ready for Courtaulds' Great Send-off Race Party on the Thursday night. A world premiere screening at Ocean Village cinema of *Carry on Columbus* was followed by a barbecue and disco at International Paint's warehouse, which was filled with sand and potted palms to resemble a Copacabana beach party. Supporters were invited to caption cartoons of the crew.

Skipper Paul Jeffes promised Courtaulds' Chief Executive, and all our well-wishers: 'This ain't no cruise. We're going out there to do the business – racing 24-hours a day.'

InterSpray's Challenge Team

PAUL JEFFES (40) Skipper

A cool man in a crisis whose style of leadership was to give a free rein to his Watchleaders, which made the circumnavigation that much more rewarding for them. Paul is a Naval Architect and Managing Director of Silvers Marine Ltd, a leading Scottish boatbuilding yard on the Clyde, which is also an International Paint Gelshield and InterSpray centre. He studied Naval Architecture for three years at Southampton College of Technology. He left his job as Technical Services Manager at Simpson-Lawrence Ltd in 1982 to set up Silvers Marine Ltd, building it into the second biggest yard in Scotland. He crewed in the 1978 Round Britain and Ireland Race, and skippered the 1982 race in *Simpson-Lawrence*. He also skippered in the 1981 Three Peaks Race and the International One Design World Championships in Maine, America, in 1987; won the Scottish Offshore Points IOR Championship in 1985 and 1987; won the Scottish Series twice, most recently in 1991. He regularly sails two classes of keel boat, his own 24ft Loch Long, and an IOD keelboat, a Frers two-tonner *Sapphire*. In Scotland he writes for *Yachting Life* magazine.

JULIAN (Awesome) WELLS (41)
Senior Watch leader and Medical Officer

Dubbed 'the Sailing Vet', responsible for amputations, organ transplants and SWEs (salt water enemas). Julian has his own veterinary practice in Shrewsbury. His specific areas of responsibility aboard were navigation and meteorology. He first started sailing in 1970, progressing from dinghies to keelboats. The Ship's Medical chest bears the legend: 'INTERSPRAY VETERINARY CLINIC: medicines for animal treatment only.' Well known for treating crew with udder cream and a bran extract for dogs, Julian was considered by friends in Shrewsbury to be certifiable to sign up for the Challenge. As a member of Shawbury and Mid Shropshire Rotary Club, he gave numerous illustrated talks on the voyage to business and social groups and Rotary Clubs at stopovers, sending regular despatches to local radio and newspapers. He had great support from his wife Trisha and daughters Jenny (15) and Emma (13). Trisha came to all stopovers and ran the shore-based support team for families, providing regular updates on race happenings.

CARLTON DODD (39)
Watch *Leader (first and second legs)*

Famous for Dodd's Doldrum Act. When *InterSpray* was hit by 40 knot tropical squalls and forked lightning, there was Carlton, silhouetted on the wheel, yelling above the shrieking wind in a rich Devon accent: 'She won't stand up to her canvas no more Mr. Onedin, the rig'll carry away. . .' Carlton's sailing experience includes half a dozen RORC Channel races in the late 1980s and crewing in the 1989 Fastnet Race. He was one of the crew for the delivery trip of the prototype training yacht, *British Steel Challenge*, to Seville for the Expo '92 exhibition. After completing the delivery trip he gained his Yachtmaster Ocean ticket. For three years he had his own 31ft Danish-built Star yacht which he sailed from the Hamble. He has a degree in business administration studies and worked in investment marketing before joining the Challenge. He lives in Stratford on Avon, Warwickshire.

JOHN (Crocodile) DAVIS (52)
Watch Leader, Rigger and ship's carpenter

The only Australian doing the full circumnavigation – hence the nickname – John has considerable sailing experience. He designed and built his own ultra light displacement 26ft yacht to comply with Junior Offshore Group rules. Aboard *InterSpray* he had special responsibility for rigging and spars, adding valuable input on route planning. John learned to sail as a teenager and competed at state and national level in Fireballs. Before joining the Challenge he raced his yacht with JOG off Sydney. He is Managing Director of Central West Petroleum, his own wholesale and retail petroleum distribution company. His wife Jocelyn was in Hobart, with son Craig (31) and daughter Rebecca (16), to welcome him at the emotional halfway home mark of his circumnavigation. John had always wanted to compete in a long-distance race. A past president of The Rotary Club of Orange, New South Wales, he gave talks to fellow Rotarians in Rio, Hobart, Cape Town and Southampton.

DOMINIC (Slick) MATHEWS (48)
Watch Leader third and fourth leg and Joint Purser

Known as 'Slick', for his slicked back hair and his suave appearance, aided by his own costume department in the tropics. Dominic put his urbane businessman away with the pin striped suits for eight months and played a few other characters. He is, after all, a member of Weavering Entertainers, an amateur drama group. Also answers to nickname 'Dom', but his real job is Managing Director of his own independent financial advice consultancy in Maidstone ('directly opposite the prison'). He lives in Weavering Street, Kent, and can claim to be the first man to morris dance around Cape Horn. Also an honorary member of Rene's Cafe, and founder member of the Exclusive Foredeck Club. A one-time gliding instructor, Dom was hooked on sailing after a flotilla holiday in the Med, eventually buying his own 36ft Beneteau, which he sailed from the Hamble. He sold her during the circumnavigation. He and his wife, Thomasina, have four children: Shereden (25), Giles (24), Keiron (22) and Hannah (12). The three eldest are all honour graduates. 'They get their looks from me,' says Dom.

PATRICK (Dump Truck) BROCKMAN (30)

Sailmaker

Star of the Exclusive Foredeck Club and the quiet man of the crew, but a very hard worker who never lost his cool. Patrick, a keen all-round sportsman, revelled in the tough conditions of the Southern Ocean, though his only sailing experience before joining the Challenge was a weekend trip to the Isle of Wight and some dinghy sailing on the Norfolk Broads. Born in Crosby, Lancashire, he lives in West Kensington, London, and runs a small building company. He spent a week at Hood Sails loft, in Lymington, and Rockall Sails in Bosham, learning about sail repairs and chafe prevention. Sometimes dubbed *InterSpray*'s 'token glamour boy'. Eats like a horse, but didn't require veterinary treatment. His girl-friend, Caroline Bird, Group Product Manager at L'oreal, followed him round the world to every stopover.

JULIET CONNELL (Fortysomething)

Ocean Vigil Watchleader,
Jill of all Trades

Known to the crew as Queen of the light weather helm and Officer IC flags. Juliet gave up her 15-year job as an Air Stewardess with Dan Air to join the race, replacing a crew member who dropped out. She had been on the Challenge waiting list for two-and-a-half years. Juliet remarried her ex-husband, Tony, in Adelaide, returning to Southampton two days later to join *InterSpray* for race training. After the race she emigrated to join Tony in Australia, having enjoyed a delayed honey-moon during the Hobart stopover. Her sailing experience includes over 15,000 miles aboard the square-rigged Tall Ship *Lord Nelson*, where she has been Watchleader and Bosun's Mate. Juliet was Assistant Purser on the final leg home and took to her role as Happy Hour hostess with more enthusiasm than that of Officer IC flags. She once ran a pub. She has two grown-up children and returned to Australia with plans to take up parachute jumping, gliding and to continue sailing.

PAUL BUCHANAN (31)

Photographer, Video Cameraman

Started out on the first leg wanting to be a bronzed sea god, and using ship's supply of precious lemon juice to turn his hair blonde. By Cape Horn he was a salty seadog threat-ening to wear an earring and tattoo in Hobart. By Cape Town it was a wooden leg and an eye patch. As Official Ship's Photographer, Paul got flak every time he appeared with his camera in a crisis: 'You always get *that* out at the wrong time,' crew members moaned at him. As he often replied, it was precisely the right time, as his pictures in this book testify. Renowned for saying things that other people think, but are too tactful to say, Paul has a promising career as a diarist. He once ran a mobile phone hire business for Securicor. He grew up in Duston, Northampton, and was a keen canoeist, paddling for his county. He lives in Ealing, London, and sailed dinghies as a teenager. Another founder member of the Exclusive Foredeck Club. A good cook (a wizard with sauces), but leaves a lot of washing up behind. Once credited with taking a picture for a Nikon advert. The crew claim he took it with a Pentax.

DUGGIE GILLESPIE (26)

Assistant Rigger and Ship's Bagpiper

Duggie was in charge of waves below deck after opening the forehatch during a Southern Ocean gale. He claimed he was 'washing out the bilges.' Also banned by the Skipper from wearing his kilt up the mast. 'We have three lady crew members, and it will be too windy round the Horn for kilts, anyway,' said Jeffes. Duggie hails from Kirkcudbright, Dumfries and Galloway, Scotland, where his parents run Brighouse Bay Holiday Park. A qualified chartered surveyor, his last job was Assistant Land Agent at Chatsworth Estate, Derbyshire, home to the Duke and Duchess of Devon-shire. He joined the yacht a month before the race, straight from two weeks at John Ridgeway's Adventure School. Having originally applied for the Challenge 1996 Round the World Race, he was offered a place in the '92 race a few weeks before it started, replacing one of the original crew who dropped out. It took Duggie two days to de-cide he'd join *InterSpray*.

Julian (Awesome) Welles

John (Crocodile) Davis

Carlton Dodd

Dominic (Slick) Mathews

INTERSPRAY'S CHALLENGE TEAM

Patrick (Dump Truck) Brockman

Paul Buchanan

Juliet Connell

Duggie Gillespie

JEFF (Mr Angry) PLUMMER (45)
Entertainments Officer and Engineer

The man who brought you Gladys, the inflatable stowaway, King Neptune, a blow-up Father Christmas and Mr Grumpy. Dame Jeffery first trod the Broads in Norfolk in his Hobie catamaran. He lives in Norfolk and skippers a 42ft Broads cruiser. He began dinghy sailing at 16, crewing in Merlin Rockets and competing to national standards. Born in London, he lived in south Birmingham and emigrated to South Africa in the late sixties, working in the car industry. He returned to Britain in 1972 and six years later went to Saudi Arabia to work in the oil industry. He now works in partnership with his brother, Raymond, mixing drilling fluids for offshore oil fields in the North Sea, when he's not joining a samba school in Rio or riding shotgun on the helm in his Stetson. His girlfriend, Carol Preston, followed *InterSpray* around the world on her own eight-month adventure.

ALISON SMITH (25)
Joint Purser and assistant medic

A keen Tall Ships sailor, Alison, took part as a Watch Leader in the Australian Bicentennial Tall Ships series (1987-88). She broke her neck when thrown off the helm in a gale in the Australian bight aboard an 85ft tall ship. She worked in the leisure industry and for an adventure holiday company before joining the Challenge. Alison has a sports studies degree from Newcastle Polytechnic and is active in climbing, abseiling and windsurfing, as well as being a dinghy sailing instructor. During the Challenge Alison, from Sowerby, Thirsk, North Yorks, undertook the arduous responsibility of victualling the yacht for the circumnavigation. She also did comparative research for the crew on cold weather clothing for the Southern Ocean before they left Southampton, ordering clothing from various manufacturers. As assistant medic, Alison attended the Royal Navy medical services training programme for paramedics. She was also the skipper's Girl Friday, typing and sending his Sat-com despatches.

RICKY SCOTT (37)
Steering Gear, Deck Equipment and Assistant Bosun

Big Ricky (17 stone) has been round world three times while serving six years in the Merchant Navy, until he left in 1978. He has 15 years' sailing experience, crewing in club races around the Humber and East Coast and across to Holland. He and his wife, Jane, an operating theatre nurse, have three children: Julie (13) Joanna (12) and Philip (10). Ricky had already signed up for the Challenge before Courtaulds announced its sponsorship of *InterSpray*. When it was discovered that one of the 120 volunteer Challenge volunteers was employed by Courtaulds Fibres – Ricky is a technician in fibre production at Courtelle in Grimsby – he was assigned to *InterSpray*. His job was kept open, but he paid his own way round the world. It was a challenge within the Challenge to work extra night shifts to raise the money. A member of Humber Mouth Yacht Club and Grimsby and Cleethorpes Cruising Association, Ricky lives in Grimsby and sails his own 26ft Telstar trimaran and a 28ft Atlanta.

BRIAN (Bilge Rat) WARR (43)
Safety Officer and Engineer

Brian learned survival techniques and first aid as an engineering maintenance fitter in the North Sea oil industry. He has an offshore survival certificate and soon took charge of *InterSpray's* safety. His engineering skills earned him the title 'Bilge Rat' – always lifting floors to check skin fittings. Brian is a keen narrow boater and designed and built his own 30ft narrow boat in 1981. He sold it to finance the circumnavigation. He has sailed the Humber and Trent Rivers for the past 27 years. Brian went to sea at seven on steam tugs with his father, a North Sea trawlerman for 20 years. Both his grandfathers worked as steam engineers on trawlers. Brian is a Cub instructor in the Scouts and a member of Strawberry Island Boat Club, Doncaster. He and his wife Janet have two children, Alex (11) and Emily (4), and live in Goxhill, Barrow on Humber, South Humberside. Brian's sailing partner is fellow crewman Ricky Scott.

One-leggers

Leg One
(5,300 miles: Southampton to Rio)
PAUL (Scribe) GELDER (46)

In three years as Features Editor at *Yachting Monthly* magazine my dreams and nightmares have been realised. I have found myself licking curry out of a dog bowl aboard *Suhaili* with Robin Knox-Johnston in a mid-Atlantic gale; eating mackerel out of Mike Peyton's all-purpose galvanised bucket aboard his ferro-cement *Touchstone*. I escaped war torn Yugoslavia while flotilla sailing (admittedly by several months) only to be boarded by armed Coastguards off Grenada while sailing in the Caribbean. Having survived Knox-Johnston's friendly bark, I was bitten a few months later by a suspected rabid dog in the Caribbean. Not surprisingly, I am most contented day-sailing with my wife, Anne, and daughter, Laura (10), aboard our a 20ft Robert Tucker Princess sloop, in Chichester Harbour.

Leg two
(9,800 miles: Rio to Hobart)
BARRY (F) FORD (31)

The 'F' stands for effing. Also famous for the perspicacious observation on Southern Ocean hygiene 'Whatever happens, you're bound to end up smelling like a dog otter.' Barry, from South Yorkshire, works for British Steel in a Sheffield plate mill as a maintenance electrician. He was one of four workers from British Steel Stainless selected for the Challenge. His previous sailing experience was limited to a trip round Flamborough head on the *Bridlington Belle*, which 'didn't count for much,' he was told. Barry can now describe himself as a professional sailor (the only one who was being paid to sail, apart from the skipper). 'The worst thing about doing this trip,' he said, 'was leaving my then nine-month old son, Matthew. He had learned to walk while I was away.' Barry postponed his studies for a degree in engineering for *InterSpray's* adventure

Leg three
(6,800 miles: Hobart to Cape Town)
ROGER PEEK (48)

Treasurer of British Steel plc, the event's main sponsor, and one of the company's two directors on the Board of The Challenge Business Ltd, the company set up by Chay Blyth to run the race. Roger lives in Haywards Heath, West Sussex, and his sailing experience before the race was zero. He was a natural to be put in charge of *InterSpray's* crew fund. Roger's celebrated quote on leg three came when he picked himself up from the back of the cockpit during a vicious squall one night, with 60 knots of wind and razor-sharp ice spray, and remarked: 'Doesn't the moon on the water look romantic?' He has two daughters, Katie (21) and Helen (18).

Leg four
(6,800 miles: Cape Town to Southampton)
RUTH COLENSO (26)

Ruth lives in Hooton, South Wirral, and works for British Steel's Shotton Works, implementing a Total Quality Programme. Born in Wirral, she took an engineering degree at Cambridge in 1985-88, followed by a year travelling in Australia and New Zealand before starting work. Ruth is a Sea Ranger leader of a crew of 10-14 year-olds, whom she takes sailing ,canoeing and hiking, as well as enjoying indoor activities. The Challenge was an opportunity to develop her sailing skills. Her family had always played around in dinghys. At the age of 17, Ruth spent a week on board the Ocean Youth Club's *Francis Drake*, her first experience of keelboat sailing. She was hooked and looking for more opportunites when the Challenge came along. She is getting married in October to Nick Wake, a graduate engineer who also works for British Steel.

Jeff (Mr Angry) Plummer

Ricky Scott

Alison Smith

Brian (Bilge Rat) Warr

INTERSPRAY'S CHALLENGE TEAM

Paul (Scribe) Gelder

Barry (F) Ford

Roger Peek

Ruth Colenso

INTERSPRAY'S RACE AROUND THE WORLD

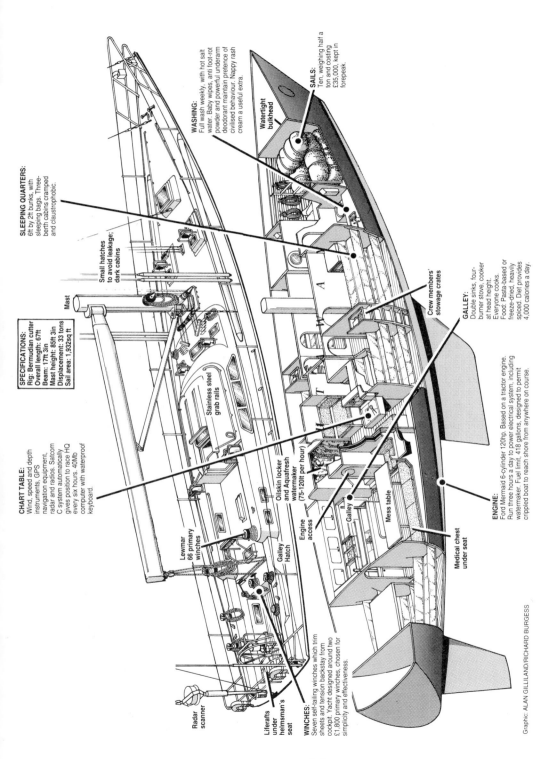

WASHING:
Full wash weekly, with hot salt water. Baby wipes, anti foot-rot powder and powerful underarm deodorant maintain pretence of civilised behaviour. Nappy rash cream a useful extra.

SAILS:
Ten, weighing half a ton and costing £35,000, kept in forepeak.

Watertight bulkhead

SLEEPING QUARTERS:
6ft by 2ft bunks, with sleeping bags. Three-berth cabins cramped and claustrophobic.

Small hatches to avoid leakage; dark cabins

Mast

SPECIFICATIONS:
Rig: Bermudian cutter
Overall length: 67ft
Beam: 17ft 3in
Mast height: 85ft 3in
Displacement: 33 tons
Sail area: 1,932sq ft

CHART TABLE:
Wind, speed and depth instruments, GPS navigation equipment, radar and radios. Satcom C system automatically gives position to race HQ every six hours. 40Mb computer with waterproof keyboard.

Stainless steel grab rails

Crew members' stowage crates

GALLEY:
Double sinks, four-burner stove, cooker at head height. Everyone cooks. Food: Pasta-based or freeze-dried, heavily spiced. Diet provides 4,000 calories a day.

Lewmar 66 primary winches

Galley Hatch

Oilskin locker and Aquafresh watermaker (75-120lt per hour)

Engine access

Galley

Mess table

ENGINE:
Ford Mermaid 6-cylinder 120hp. Based on a tractor engine. Run three hours a day to power electrical system, including watermaker. Fuel limit, 418 gallons, designed to permit crippled boat to reach shore from anywhere on course.

Medical chest under seat

Radar scanner

Liferafts under helmsman's seat

WINCHES:
Seven self-tailing winches which trim sheets and tension backstay from cockpit. Yacht designed around two £1,800 primary winches, chosen for simplicity and effectiveness.

Graphic: ALAN GILLILAND/RICHARD BURGESS

Leg One

Flying Down to Rio

Start Saturday, September 26,
Southampton to Rio de Janeiro, 5,300 miles

O ur instructions couldn't have been simpler: 'The course for the race is round the world, leaving Cape Horn and the Cape of Good Hope to starboard and the following to port: position 52°S and 120°W and the Kerguelen Isles.'

It's an old axiom among sailors that no matter how much time is spent preparing a yacht, she is never completely ready to set sail. As an early morning drizzle shrouded Ocean Village on Saturday September 26, we were as ready as we would ever be.

Crew, with wives, girlfriends children and family, had begun arriving around 0700 to put personal gear aboard. There was tension in the air, and underlying the anticipation a strange sense of solemnity which the crew's usual casual banter couldn't disguise as the crowds grew around the yacht.

Each crew member was allowed two plastic boxes in which to keep worldly possessions for the next 28,000 miles, plus a contribution to the yacht's library of couple of books and cassette tapes. There were a few laughs as bulging sea bags,

straining at the seams, were heaved down the companionway. There were a few more at the convict haircuts sported by some of the crew. Christmas and birthday presents (and cakes) had been secreted away, together with some odder parcels of bells and balls. Dominic Mathews was planning to morris dance at Cape Horn, providing his bells didn't freeze. And why not? We'd seen a *Hofbrau* crew member water skiing from the transom during training with a harness fastened to a spare

We gybed the spinnaker 14 times as we ran down the Solent

halyard. Paul Buchanan was going to do a juggling act at the Horn. Mascots and St Christophers and other lucky charms were handed over. One-leggers Barry Ford and Ruth Colenso were still working at odd jobs down below, where a sprig of white heather decorated the galley along with cards and letters from schoolchildren who would be following *InterSpray*.

As precious minutes ticked by and we bid our final farewells, the carnival atmosphere and the sound of marching bands on the quayside seemed a million miles away. Tears may have been shed in private, but there was still a collective swell of emotions to match the swell of the beckoning Solent. There was guilt, too. For some it was the last time they

would see their families for eight months.

When Duggie Gillespie slipped below to gather his bagpipes we knew the moment had come for *InterSpray* to slip her lines. Barry and Ruth wished us luck and reluctantly disembarked. It was affecting to see people who had been tough mates for the past months revealing a softer, more vulnerable side to their natures. Barry would have to wait until Rio before his adventure, sailing to Hobart. For Ruth

it would be Cape Town for the leg home. Roger Peek, sailing the third leg from Hobart, had permission to stay aboard for the start – providing he didn't give the crew any assistance.

With the haunting strains of *Mull of Kintyre* echoing across the water as Duggie played his pipes on the foredeck, *InterSpray*'s 120hp engine was fired up and we cast off from the crowded pontoon at 0745 to brave cheers and a few tears. We were the first yacht to leave Ocean Village Marina, saluted by the old steam ship the *Shieldhall*, who gave a rousing blast on her siren, signalling the start of a chorus of foghorns and applause from other Challenge yachts and spectators ringing the docksides on this misty morning, including a fanfare from the band.

'Starting the adventure of a life time crying, was not what I expected,' said Alison, wiping away the tears. Leaving for the unknown was one thing, but leaving behind loved ones proved tougher than most had expected, especially since, up to this moment, most had been equal partners in our adventure, sharing the burden of frustrations, fears and hopes.

Standing on the end of the RSYC jetty, by the entrance to Ocean Village, was Sipko Huismans.

'Three cheers for Sipko!' called Ricky for his boss. Silence hung in the air for a few seconds as the crew wound Ricky up before hoorays resounded.

Around the corner, it was the turn of Jeff Plummer's sister, Lorraine, who was standing on a piece of dockland waste ground with a knot of cheering relatives. It was her 40th birthday. The crew lined up on the starboard rail to sing 'Happy birthday' to her.

'Just make sure you're back for the next one!' she shouted across the 50 yard gap to Jeff.

Heading down Southampton Water, on a damp, overcast morning, the crew were in reflective mood. Twenty-two years ago, on an October Sunday, upon this same stretch of water Chay Blyth had boarded his ketch *British Steel* in the Hamble to start his solo circumnavigation:

'People ask you what you feel like when you have cut the last links with home and family and realise you are on your own for ten months or more,' he reflected later. 'The honest answer is that you don't feel anything. At that moment you are beyond feeling. . . You have a vague feeling of thankfulness that something you have planned, worked and dreamed for has actually been achieved.' Blyth also recalled that he was pretty exhausted when he left. . . 'more like a zombie than a human being.'

We knew what he meant.

There was one last job to complete as we uncovered the mainsail to mount Courtaulds' logo on the top panel. Light winds were forecast, but it was going to be a downwind start with one of the fastest running tides of the year at full ebb underneath us. Out in the Solent we practised a few spinnaker peels and gybes before Paul Jeffes gathered the crew into the cockpit for a last briefing session. He didn't need to explain what he expected of his crew, who had slept and eaten the race for the past 30 months. But a good result on this leg would set us up for the rest of the race. He explained his theory of NTT (Nervous Tiddle Time), which roughly translated for the men as: 'Go now or forever hold your piece.'

The sun was breaking through grey clouds as the spectator fleet grew into an armada of some 2,000 craft of all sizes, and descriptions, from Channel ferries, to Tall Ships, small inflatables, jet skis and even a canoeist. Blyth's original *British Steel* was there, too. Courtaulds' had hired the ferry *Solent Enterprise* and the *Soren Larsen*, star of the *Onedin Line*, for our families and supporters.

We threaded our way through the churning white water rapids of the spectator fleet to the start line, off Gilkicker Point. The race 'corridor' was awash with small craft, despite policing by fast patrol boats.

The start was delayed by five minutes to accommodate a live BBC radio broadcast, but no one seemed to have told *Commercial Union*. When the Princess Royal fired the start gun at 1205 from Brittany Ferries' 700-passenger *Armorique*, chartered for VIPs, Will Sutherland's yacht had already crossed over the line by several minutes. *Group 4* overshot the line 10 seconds early, while *Heath Insured* had her rudder snagged around the anchor line of a buoy marking the outer limit of the start line. To make matters worse, she was towing it across the line in front of *InterSpray*. Pandemonium broke loose. *Group 4*, caught in a posse of spectator boats, ignored the recall and followed the fleet. Commercial Union attempted to stem the fast-flowing tide, but failed to recross the line. Both yachts could expect a two-hour time penalty.

The Sunday Times sailing correspondent called it 'stage fright'. Danger at the start line was less of a problem than nerves, he reported.

We crossed in eighth place as the ten 3,780 sq ft spinnakers, nine of them emblazoned with sponsor's logos, blossomed in the forest of spectator boats which engulfed the Challenge fleet. *Heath Insured* did a 720-degree turn as her punishment for getting entangled with the line buoy.

'The most impressive yachting spectacle since the Aussies took the America's Cup,' reckoned Jeffes.

Running downwind in the 12-knot breeze meant it was a case of follow the leader through the Solent, gybing the spinnaker 14 times along the way. *Pride of Teesside*, flying her lightweight plain white kite, was first through the two start gates marked by the Tall Ships *Malcolm Miller* and *Winston Churchill*, winning £4,000 prize money.

Before we got to Hurst Point, Roger Peek reluctantly jumped ship, leaping aboard an inflatable boat. At the western end of the Isle of Wight we were caught by a sudden gust of wind funnelling through Hurst Narrows and it was a case of 'all hands' to pull down the spinnaker, streaming at the end of its halyard and threatening to turn into a kite in more ways than one.

It was not the last sight we wanted our

families to remember for the next 5,300 miles, but by the time we'd got the beast under control, the *InterSpray* supporters' ferry had abruptly turned for home and was a smudge on the horizon. A launch chartered by staff from *Yachting Monthly* magazine, official supporters of *InterSpray*, followed us for a while but once past the Needles we were on our own. Goodbye England, hello world.

We had finally cut the cord. It was difficult to believe that more than two years' preparation were over and we were off on the adventure that promised to change lives. The send-off had been spectacular, but we were all relieved to banish the emotional pre-race blues and leave behind the cynics who said we were crazy. For the next month life would be a series of lessons with no time to practice. Experience would be the name we gave to our mistakes.

Heath Insured, meanwhile, explained their attachment to a certain buoy in their own inimitable fashion. 'The thing is at the last minute we got homesick and decided to take a memento of Ol' Blighty. The buoy was the nearest thing to hand, but we didn't know what to feed it, so threw it back.'

During the next 24 hours the fleet closed on Ushant, still led by *Pride of Teesside*, as we settled into our watch system. The wind died temporarily early on Sunday morning and the log records: 'Passed two gannets and a lone cross channel swimmer wearing a black helmet and going quite a lot faster than us.'

At 1800 on Sunday we crossed tracks with *Commercial Union*, lying in joint ninth place. As we sailed alongside each other, Jeff came on deck to throw the galley slops overboard and give an all too convincing imitation of seasickness before we bore away. He wasn't Entertainments Officer for nothing.

InterSpray's routing information came from the commercial London-based weather forecast service of Noble Denton.

Above and right: see you in eight months time! Final farewells before the starting gun from the families of InterSpray's *crew and supporters on the ferry* Solent Enterprise. *Below: the spinnaker threatens to turn into a proper kite as a gust of wind catches* InterSpray *at the western end of the Isle of Wight*

INTERSPRAY'S RACE AROUND THE WORLD

Hurricane Charlie was supposed to dissipate on the way over the Atlantic, but by Sunday night we were recording 28 knots of wind and tramping along to the west of the fleet on a close reach at 9-10 knots. Finisterre was 395 miles away. Two of the five crew members on stand-by (mother) watch were suffering seasickness and three out of four crew were seasick on the watch they were 'mothering'.

The Bay of Biscay lived up to its reputation by Monday night as the fleet caught the vicious lash of the tail end of Hurricane Charlie, with winds gusting to 45 knots. Getting dressed, drinking coffee, simply moving around, was an athletic feat and an acquired art that hadn't been acquired by everyone. Hot coffee showers and frequent bruisings were commonplace as crews got to grips with living at an angle of 45 degrees. The doors on the heads had been replaced by curtains, for safety reasons, but there was a danger of being hurled into the companionway with trousers round ankles.

Loose objects down below became lethal missiles, including spare winch handles, knives in the galley and mugs of scalding tea. It proved we didn't have to be in the Southern Ocean for it to be dangerous.

At the height of the storm Ricky shouted across the deck 'you want some heavy metal music with this lot' – to accompany the sound of steel hitting waves. Jeff Plummer announced a fortune teller had once told his mum one of her sons would sail round the world. 'She was wrong. After this lot I'm getting off in Rio!' he joked. Several crew were swept off their feet on deck and John Davis, swept into a dorade vent, had the honour of presenting himself as the first patient at the vet's animal clinic.

InterSpray already had three bent stanchions and a loose guardrail wire. She had taken a hammering which shook the polystyrene hull insulation into the bilges. On *Hofbrau*, to the west of us, Pete Goss reported the deck had disappeared underwater as a big wave swept her from stem to stern. The jockey pole, two winch handles and a danbuoy disappeared overboard. *Pride of Teesside* had a torn No 1 genoa.

Foresail changes in these conditions were a very wet affair as the foredeck submarined through the waves. The self-inflating lifejackets (a DoT requirement) had popped off so often that we thought we would run out of water-activated cartridges. Paul Jeffes was thinking of organising a competition with the manufacturer for the most lifejackets inflated *en route* to Rio.

Wearing the Henri-Lloyd one-piece dry suit, I discovered it had been worn by someone else – the distilled essence (or 'ming' as the skipper said) of eau de dog otter was overpowering, as everyone approaching from downwind said. Jeffes threatened to set me adrift in the suit off the Spanish coast, except it might alert a Sécurité message. It was packed away for cleaning in Rio.

After 15 hours the wind had dropped to 18 knots by Tuesday mid-morning and we had moved up to seventh place. The gale had blown away the cobwebs and everyone's sea legs were sorted out, apart from the person who wrote the log entry: 'Starboard head covered in misdirected puke, quite a lot of which was carrot.' The gale had washed oil and tar balls on the deck, foresails and sheets. We parcelled the oil-covered sheets with strips of plastic sticky tape.

By noon on day four, after nearly 600 miles of racing, eighth-placed *Nuclear Electric* was in sight two miles off our port quarter. *Group 4* was lying ninth while *Commercial Union*, which had perplexed race officials by apparently heaving to on Monday night and falling 40 miles behind, was now lying tenth. *British Steel II* had taken the lead from Ian MacGillivray. Yachts in the middle of the fleet were trading places by the hour.

LEG ONE

With plenty of shipping around at night we used a powerful searchlight to illuminate the sails and show our presence on a couple of occasions. Some ships acknowledged by flashing a signal in reply and Ricky tried communicating with morse code remembered from his Merchant Navy days.

Back home race followers had been calling the fax data retrieval system at a rate of 200 calls an hour. British Telecom had doubled the number of lines to 32.

The morning of day five found us off Cape Finisterre with a school of pilot whales and dolphins playing around the yacht. The crew caught up on missed, or mislaid, meals with chicken curry and strawberry cheesecake, and the pursers discovered a miscalculation on sugar supplies and toilet paper. It was to be rations all the way to Rio. By now days of the week became meaningless as time was measured in three four-hour night watches and two six-hour daytime watches. These divided into sail changes and turns on the helm.

Two focal points every 24-hours were the radio round-ups, or chat shows, when yachts relayed their respective positions to the duty yacht and the crew huddled around the chart table to see if we had climbed or dropped places on the leaderboard. It often set the mood for the day.

We began the luxury of hot water showers every three days, since we had to run the engine to re-charge batteries and make water for the dehydrated food. At mealtimes there were two sittings of seven.

Yachts began to experience the first of the weatherfax problems. John Chittenden on *Nuclear Electric* announced on the chat show that they had problems with their Satcom-C computer and their weatherfax was 'up the spout.'

'At least the cupboard keeps the crisps dry – about all it's useful for,' said Chittenden. Having consumed the last bottle of whiskey aboard the previous night, Chittenden's crew were going to put a message in it for Spencer Drummond at RHQ – it seemed a more reliable method of communication.

We finally mastered our weatherfax, but the maps it produced prompted a telex back to RHQ saying 'they seem about as much help as asking Michael Fish which day of summer is best for a barbecue.'

We heard on the chat show that Mike Martin on *British Steel II* had proposed to his girlfriend Carol McBean over ship-to-shore radio. They were getting married in Rio and the fleet's entire crew were invited to the wedding.

There was eight miles dividing the first three yachts at noon, with *InterSpray*, listed in 5th and 4th place, depending on which position check was taken. We were 26 miles behind *Pride of Teesside*, who were leading the fleet again.

Winds were light and variable. By evening, *Coopers & Lybrand* were within hailing distance, having been forced to tack westwards to clear Cape Finisterre, along with *Heath* and *Rhone-Poulenc*.

Paul Buchanan, who was prone to seasickness, was still suffering badly. After two mouthfuls of supper he threw up over the transom and announced: 'Well, so much for the first course, what's for dessert?' The *InterSpray* brand of humour lived on.

We drifted around off the Spanish coastline looking for fickle breezes. At sunset, while we lay becalmed off the loom of Cape Finisterre lighthouse, Duggie was standing sentinel in the bows playing the bagpipes to appease the wind gods. The first time some of us heard him tuning up his pipes, in the English Channel, we thought it was a squeal from a ship's rat in the bilges. Nothing had changed, according to some Sassenachs. A solitary Spanish fishing boat motored past on the oily swell, its bemused crew waving at the mad Scot and Englishmen

Catching the tail end lash of Hurricane Charlie: John helming, Jeff riding shotgun

out in the setting sun as the incongruous sound wailed across the waters.

Half an hour later Duggie was being congratulated for successfully piping up a breeze. Most of the fleet were 50 miles west. Jeffes, having decided there was great big area of nothing to the west gambled on sticking close to the shore, hoping for a land or sea breeze effect. We ghosted along the coast at 5 knots under moonlight like a stealth bomber. The smell of eucalyptus trees and land five miles away was in our nostrils. It was slow and frustrating as the wind filled in and died.

Dawn on day 6 found us totally becalmed off the Portuguese coast near Vigo and going backwards. We had slipped to ninth place again. The log had optimistically recorded: 'With luck the dawn will bring some breeze. Beef in Guiness certainly did, and with it some deck frogs who croaked till dawn.'

To keep themselves occupied in the calms crews on other yachts resorted to guitar lessons and canvas work – Valerie Elliott on *Rhone-Poulenc* made a canvas bucket, but planned to wear it as a hat at the Equator. Jeff tried serenading the wind gods with his mouth organ and by mid-morning John Davis took a trip up the mast to check for chafe. In preparation for all the spinnaker work ahead we decided to reduce chafe by running the spinnaker halyards outside the mast, through plastic pipe sections taped to the spreader roots as fairleads.

By afternoon someone noted in the log: 'Scots git up the mast dropping spanners all over the deck.'

The noon to noon run was a pitiful 80.8 miles. Trying to get the boat moving with the lightweight spinnaker we put a tiny tear in it as it caught on the end of the spinnaker pole. The crew's frustrations were evident when sailmaker Patrick was anxious to get the kite down before it split. John Davis pointed out in no uncertain terms that we were racing and already behind. '. . . at this rate we'll never get to Rio!'

The sail stayed up and mercifully intact. By afternoon a breeze had sprung up sending our al fresco luncheon party spilling across the cockpit. The off watch

Spinnaker trimming and teamwork improved all the way to Rio

sat around at lunchtime and John decided that we all had a gift from the Gods with 2,000 miles of tropical sailing ahead.

By late afternoon there were four dolphins played on our bow wave. *British Steel II*, some 60 miles west, were finding conditions calm and staged a table tennis tournament aboard.

A telex from Chay said: 'I'm meeting a couple of journalists over the next few days. Can you tell me how you managed to race across the notorious Bay of Biscay and still be so close together, especially as we are told that you are all a bunch of amateurs who can't sail.'

The fleet was spread across the 42nd parallel, from the Portuguese coast to some 150 miles west, as skippers followed different hunches, theories and old wives' tales interpreting weather information. The weather was predominantly high pressure to the west and south so Jeffes opted for eastern side of the course, admitting: 'I am not comfortable being exposed on the edge of the fleet at this stage in case something develops on the other edge.'

There was no let up in sail trim. Adjusting sheets, luff tension, outhauls and tweaking kicker tension. 'Spinnaker sheets should never be still. If they're not moving they're not working,' said Jeffes, ordering the mainsheet be winched in a 'thrang' – some Scottish word for fine tuning, he claimed.

We continued to live dangerously, shadowing the coast under spinnaker and a crescent moon and hoping yachts to the west were struggling.

Spain finally produced the low pressure area we'd hoped for. We had a tail wind and being closest to the shore we got it first as the offshore yachts ran out of wind. Overnight we were trucking along under our spinnaker staysail combination at speeds touching 12 knots.

North Sails Guide to Trimming didn't give everyone confidence at steering downwind: 'If you can balance a broomstick on your nose while running at top speed over seaweed covered rocks, then you understand the principle behind corrective steering,' it stated.

On John Davis's watch from 2200, with

Ricky and Juliet, we covered 27.9 miles in three hours – one of our best runs of the race so far. Helming 40 tons of yacht at these speeds under a starlit sky with the big kite flying gave us all the buzz we'd been looking for.

We moved up five positions in six hours overnight to third place overall, three miles behind race leader *Hofbrau*, who reported: 'Ocean sailing is a game of chess, unfortunately without any weatherfaxes we are only allowed to see half the chess board.'

It wasn't the weatherfax that had helped us, though. It was simply a gamble that paid off.

At 0400 a telex from the Petersfield RHQ asked: 'How are you going so fast?'

Our 24-hour run at noon on day seven was 196.3. We were all very elated. On the afternoon chat show we learned we had taken the lead from *Coopers & Lybrand*. Telexes were coming in saying 'How on earth did you do it?'. David Hodgson at International Paint was brief: 'Brilliant!'

The afternoon of day 7 the log recorded 13 knots with 'Slick' Dominic at the wheel. At sunset the skipper bought out the champagne, pouring a libation to the sea gods, and we toasted our success. It was Happy Hour and the log added 'and boy are we happy!'

By now we were hoping to pick up the Portuguese trades. During our rapid progress south the Spectra spinnaker guy had parted twice through chafe in the pole jaws. It sounded like a pistol shot. We dropped the spinnaker, put up the genoa, re-packed the spinnaker, repaired the frayed guy and rehoisted the spinnaker within 30 minutes. The teamwork was finally coming together.

We devised a new method to secure the spinnaker clew to the pole jaws, using a short strop with a snapshackle as a 'fuse'. It cut down on the chafe.

Next morning Julian got his second patient – himself – when he trod on some glass from a broken champagne bottle from last night's celebrations. He also treated Paul Buchanan when he scalded himself with a cup of soup.

InterSpray's medical chest bore the legend: 'INTERSPRAY VETERINARY CLINIC: medicines for animal treatment only.'

Julian was always eager for new challenges to advance his skills and was well known for treating crew ailments with udder cream and a high fibre bran extract called 'Nutrifyba'.

Some of the crew were south of Rio before they read the package:

'1 level measure for cats and toy dogs; 2 level measures for medium sized dogs; 4 level measures daily for large dogs.'

Duggie used to go for Scottish terrier dose. Dump Truck went for the wolfhound portion.

The vet's cream certainly reached the parts udder creams fail to reach. It proved highly efficacious in the treatment of gunwale bum, chapped hands and other skin ailments. *Hofbrau* were also using it and by the time *InterSpray* got to Hobart *Coopers & Lybrand* were udder cream converts, too.

A school of dolphins being chased by killer whales and leaping out of the water in a state of obvious agitation provided an amazing spectacle for those on deck the following afternoon. But we had started to run out of breeze. Day eight's 24-hour run was 211 miles – our best so far – but we were being chased by *Coopers & Lybrand*. Vivien Cherry, who had stuck to the shore, had kept the breeze.

We had also run out of something else. Ship's pursers Ali and Dom took a lot of flak from the crew when a teabag shortage was discovered, to add to the sugar rationing. The curtain rose on the Great Teabag Tiff as Ali lectured the crew members, including those old enough to be her father, on the use (or misuse) of provisions and the merits of tea rationing. Jeff was in full flow with his Mr. Angry act before Ali's exit stage left with the parting shot: 'Well, I did my best!'

A minor disagreement on the course between Julian and Jeff

Jeff was enough to reduce the crew to tears at the best of times.

Ali continued to put in a huge amount of effort and the appreciation wasn't always as evident as it should have been.

The early hours of day nine found us 400 miles off the coast of Morroco and engaged in a midnight match race at 10 knots under spinnaker with *Coopers & Lybrand*, whose masthead light had been spotted at 0100. She crossed our bow on starboard gybe heading WSW. Jeffes was woken and was tracking Vivien's yacht on radar when she called him up on the radio.

'Good morning Paul, I think it's time to take off your yellow jersey,' she said. 'By my calculations we are now ahead.'

'We must stop meeting like this, or they'll all be talking about us,' replied Jeffes, suggesting a race to.Porto Santo, in the Madeira islands, followed by a beach barbecue.

Jeffes admitted: 'It's nice to have company after 1,200 miles, but I must get back to making my boat go faster, I've got a racy lady in front of me.'

'You know it's always ladies first,' said Vivien, having the last word.

Coopers & Lybrand became the fifth Challenge yacht to take the lead in the race, crossing us that evening on opposite gybes less than half a mile ahead. The tail-enders were still 118 miles behind.

'It's question of playing the course or playing the weather, and right now we're playing for the weather,' Jeffes told the deck watch. 'I'm in the business of beating her over the next 5,000 miles not the next five-minutes.'

Plotting the tracks of yachts behind us showed that those furthest east were getting the best breeze. We were trying to get inshore to get the breeze off the African coast while laying a course through Canaries to our chosen crossing point at the ITCZ, 26°W.

By 0400 on day 10 there was a touch of mayhem on the foredeck as we gybed the spinnaker in 20 knots and found the guy wouldn't release from the dipped pole. Much shouting and confusion went on between the cockpit team and foredeck. Having rigged a main boom preventer, a pole brace, spinnaker guys, downhaul, and staysail sheets we'd simply run out of winches in the cockpit and the lines were all bar taut. At one point the boom swept the deck three times with the preventer hanging loose and threatening to scythe someone's head off, or the steering pedestal. Tired people easily make wrong decisions.

Four hours later we had a spinnaker wrap. We'd damaged the wrap net, but saved the lightweight spinnaker, which had a small tear. In 25 knots of wind we put up the starcut kite (a stable, steady sail with smaller shoulders than the corporate kite) and flew it very high with the staysail tacked to the starboard rail. The combination gave us tremendous boat speed. Within two hours the repaired net was back up as we ran over Seine Seamount with the wind gusting to 25 knots. By Sunday evening Vivien was sighted again three miles ahead and we crossed tracks again the following morning.

The fleet was now spread across a 350 mile-wide flank, with *Group 4* furthest west and *Heath Insured*, furthest east. *Heath*, lying eighth, had claimed a record run of 245.1 miles noon-to-noon between October 3 and 4. We were 300 miles offshore.

Weatherfax maps from Senegal and Toulouse suggested more wind on the African Coast than out to sea, but the pilot book talked about the Canaries' land breeze effect. The plan was pass through the Canaries between Gran Canaria and Fuerteventura.

During a picnic lunch on deck, Brian, our safety officer, did a briefing about the onboard fire fighting systems. On the afternoon chat show *Rhone-Poulenc* reported blowing their corporate spinnaker. With no sewing machines aboard, under race rules, someone was going to be busy hand-sewing.

Duggie meanwhile was busy in our galley making scones for tea. 'They'll come in very useful as diving weights,' was the villainous verdict of the vet.

Soon after midnight on day 11 we sent a telex cancelling the Madeira beach party due to rapid progress south and, after John's calculations suggested a shorter route, we gybed to take a course splitting the Canaries between Gran Canaria and Tenerife, where the party was relocated 'on one of the topless beaches.'

We had a magnificent run in the early hours of the morning, catching the notorious wind acceleration zone which funnelled through the passage between the two islands. The wind here can increase from 10 to 30 knots in a matter of seconds. The local blasts are named 'mosquitoes' because they are only heard when about to bite. In daytime the gusts can be predicted as the wind ruffles the water and changes it to a darker colour.

'We're cooking with the gas now, keep those numbers coming up,' Jeffes told the helmsman as the log registered 8.9, 9.5, 10.6 and 12 knots. We shot through the gap as huge masses of air carried by the tradewinds squeezed through the channel separating the islands. We switched on the deck floodlight to illuminate our Courtaulds' spinnaker logo. It would have made a spectacular picture. Where were the photographers when we needed them? The twinkling lights of Las Palmas beckoned, but the beach party turned out to be a figment of the skipper's fevered imagination. It was a pity only one watch at a time could enjoy the spectacle. The good news was that we'd regained the lead as *Coopers & Lybrand* were forced to bear off to avoid the island of Gomera. Vivien lost 30 miles to our overnight run of 90 miles. *British Steel II, Pride of Teesside* and *Heath Insured* were now the threat to our east. But still only 102 miles separated us from 10th placed *Rhone-Poulenc*.

The bad news was that Ricky got a nasty rope burn on his right hand, with instant blisters the size of ping pong balls, when he instinctively grabbed a runaway spinnaker guy as it whipped off a winch.

The skipper, naturally, was concerned about chafe on the Spectra halyards. 'At least your skin will grow again,' he told Ricky. The vet's clinic was busy with another suitable case for treatment. The problem then was to stop Ricky using his hand. Impossible.

We had been flying down to Rio under spinnaker for six days and nights. It was being constantly trimmed with every ounce of drive extracted. The sea temperature was 74°F. This was where the butter melted and you were supposed to turn right, for the Caribbean. But by 0700 we were clearing the islands and reeling off the miles on a direct course for Recife, at the north-west corner of South America. To port the impressive jagged mountain range of Gran Canaria was silhouetted against the dawn sky.

Our first flying fish landed on deck, together with a baby squid. *Calamari a la InterSpray* was not to be on the menu. Paul Buchanan trod on the squid and Ocean Vigil Watchleader Juliet threw the flying fish back to sea, to the exasperation of the hungry breakfast brigade. Two whales were breaching to starboard half a mile away.

Tropics here we come. Out came the *InterSpray* Supporters' Club products – Bergasol's sunblock, Factor 15 suntan cream and lip salve.

This was a strange time for the double-glazing man to call, but in preparation for the Southern Ocean we took the opportunity to double-glaze the dog-house windows with Perspex sheets brought along specially for the purpose.

One of the ship's mascots, Garfield, was 'incarcerated between layers of Perspex in perpetuity,' we telexed home, adding: 'We are confident we'll feel a lot more comfortable in the Southern Ocean and will certainly feel the benefit once the loft insulation and open fire are installed in Rio.'

A great topic of conversation as we headed down the African coast to the Cape Verdes was how different life would be in the Southern Ocean. Tales of terror of sailors strapped in their bunks to stop themselves being thrown around were retold at meal times.

Day 12 saw the fleet split in two – one half (*Hofbrau, Rhone-Poulenc Nuclear Electric Group 4* and *Commercial Union*) heading westward ho' and the rest, including *InterSpray*, keeping close to the African coast. At one point we were just two miles ahead of *British Steel* II. We'd had our worst 24-hour run for six days – just 140 miles. By now we were doing spinnaker peels and gybes with just three or four crew on deck. Fewer people made it much easier with less shouting. 'Every time the spinnaker collapses we lose 10 boat lengths,' the helmsman was told.

In the interests of keeping the boat going faster, the skipper cancelled the lunchtime deck picnics. 'We have a lot of smart guys on our tail and we have to concentrate.' Lunch would now be served in two sittings to the new on watch and off watch in the sweltering galley. The cockpit was becoming a hazardous picnic spot anyway, deck frogs not withstanding.

On the radio show *Coopers & Lybrand* admitted dropping their deck scrubbing brush overboard and since they were going so slowly someone jumped over for it – only to find they couldn't swim fast enough to keep up with the yacht. Vivien had to drop the spinnaker to go back to rescue them in virtually no wind. They did 25 miles that day.

The adverse current encountered in the Canaries Current area suddenly ceased at 1351. 'This is worth noting,' wrote someone in the log, 'because it coincided with a large area of bubbles on an otherwise flat sea.'

Jeff, desperate for something to get his teeth into other than the dehydrated menu of 'five flavours of porridge', emerged on deck with limb-sized sticks of biltong (dried beef jerky). We all thought

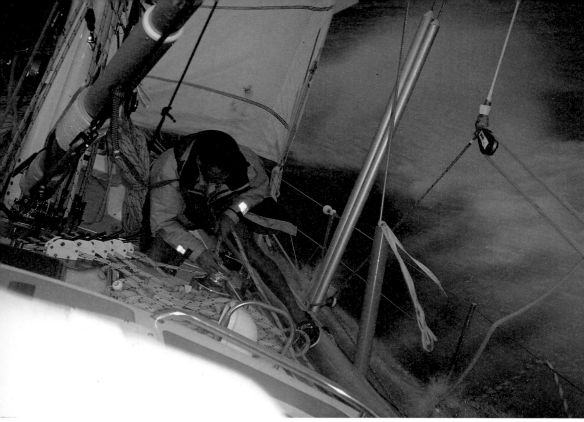

Duggie puts in a reef in the midst of a tropical squall

it looked suspiciously like a mummified corpse – Plummer's perfect murder? Or a DML dockworker discovered behind the cabin lining?

John Davis, meanwhile, nicknamed Crocodile (was it his Aussie accent, or the way he sank his teeth into the McDougalls food?) was sitting in the dunny on dawn standby when he spotted the spinnaker halyards crossed at the masthead. Ten minutes later, having been hoisted to the masthead, he was standing on deck holding one badly chafed halyard. It could have parted at any time, sending our kite on a costly flyer.

Duggie, the other half of the rigging team, was also ascending the 86ft mast as part of the daily chafe patrol. There was no truth in the rumour that it was the only place he could practise his bagpipes.

Two well known sayings entered the language of *InterSpray* at this time: the 'Inner Sanctum' was coined by Paul Buchanan and began to appear in the log book, drawing the attention of the skipper and watch leaders to priority telex messages. There was no Outer Sanctum, however.

The other phrase was Julian's tropical greeting in the heat of the day to the standby watch: 'Barman, a pint of your coldest lager, please!' He got powdered Refresh with reconstituted sea water and was grateful for it.

The discovery of the day was a 15th crew member – a 'glamorous' blonde called Gladys, smuggled aboard by Jeff. Her inflated ego and buoyant personality were put down to the fact that she had a blow-up valve in her back. We worried about Jeff sometimes.

Meanwhile, financial consultant Dominic had put the businessman in the closet for eight months, together with his pin-striped suits, and let out the comedian. As joint purser he was also raiding the stores and running a blackmarket in chocolate bars and wine gums during the night watch. Clandestine moonlit munching sessions were conducted on the afterdeck, where evidence could be disposed of quickly. Ali, meanwhile, was on the hunt for the phantom teabag snatcher. Our ration of 180 teabags per week had run out after four days.

On our 13th day out from Southampton, October 8, we crossed the Tropic of Cancer at 23°30'N 16°57'W. We celebrated with a group photo and also celebrated our fourth day at the head of the fleet – the longest spell so far of any of the five yachts which had held the lead.

British Steel II was still snapping at our heels 12 miles away, her spinnaker visible on the horizon. In the afternoon we eavesdropped on *British Steel II*'s Giles Trollope being interviewed on the Ed Stewart radio show. It was a yawn as Giles laboriously read out his entire crew list. No mention of *InterSpray* in front. Paul Jeffes gatecrashed the airwaves asking indignantly: 'What about the rest of the yachts?' Trollope had to admit his yacht was no longer in the lead. Stewart was delighted with the spontaneity of our unorthodox broadcast and the BBC asked us to stand by for an interview. Even the Portishead operator, ignoring the fact we'd interrupted private radio traffic, was amused as *InterSpray* stole the show. It certainly added some needle to the competition between us.

Our noon-to-noon run was just 117 miles. At 1600 the entire crew went to the bow to improve boat trim. 'Is this a rebellion or just a weight adjustment?' the log asked. Either way it didn't make any difference.

The skipper, meanwhile, had developed a back problem. Bedsores, said the unsympathetic. The vet devised an orthopaedic bed with plywood storm boards (intended for the deckhouse windows) under his mattress. Having bored the crew rigid with tales of his stiff back the skipper took to his rock hard bunk for his best night's sleep to date.

Trading places in the trades

It was now so hot as we headed towards the Equator that off watch crew were sleeping in the forepeak sail locker. It meant a rude awakening during a rain squall or sail change. We tried rigging a wind scoop with a sail bag over the forehatch to try to and circulate air through the boat. A couple of the crew had small battery-powered fans over their bunks.

The tranquillity and enchantment of the ocean in these conditions worked its spell from sunrise to sunset and by moonlight. Those on deck never tired of contemplating the line where the sea met the sky. Multitudes in towns and cities looked forward every year to their annual escape in the sun lying on a beach. We felt

Great Scott! Ricky adds his pulling power at the mast

privileged to have it all to ourselves for days on end, though there was often shipping around during the night, small fishing vessels as well as bigger ships.

Day 14 found us trucking down the African Coast, 30 miles off Mauritania, under a light spinnaker in 12 knots of breeze. With 1,000 miles-plus to the Equator, we needed to start breaking away from the coast soon to cross the doldrums – the dreaded airlock around the Equator between the northern and southern hemisphere trade winds.

Although our tracks were 20-30 miles apart, the evening chat show revealed *British Steel II* just a mile ahead in terms of distance to Rio. But we weren't giving our lead up easily. There were still 2,993 miles to the finish and it could all change when we hit the brick wall at the Equator.

To prove the fleet's fluctuating fortunes, last-placed *Coopers & Lybrand* had managed only 25 miles in 12 hours and were now 170 miles behind us, having led the race a few days ago.

Richard Tudor came on the radio inquiring: 'What's your boat speed?'

'Ah yes, which dial is that?' queried Jeffes. 'Do you have any current where you are?'

'Only sultanas,' replied Tudor.

'Any Spanish speaking crew members?' quizzed Jeffes. 'We could do with a translator for weatherfaxes.'

'Only one Welshman,' came the reply.

'You'll be alright when you get to Patagonia then,' added Jeffes.

Tudor had been studying his charts and found a place called Alcatraz in the Cape Verdes islands.

'Perhaps they could lock you up for a couple of days,' he inquired hopefully of our skipper.

Our GPS was giving us an ETA for Rio of 0600 on October 22.

A focus of interest among Challenge crews was the Ocean Vigil project, with *Pride of Teesside* spotting turtles and *Group 4* sighting seven sperm whales

alongside, as close as 10ft. *Rhone-Poulenc* were on a fishing expedition – catching seven fish.

That night, 80 miles off the African coast in shorts and T-shirts, we revelled in some of the most memorable and magical sailing of the trip so far. A pastel shaded sunset of magenta and gold, with a 20-23 knot breeze and a water temperature of 84°F. An unexpected splash alongside the cockpit revealed a pair of dolphins glistening like sleek black torpedoes and racing our hull through the silver, moonlit waters. Swooping and gliding, they trailed their own glowing lights beneath the water.

Standing in *InterSpray's* pulpit as she ploughed her thunderous bow wave down the Atlantic, the surge of power felt awesome as the bow rose and fell through 12ft, the helmsman a silhouette in the glow of the compass.

The yacht's phosphorescent wake was 'a trail of sparks from the friction of our hull', according to Dominic, who tried to convince Duggie of this strange law of physics.

At dawn there were flying fish on deck and the smell of fresh bread rolls being passed to the watch on deck through the galley hatch – and the prospect of another perfect day's run in the trades.

Buchanan wrote: 'Paul's theory is that only a small percentage of people in the world go sailing. And a smaller percentage of them ever experience such perfect conditions for so many days. So we are experiencing something very rare.'

InterSpray's run for that night was 110 miles to *British Steel II's* 103. We had the lead back by the slimmest of margins. But later on the morning of day 15 Richard had his own dramas aboard. He put out a medical alert after crewman Rob Haines lost the top third of his thumb when it was caught in the spinnaker tripping line as he tied a bowline and the spinnaker guy came off a winch. Julian offered medical advice over the radio, but they were already administering pain killers. Richard Tudor reflected that as accidents go at least it made people aware of the power of their machines.

Calculations at the end of the day showed the gap between *British Steel II* and *InterSpray* was 42 miles, but the distance between us to Rio was only nine miles. It really had developed into a two-yacht race with the third yacht, *Heath Insured*, 50-60 miles astern. The rest of the fleet were trailing us 200-300 miles away. We celebrated being back in front with a can of warm beer on deck and wine with dinner.

Vivien Cherry was now some two and a half days behind us, with 3,114 miles to Rio, six days after leading.

On day 16 the duel continued as we exchanged the lead with Richard's crew and crossed the halfway mark to Rio. Even Richard claimed: 'We're going to have to stay together , this is becoming a match race.'

East of the Cape Verdes and off the African coast of Senegal we recorded our best noon-to-noon run of 215 miles so far. It was a critical point of the race for us, since we believed that the first yacht out of the doldrums and into the south-east trades would undoubtedly win.

Nuclear Electric was still having problems with their Sat-com and reported: 'I hope they give us a couple of crates of pigeons for communications when we get to Rio. That way at least if *they* don't work we can eat them!'

The flying fish patrol found five more on the foredeck. During the day you could see squadrons of flying fish – whole flocks of them – erupting from the sea and skimming across the wave tops at 30mph, banking left and right. These little creatures, some 9ins long, swam below the surface with folded wings and when danger approached (like *InterSpray*, or a predator) they launched themselves out of the water like Polaris and remained airborne for what seemed like a minute,

gliding distances of up to 300ft. Their Latin name is exocoetids and the French named the Exocet missile after them. As they did their fly pasts while we were sandbagging on the weather rail, we used to whistle the theme from the *Dam Busters March* and salute them.

It was now so hot and sticky that most of the crew had taken to sleeping on the foredeck. No one wore more than shorts, except the girls. The log recorded after midnight: 'JP (Jeff) no longer asleep on foredeck. No splash heard so inspection of boat carried out. He had obviously fallen through the open hatch and is now asleep in the sail locker . . . noisily.'

With no shade on deck and temperatures topping 40°C the deck was too hot to stand on and the Mars Bars below were melting. A man could easily lose several pints of water a day and dehydration caused a loss of muscular potential – no good for the winchmen. Some folk said the biggest enemy at sea was boredom and monotony. But with sail trimming, repairs, cooking, watching dolphins and flying fish, putting the world to rights and writing up journals, there wasn't time to be bored.

Our community of fourteen had grown into a close-knit team, totally concentrating all our physical and mental efforts on the race. With two deck watches and a standby watch, crew came and went like ships in the night. The saloon was rarely crowded, since people were either off watch asleep or working on deck. Only at mealtimes did we all come together.

InterSpray's community was self-contained and included several cooks, a couple of engineers, a ship's doctor, a waterworks manager, a Sat-coms operator, and even an ecologically-aware garbage collector, who came on deck at night to dump his biodegradable rubbish overboard. The plastics and tin cans were washed, compacted and stowed for when we reached Rio. The standard of hygiene on board was very high, thanks to Julian's

INTERSPRAY'S RACE AROUND THE WORLD

Above: concentrated sail trimming with Dominic and Julian, while John helms.
Below: crossing the tropic of Cancer, complete with homemade signpost

Above: Neptune (Jeff Plummer) is returned to the deep on the end of a spinnaker balyard. Below: Paul Buchanan gets 'dunked in the gunk'

training. The yacht was cleaned and disinfected below every day from sail locker to stern.

Over the next two days we continued our intensive match race for pole position within shouting distance of *British Steel II*. *The Times* headline back home was 'InterSpray takes lead in transatlantic tussle'. *The Daily Telegraph*'s sailing correspondent thought that the two crews must have come to a gentleman's agreement, so regularly were we swapping the lead

There was a great kerfuffle on deck on day 18 when Ricky sighted a big fin. It turned out to be a large red, unmarked steel buoy floating past in the middle of the ocean. A surreal sight. It had probably been drifting around out there for months, even years. We were glad we weren't sailing a plastic or wooden boat. Strangely, the depth sounder registered 6.5 metres at around the same time. An uncharted shoal patch in mid ocean?

Richard Tudor did hit something around this time – a basking shark.

We could not get any weatherfax maps from Senegal or Dakar (we may have been too far away) and Olinda, at the north-east corner of Brazil, didn't seem be to transmitting either. Race HQ were sending weather information through for those whose fax machines were playing up.

We were now some ten degrees north of the Equator in the region of the doldrums with its oppressive heat, heavy black skies streaked with forked lightning and 40 knot squalls. Even the Portishead Radio operator, who had heard tales of stowaway Gladys, inquired about how she was coping with the heat. By the time of the first daylight watch change at 0600 it was already hot.

This watery limbo between the two hemispheres seemed a desert as far as far as marine life was concerned. The fear of being becalmed for days on a vast, motionless mirror played on everyone's nerves. Jeffes announced that he was holding his breath for the next 300 miles. 'The longer we sit in this latitude the more it spooks me.'

Instead of calms we got black squalls. It was like sailing off the edge of the world. Thick cloud cover blotted out the horizon. The phrase 'as black as the inside of a cow' took on a new meaning for the vet. The deck floodlight had to be switched on to see the spinnaker to trim it. We peeled from the lightweight kite to the heavyweight just in time as Jeff was pulled across the deck holding the spinnaker sheet with three turns around the winch.

Quotes of the night.

Skipper: 'My job is to reduce the risks.'

Crew: 'That's why we're flying the spinnaker in 40 knots?'

'For a place that supposed to have no wind this is bloody exciting,' said Jeffes as a 45 knot squall passed over us. 'No wonder ancient mariners thought there were wind and sea gods with these elemental forces at play.'

Carlton was doing his theatricals, yelling above the shrieking wind in a rich Devon accent; 'She won't stand up to her canvas no more Mr. Onedin, the rig'll carry away. . . '

Julian came on deck to announce that the weatherfax man at Toulouse said we were the middle of the ITCZ (Inter tropical convergence zone) and it was tracking north. At this rate we thought we might creep through before it even noticed us.

'We make hay while the lightning strikes,' said Jeffes, altering our crossing-the-line point from 023° 30'W to 026°W. 'We are halfway through a minefield, except the mines don't explode, you just lose the wind instead.'

On day 19 in another electrical storm we dropped the spinnaker for first time in 14 days and dumped it straight down the forehatch – much to the consternation of Jeff, sleeping there. Then came the rain – 'not so much stair rods as railway sleepers,' claimed Buchanan. It was a novelty changing to hanked on foresails and sailing to windward again under No 1 Yankee and staysail. The crew's washing got another rainwater rinse as *InterSpray*'s Chinese laundry headed south-west with a small hitch-hiker – a hawk exhausted by the winds and blown off course from the African coast. It fluttered down from the first set of spreaders to land on the boom above *InterSpray*'s logo – perfect for Jeff's photograph.

That evening we were being headed by fluctuating breezes and made the decision to tack, going almost from west to east. 'Is this the tack that ruins my career?' speculated Jeffes idly.

The tack brought us to a standstill, wallowing with that painful, familiar sound of the slatting mainsail. It took almost an hour to get her moving again. 'Any fool can sail in a gale or heavy wind, but it takes a genius to sail in light airs, let alone get a 40 ton yacht moving in eight knots of breeze,' said the skipper.

By day 20 it appeared, touch wood, that we'd almost got through the doldrums unscathed, with just 45 minutes becalmed and, hopefully, the door slammed on the opposition astern. *Heath Insured* was now firmly established in second place, having pulled up to within 15 miles behind us. In the morning we received notification that *Hofbrau* had transmitted a distress signal and after several hours of wondering were advised that it had been an accidental alert.

British Steel II seemed to be taking a wild flyer, heading south-east. She was now 100 miles east of us and we guessed she was hoping to get through the ITCZ quicker and into the SE Trades sooner, so she could come back at us with her spinnaker up. We had less than 2,000 miles to go and the mood was buoyant with a noon to noon run of 164 miles and going like stink. Quote of the watch: 'We have a morale problem – it's too high.' The vet was doing 40 press ups by moonlight across the cockpit seats.

Next day we had a cockpit council of war as Richard Tudor's gamble appeared to be paying off. He had broken through the doldrums first and picked up the south-east trades already and our lead was being reduced hourly. He had almost eliminated all of the loss that he took to go east. It was going to be a straight line drag race for the next 750 miles before land and current considerations came into play.

'We've got to sail this boat faster than we've ever sailed it before for the next 1,800 miles,' Jeffes urged. We had 180 miles to go to the Equator.

Distances on the rhumb line to Rio at the 1830 radio round-up showed Richard 23 miles astern and Adrian Donovan 19 miles astern. Furthest away was luckless Will Sutherland, 396 miles back.

The mood of the crew, including the skipper, had become shadowed with pessimism. But John was still hopeful. During the night the skipper had crash trimming and helming courses for crew. It was a cliff hanger but we pushed the boat hard all night with the off watch crew clipped on and sleeping on the weather rail. Jeffes was convinced it was crucial to get to the South American coast to stay in touch with Richard.

From Recife down the coast of Brazil to Rio, it looked from the weather info we had as though it would be a soldier's race with wind and currents behind us.

On day 22, Saturday October 17, Richard crossed the Equator at 0700 local time, but we were further west with 25 miles to go. We passed to starboard two little dimples of rock barely visible in the distance, the tips of underwater mountains, called St Peter and St Paul, that stick up in the middle of the Atlantic, halfway between Africa and South America. By noon we'd covered 182 miles in 24 hours. It was difficult to believe how flat the sea was and the flying fish were back, a sure sign that we were back in the trades.

That evening *InterSpray* finally crossed

the Equator at 2055, counting down the metres on the GPS as we flew along in 23 knots apparent wind with the waves washing the sacrificial patches off the genoa. The champagne was ready to toast Neptune under the tropical moon. The real Crossing the Line ceremony was postponed for daylight. Meanwhile, the off-watch were still hot-bunking, or sandbagging on deck, to keep weight on the high side. Leeward bunks were declared out of bounds with Richard, still in second place, just 9 miles further from Rio and *Heath* 36 miles astern.

That night we had the company of two large seabirds which soared on the updraught from our mainsail like phantoms, lit by the glow of our masthead light. They hovered for six or seven hours and were identified by Julian as Great Shearwaters. 'Neptune's Messengers and Scouts,' claimed King Neptune-Plummer, as he disappeared below to prepare for tomorrow's entertainments.

The following morning there were devilish chuckles, sickly groans and retching sounds coming from the galley as Neptune's slaves gloated over their

Facing page, top: Duggie is christened with the ocean potion. Below: Juliet gets some early morning exercise. Above: tropical trimming – Jeff on sunset spinnaker duties. Below: rolling down to Rio under spinnaker for 14 days

cauldrons preparing the ceremonial Sea Sperm for the Crossing the Equator Ceremony. Julian was invited to pass a medical opinion on the evil-smelling brew which had been festering in the depth of the engine room in a saucepan for seven days. 'I also wanted to see if anyone could stand to look at it without passing out,' admitted Jeff.

Julian suggested dividing it into two blends – one, a sort of week-old salt water custard, with added spaghetti and baked beans, for the baptism, and the other the 'cleansing cream'. That way we all got dunked in the gunk twice. The idea seemed to appeal to Neptune.

Dress for the Ceremony of the Ancient Order of the Deep was optional – swimming trunks advisable. Jeff made a very stagey entrance wearing a silver crown, bearing the words 'Boss of the Sea', with a fetching blue fishnet veil. He was patriotically wrapped in a red ensign. We weren't sure where he had purchased his underpants from. The same place as Gladys, we guessed.

Ricky Scott in eye-patch was Neptune's henchman, Captain Black Beard, who prodded reluctant victims with his trident.

Each crew member who had not crossed the Equator was expected to present Neptune with a gift (sweets, pencil case, condoms) before being christened with the ocean potion.

At the end of the ceremony, at the suggestion of the skipper, the crew got their own back as Neptune was 'returned to the deep' – attached to a spinnaker halyard.

InterSpray romped along at 10 knots heeled well over as Jeff was flying over the wave tops in a series of spectacular 30mph swoops 30ft out from the yacht, his red ensign cloak streaming in the wind. Simultaneously, while clutching his disintegrating crown and holding onto his shorts, he was performing an eloquent monologue on the perils of the deep. We finally dunked him in the waves and his shorts were ripped off by the force of the water.

For those of us venturing into Southern Latitudes for the first time it was a memorable occasion. Jeff received a standing ovation for his Oscar-winning performance. His next engagement would be deep in the Southern Ocean, after rounding Cape Horn, as Father Christmas.

It took almost the rest of the day to clear up the yacht and ourselves and the celebrations were overshadowed by the news at the end of the day that *British Steel II* were overhauling us and were three miles closer to Rio.

Next morning (day 24), Richard had retained his slender lead, despite our best noon to noon run on the leg so far of 216.5 miles. Our doldrums, it seemed, had come after the real doldrums, as we fell into pockets of frustrating light air and watched as *British Steel II*'s lead built over the next five days from a slender 10 miles to a seemingly unassailable 100 miles.

That night we discussed our game plan in the cockpit examining the charts and swapping strategy under the southern hemisphere stars.

Soon after midnight we witnessed the most spectacular meteorite shower. It was so bright that at first we thought it was a flare astern. The sky was lit up by a green and white light which left a trail as it appeared to fall into the sea somewhere behind us. *Heath Insured*, 35 miles astern, also reported on the radio that they had seen it.

With no weatherfax information coming through, the only forecasts we got were what we picked up from Spencer Drummond at race headquarters. We tried to think of everything we could to make the boat go faster. The off watch and standby watch were summoned to 'sandbag duty' – human ballast, clipped on to the weather rail, we catnapped to keep cool and keep the yacht upright.

Jeffes assured us it could make a difference of a tenth of a knot. 'Big deal,' thought some, 'What difference is that?' By the end of the leg the doubters would have their answer. Over the course of 5,000 miles from Southampton to Rio it could make a difference of 70 miles, or 10 hours' sailing – the margin by which we would be beaten to first place. It was a mistake we wouldn't make again.

By now we had switched charts to one that showed Rio, which increased every-one's sense of anticipation and adrenalin.

Quote of the watch: 'It's difficult to stay level-headed when everything else is tilted.'

Paul Buchanan on helming: 'It's worse when the skipper and two watch leaders are on deck. We've already got at least six skippers on this boat.'

Over the next two days, from day 25 (October 21) Richard Tudor stretched his lead in increments from 27 miles to 39 miles, 63 miles and 99 miles *Commercial Union* were still languishing in the dol-drums more than 1,000 behind us. 'We've run into a hole,' lamented Sutherland.

There was a predicted lull in the wind near Rio which was expected to slow down the leaders. With *British Steel II* 70 miles offshore, it was thought by RHQ that *InterSpray*, 50 miles further out, might overtake him. No such luck.

The unrelenting heat continued to be a catalyst for bizarre fashion displays by male crew members. Brian Warr, with a T-shirt wrapped around his head, was either a Lawrence of Arabia look-alike or a stand-in for Ghandi. Dominic's bottom-less wardrobe (in both senses of the word, if you like to include gunwale bum) continued to amaze; there were his Turkish trousers, his fetching long-sleeved Laura Ashley-style blouse and neck scarf, all crowned by a very English floppy cricket hat. His outrageous tropical outfits gained him the nickname Klinger, from MASH.

Carlton, meanwhile, known as Horatio, was sporting a pink eye-patch, after poking himself in the eye with his sunglasses, and practising for Rio's beaches with his pants caught between clenched cheeks.

Around this time Rene's cafe opened for business in the galley, under the proprietorship of Monsieurs Plummer and Gelder. French accents and characters abounded. The *'Allo 'Allo* cafe party lasted for days and the crew voted to ban dumplings and suet pudding from the tropical menu. The best cooking by now was being done in suntan oil.

The food smelled like school dinners and tasted like cardboard. The bread, pasta, powdered milk and fruit drink were fine. Richard Tudor's crew were report-edly eating their way through tinned food (hardly a McDougalls meal in sight) and meal times were a high spot. They would arrive a better fed crew and by the time they neared Rio the extra weight (of tins) was no longer a concern.

On day 28 with just 500 miles to go ('only the equivalent of the Orkneys to Ramsgate,' said Jeffes) there was good news and bad news. We sat in a hole for half a day while *British Steel II* romped along. The good news was that when we found breeze, *Heath Insured* fell into the same hole and were now 63 miles behind.

That night three Wilson's storm petrels took up residence on the deck and we tried to put them in the temporary shelter of the dorade vents as we hit rain squalls with thunder and forked lightning. The wind seemed to be sucked out of the sails. One petrel was named Horace and made an honorary Wind God. He was fed biscuits and honey and housed in a Kit-Kat box. Life can be precious out on the ocean. But next morning Horace was found on his back and was buried at sea with great ceremony. 'But he was only sleeping after the storm', insisted the Birdman of *InterSpray*.

Dawn revealed a steel-grey sky and a sea as still as a graveyard with black storm clouds astern. We had the fastest packing of the genoa yet. We also received a telex

Above: under a threatening tropical sky, John, Duggie, Alison and Brian try to whistle up some wind. Below: Chay Blyth shakes hands with the Scribe as InterSpray arrives in Rio. Facing page: sandbagging duty on the sidedeck. We catnapped to keep cool and keep the yacht upright.

from Chay Blyth to call Rio Yacht Club when we were within 300 miles.

Richard Tudor was giving gave his ETA at 0700 local time tomorrow, Sunday – 15 hours for a distance of 165 miles, showing an average speed of 11 knots. It turned out to be optimistic.

Our ETA, with 260 miles to go at 8 knots, was 32 hours away at 0100 hours Monday. We managed to improve on it.

The worry now was that we might lose the breeze close to the coast of Brazil while the rest of the fleet caught up with us.

On day 30, Sunday October 25, Richard Tudor crossed the finish lines at 1143 local time while we still had 70 miles to go. Our target now was to get in on the same day. Alistair Hackett, Fleet Manager, came on the radio from Rio Yacht Club to advise us to fill our water tanks before coming in because the water in the harbour was so polluted, but the skipper was not about to jeopardise our speed by taking on extra weight.

As the coast of Brazil and some impressive verdant islands appeared through the Sunday afternoon heat haze, a fantastic breeze kicked in and we had some our most spectacular sailing of the leg along the Brazilian coast, past Cabo Frio, surfing at up to 13 knots in 30 knots of following wind. It went on all afternoon and even after sunset. It was our first sight of land since the Canaries.

The course to the finish line off Copacabana Fort took us inshore, past the famous conical rock of Sugar Loaf mountain, to a lit buoy, and along Copacabana Beach. Gybing for the buoy in the darkness seemed fraught when we couldn't find the mark, so we dropped the spinnaker and with it lost the wind as we continued, ghosting along under genoa.

The log at 2000 stated: 'Can't find bloody marker buoy anywhere!' That was because it wasn't lit. Eagle-eyed Alison spotted its silhouette blocking a strip of beach lights.

The illuminated Statue of Christ the Redeemer, arms out-stretched, watched us from 2,300ft high up on Corcovado mountain. Below the thousands of lights of favelas (shanty towns) shimmered on the mountainsides behind Ipanema. The girls from Ipanema were somewhere ahead, with the flashing lights of night-clubs, bars and restaurants.

We finally crossed the line at 2332 GMT (21.32 local time), having taken 29 days 12 hours and 27 minutes to sail 5,107 miles from the start line in the Solent. InterSpray had a useful cushion for the long haul to Hobart.

It seemed almost an anti-climax. In the darkness there were no searchlights, no foghorns or klaxons, no one to greet us. We dropped the mainsail, for the first time since Southampton, and started the engine to motor back to Sugar Loaf and the exclusive Iate Clube do Rio de Janeiro some 10 miles away.

Soon a launch appeared alongside with some cheering Brazilians who didn't speak English but began singing. Jeff started doing a samba on the foredeck. Duggie went below to get his bagpipes. If that didn't confound them nothing would.

As we came in Botafogo Bay, Chay and the Challenge team, with Greg Bertram, arrived alongside in a launch with club officials and champagne. We dropped anchor under the shadow of Sugar Loaf, half a mile from Rio yacht club for a deck party that went on after midnight.

For some, it was difficult to comprehend that we'd sailed over 5,000 miles. The Rites of Passage to Rio, the longest voyage any of us, including the skipper, had undertaken, were a curtain raiser to the next act, the psychological Everest of rounding Cape Horn.

But even the fact that British Steel II had arrived 10 hours ahead of us couldn't mar the thrill of the finish. We had tasted a kind of victory, with InterSpray leading the fleet for some 12 days from Spain down to the Equator.

We had only been at sea for 30 days, but it could have been a lifetime. We had lived in our own time capsule racing across the ocean, oblivious to the outside world, as remote as if we were on a spacecraft orbiting the moon. The news that Conservative ladies in Cheltenham had been marching in support of miners threatened with redundancy by Mr. Heseltine, and the pound crisis that had rocked the City of London, was met with consternation by a few and indifference by most. Drinks ashore on the yacht club verandah were what interested us. It was too late tonight for steaks, or hotel beds but we toasted our success with beers and with the crew of *British Steel II*, who told us they had been sitting in a hole for four hours before they crossed the line watching as we shortened their lead.

Jeffes had kept his promise and 'made a nonsense' of his own prediction of the time taken to sail the first leg – 33 days 7 hours and 29 minutes – part of a Courtaulds' competition for employees to better his guess and win a free round-the-world trip.

Among those who greeted us that night in Rio was Steven Sharpe, manager of the trade and retail paint division at Courtaulds International (Brazil), and his wife Roberta. They didn't know then, but they had won the round-the-world trip, as had Don Smith, export manager of Courtlands Coatings in New Zealand, and his wife Barbara.

Our first night in Rio we slept on the yacht. We were two days ahead of schedule and Rio yacht club were not ready for us when we took water taxis ashore for breakfast. The waters of the green capital of the world looked and smelled decidedly murky. An open sewer.

Ashore at the dock workers' cafe we savored fresh orange juice, toast with butter and Brazilian coffee. After hot baths at the Luxor Hotel Continental, off Copacabana beach, our first dinner ashore was at Marius, one of Rio's most popular *churrascaria rodizo*. Here an endless selection of barbecued meats were sliced from the skewer straight on to your plate, with a mouth-watering array of side dishes. You could regulate the speed at which courses kept arriving by using flip cards on the table directing the waiter to be 'fast', 'slow' or 'stop'. But Rio hadn't reckoned on 12 starving sailors, plus Dump Truck Brockman and Big Ricky, who could eat a South American cattle herd between them. And practically did.

Early the following evening, *Heath Insured* sailed in to take third place, with a time of 30 days 9 hours and 54 minutes.

Two days after *InterSpray*'s arrival there was a photo finish between three yachts off Copacabana beach. After more than 5,000 miles of ocean racing, 59 seconds separated *Pride of Teesside*, who had destroyed a spinnaker in her last push for the coast, and *Group 4*. *Hofbrau*, less than 100 metres behind, finished nearly two minutes later. On corrected time, *Hofbrau* moved into fifth place when *Group 4*'s half-hour time penalty was applied for being early over the Southampton start line.

'It was an amazing cliff-hanger. The skippers must be nervous wrecks,' said Chay Blyth.

John Chittenden and *Nuclear Electric* had an exasperating finish the following morning, becalmed within sight of the finish line after blowing two spinnakers in a bid to catch the yachts ahead. One mile from the line the wind had died and for some seven hours the crew waited and watched while *Rhone-Poulenc* and *Coopers & Lybrand* eroded their 50 mile lead. At one point the crew – their 'L' plates still attached to the yacht's stern – had to drop anchor for fear of being blown on to Copacabana beach. At 0645 local time, *Nuclear Electric* crossed the line to hold on to her seventh place, though less than 12 minutes separated her from *Rhone-Poulenc*. Eight minutes later *Coopers & Lybrand* were over the line.

The Challenge fleet was one big family, but no one would be happy until the troubled tenth yacht, *Commercial Union*, arrived six days later.

Before midnight, John Davis and a scratch crew of eight took *InterSpray* out to meet *Commercial Union*, in a gesture of solidarity. *Hofbrau* and *Pride of Tees-side* went, too. 'We knew the skipper and crew had been through a difficult period and had more than their share of bad luck. We also realised that there but for grace of god go I,' said John.

Typically, *Commercial Union* were becalmed when *InterSpray* met them. But at 0258 local time, after a record number of days becalmed, first in the doldrums and later off the Brazilian coast, she crossed the finish line, nearly nine days behind the leader. Will Sutherland, skipper of the yacht, whose sponsor had the ironic slogan in the Official Race Programme 'We're right behind you all the way', had a mutiny on his hands. Things had got to the point where the crew had conspired, while Sutherland was asleep, to telex Race HQ with a plea for his dismissal on arrival in Rio.

Troubles between skipper and crew had begun before the yacht even left the Solent. They had suffered a four hour penalty for crossing the start line early and the crew had expressed to Chay Blyth after the Ushant-Fastnet race a crisis of confidence in their skipper's abilities. Blyth reportedly convinced the crew to give their skipper another chance. He also told Sutherland he had to get the crew on his side by the time he reached Rio.

As dawn broke over the city, two crew members performed a mock execution on *Commercial Union*'s deck. One, wearing dark glasses and a balaclava marked 'tactician', tapped a white stick and led his crew mate with a rope around his neck and a bag over his head, marked 'navigator'. *The Times* yachting correspondent, Barry Pickthall, observed 'the navigational duties fall to the skipper in this race.' An effigy in oilskins was hoisted on a halyard. It was a macabre sight.

Sutherland, who had left the yacht at dawn, faced with the crew's loss of faith, was forced to resign. The official press release referred to 'communications problems between the skipper and crew'. Later that same day Sutherland was wishing success to his replacement, Richard Merriweather, at 27 the youngest skipper in the fleet.

Chay's Challenge sailed into troubled waters once again, five days later on November 9. Jinxed *Rhone-Poulenc* found their skipper, John O'Driscoll, himself a last-minute replacement for Alec Honey, had also decided to withdraw from the race 'because of other pressures'. It was just a week before the fleet was due to set off for the hazardous second leg, around Cape Horn and into the Southern Ocean.

O'Driscoll's official reason for quitting was that he wanted to return to England to concentrate on his career after retiring from the Navy. But the decision was made amidst reports of personality clashes on board, not helped by the presence in Rio of French Whitbread winner, Lionel Pean, who was assisting in crew training.

Pean had already declared: 'From this race will come fantastic stories, both triumphant and incredibly sad.'

That Blyth had to replace two skippers at the first stop-over of his round the world race was an extraordinary state of affairs. His judgement in selecting skippers was being questioned in some quarters. This time he drafted in his old friend and rival Peter Phillips (57), a professional multihull racer and larger than life ex-policeman.

Phillips, who has sailed a quarter of a

Journey's end under the shadow of Sugar Loaf mountain

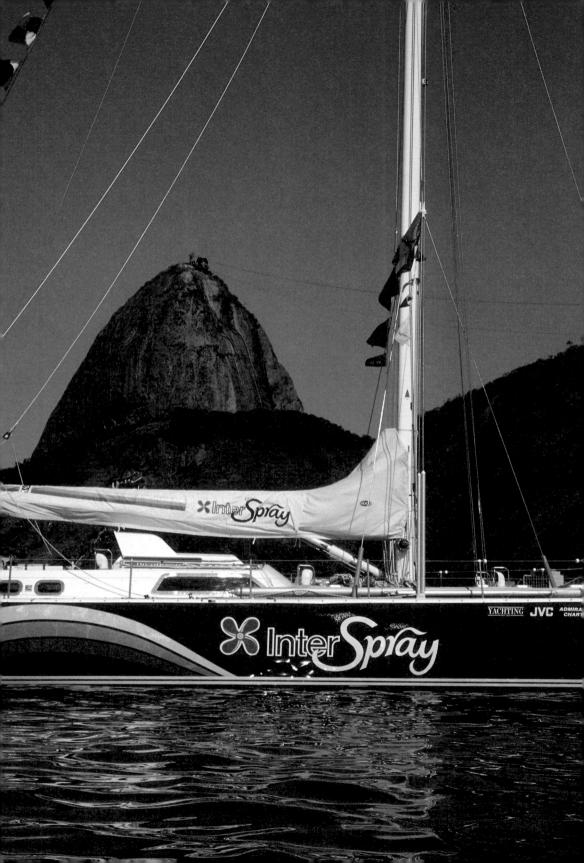

million miles in ten years, met *Rhone-Poulenc's* crew and declared: 'I told them I would be with them all the way to the finish. If anyone's getting off this boat it will be them, not me!'

Blyth also predicted that: 'Barring accidents the skippers we have now are the ones who will finish the race.'

It was ironic that the professional skippers' drop-out rate so far had turned out to be double that of the so-called amateur sailors – whose tenacity cynics had doubted. David Johnson (56), who had suffered chronic seasickness on *Nuclear Electric*, was the only crewman to withdraw from the race at this point. And even he would be back for the final leg home.

Race Leg 1 Southampton to Rio de Janeiro

Placing	Yacht Name	Arrive	Time GMT	Days	Hrs	Mins	Secs
					Leg Time		
1st	British Steel II	25 Oct	13:43:26	029	02	38	26
2nd	InterSpray	25 Oct	23:32:25	029	12	27	25
3rd	Heath Insured	26 Oct	20:59:20	030	09	54	20
4th	Pride of Teesside	27 Oct	19:06:04	031	08	01	04
5th	Hofbrau Lager	27 Oct	19:08:55	031	08	03	55
6th	Group 4	27 Oct	19:07:03	031	08	32	03
7th	Nuclear Electric	28 Oct	08:45:26	031	21	40	26
8th	Rhone-Poulenc	28 Oct	08:57:03	031	21	52	03
9th	Coopers & Lybrand	28 Oct	09:05:55	031	22	00	55
10th	Commercial Union	03 Nov	04:58:45	037	19	53	45

Sambas, spinnakers and silk underwear

Here we were in the sunshine land of the samba, carnival, nightclubs, Ronnie Biggs, and dental floss – that's what they call the minimalist bikinis, posing pouches and thongs which adorn the Brazilian body beautiful.

'Carry as little cash as possible. Only take what you are prepared to lose. Expect your bags to rifled while you're away from the hotel. Don't carry any valuables and don't fight back or give chase,' cautioned a note to *InterSpray*'s crew, adding: 'Children carry out most muggings.'

'Rio,' said Paul Buchanan 'has the culture of the bottom. Everywhere there are rear ends that would stop the traffic in London.' Paul claimed to have discovered something he called 'the three second rule.'

'In Brazil few women make eye contact with you. If they do, they are checking you out. If they do it for three seconds you're fixed up,' he claimed. We never found out if the goggle-eyed Buchanan ogle had worked.

Meanwhile Rio yacht club turned out to be a miniature town, employing 408 staff (a lot of them security guards). It had 3,000 members, most of them non-sailing social ones. Its facilities included a sauna, manicure and hairdressing, swimming pool, and air-conditioned restaurants.

But from the crew's point of view the shore-based organisation for the Challenge was a shambles. In spite of lists telexed a week before arrival, spares were not produced as needed. Brazilian bureaucracy lived down to expectations. Customs men were first on strike, then on a go-slow, and finally bribed into a grudging release of goods.

International Paint's local contacts gave helpful advice and the friendliness and welcome of the *Cariocas* (Rio inhabitants) compensated for the lack of facilities.

Being anchored off the club in the bay was a nightmare. The water taxis were unreliable and, with no direct radio contact with Challenge shore-base, the simplest jobs took an eternity.

There were compensations: crew visited nightclubs and flew off with wives and girlfriends to explore the Amazon and the unspoiled *Costa Verde* (Green Coast). Trisha, Carolyn, Carol, Thomasina, and

INTERSPRAY'S RACE AROUND THE WORLD

Crew relax on the schooner **Black Caesar,** *after their coach hijacking adventure*

Caroline had arrived in Rio, and there was a surprise visit by Duggie's mother, Jessica, and sister, Julia. Dominic's boys, Giles and Keiron, were on the Rio rampage.

Dinner in Ipanema's top fish restaurant left us dividing up a bill of national debt proportions. Inflation in Rio must go up by the minute and by the time Carlton had worked out his share of the bill in *cruzados* and *cruzeiros*, Paul Buchanan claimed he needed to negotiate a new exchange rate for his travel cheques.

As first-legger, it was my turn, reluctantly, to jump ship with an autographed Rio de Janeiro Yacht Club T-shirt, signed by all the customers and staff at Rene's Cafe. Monsieur Dominic, who made the presentation speech, demonstrated an eloquent 'gift of zee gob'.

Our 'walk in the sun' to Rio (as Peter Phillips called it) had been exhilarating, and whilst I wasn't going to miss the dehydrated five-flavoured porridge, the twilight spinnaker peels, or sleeping on the weather rail, I *would* miss the companionship and humour of my shipmates,

who were about to enter a different dimension of the race. They would need their sense of humour in the Southern Ocean.

As Barry Ford, our second-legger, set foot in Rio, Alison tripped and broke a bone in her foot in Copacabana. *InterSpray* acquired an extra one-legger.

The high spot of the Rio stop-over was the crew's outing aboard the pirate schooner *Black Caesar,* which involved hi-jacking a coach and running a police road block.

The coach to take the crew to Brazil's palm-fringed beaches failed to turn up. Then the replacement coach broke down outside a cafe, where an old man sat by the lavatories selling toilet paper, and tut-tutting loudly if more than a foot was requested. As the driver disappeared in search of a replacement coach, with our co-host for the day, International Paint's representative Steven Sharpe, *InterSpray*'s mechanic went into action. 'Bilge Rat' Brian dived head first into the engine compartment to hot-wire the ignition. In seconds it fired . . . and then stopped.

In a scene reminiscent of the Keystone Cops, the crew tried push-starting the 52-seater coach. First backwards, with Brian half in the engine bay, and local traffic diving for cover. Then forwards, with Brian entirely inside the engine compartment getting to grips with the ignition. (It wasn't a good advert for *InterSpray*'s safety officer.) Then backwards, as Brian attached a piece of string to the solenoid. Finally, triumphantly, forwards as the engine rumbled into life.

The other co-host, Johnnie Faharri, a larger than life presenter of sailing programmes on Brazilian television, took the wheel as the *InterSpray* roadshow headed south, behind schedule. Steven had literally missed the bus. He arrived back at the empty car park with the driver, head in hands, lamenting the hijack of his coach.

Johnnie, meanwhile, casually warned his nervous passengers there was a police check point ahead and the coach would be stopped, unless the cops were asleep or having lunch. They were and it wasn't.

Arriving at Paroti, the crew spent the day in deserted bays, swimming from the schooner and eating fish fresh from the fisherman's spear and cooked by a local restaurant. It turned out to be quite a birthday for Julian, who finished up playing doctor to Trish when she gashed her leg climbing up a ladder after swimming.

Steven managed to catch up with the bus in his car, but Duggie missed the trip entirely. As unofficial Piper-in-Chief to the fleet, he had received from Chay a three line whip, to play at the *British Steel II* wedding of the year between Mike Martin and Carol McBean.

At another crew outing, for the Challenge prizegiving in Rio, Jeff Plummer won the unofficial Challenge Dance Trophy when he joined a local samba troupe in their cabaret performance.

The great weatherfax cliffhanger

Rio was proving to be a watershed for the Challenge project when the Great Weatherfax Cliffhanger loomed, adding to the turmoil over the resignation of two skippers. For a while the two events overshadowed everything else. Some pessimists thought the project's credibility was in the balance.

But Chay had weathered as many storms ashore as he had at sea. Confronted with a crisis, he was predictably pugnacious.

Discontent by some yacht crews over their weatherfax equipment led several sponsors, including *Hofbrau*'s brewers, Hall & Woodhouse, and the Teesside Development Corporation, to take legal advice before finally ruling out an appeal against the results of leg one.

There was an absurd suggestion at one point that the results of the first leg should be declared null and void and the race should start again from Rio on equal terms.

The suggestion that the first three yachts into Rio had an unfair advantage was nonsense as far as *InterSpray* was concerned. The success of our game plan (including sticking to the Spanish coast and our course through the Canaries) was based on a hunch and a gamble.

Skippers signed a statement to the effect that no yacht was satisfied with the standard of weatherfax information and the results of leg one should stand. The ethos of the Challenge was to promote seamanship skills, which should not be compromised by protests over equipment failure, part and parcel of ocean sailing.

There may have been an element of

computer illiteracy among some crews. They hadn't all studied the instruction booklet. The weatherfax machines had, after all, been delivered to yachts the night before the Southampton start.

Mike Golding, skipper of *Group 4*, was vociferous about his lack of weatherfax maps on leg one, but race organisers were rumoured to have found faults on only two of the ten fax machines – but they wouldn't say on which yachts. *InterSpray*'s had worked adequately, and we got second place. *Coopers & Lybrand*'s worked fine, and she came ninth.

The controversy was to roll on until the last minute.

Each yacht's weatherfax computer hardware was replaced for leg two and Chay, wanting to avoid any repetition of controversy, sought agreement from all ten skippers in Rio that the machines had been installed in working order and there could be no redress if they subsequently failed.

Hours before the start of leg two, he called a skippers' meeting and gave an ultimatum that unless skippers unanimously signed a declaration to that effect, the weatherfax machines would be removed from the yachts. Mike Golding declined to sign. He still hadn't managed to obtain a decent weatherfax map.

Andrew Roberts announced that there wasn't time to take the fax machines off the yachts. Chay suggested they should disable the machines – one suggestion was to put Sikaflex sealant in the interface sockets.

Finally, at the 11th hour, a *Group 4* crew member appeared waving a piece of paper, like Chamberlain with his 'peace in our time' message. It was a weatherfax map. Golding was ready to sign the declaration.

Now it was a question of finding Roberts before he Sikaflexed all ten machines.

Another protest from rival skippers forced Richard Tudor to remove a GPS cockpit repeater which he had used in the first leg aboard *British Steel II*. Tudor had written permission from the Challenge management team to install the repeater, but it was felt that it compromised the spirit of the one-design race, in which all boats had equal equipment. Paul Jeffes also had permission for a handheld GPS set, as a back-up. But it hadn't come out of its box and was sent home.

By the end of the first leg, at least three yachts had seriously damaged their corporate kites. Asymmetric spinnakers had been introduced late in the training programme, due to the amount of damage to symmetrical spinnakers by inexperienced crews. On the second leg they would replace the corporate kites.

Countdown for Cape Horn

If the first leg had been a sparring round, the real bare-knuckled boxing match was expected in the 8,800-mile second leg to Hobart. Rounding Cape Horn was the ultimate credential for any seafarer, said Robin Knox-Johnston.

In Rio's benevolent spring sunshine, the prospect of icebergs and meteorological monsters at the bottom of the world created a mood among the crew that varied from the philosophical to the apprehensive. Jeffes put things into perspective by examining the detailed chart of Cape Horn and discussing a contingency plan for heavy weather with *Hofbrau*'s Pete Goss, who was sharing weather information. Goss had consulted three-times Whitbread race yachtsman Skip Novak, who had in-depth knowledge of waters around the Horn, having sailed the high latitudes in his own yacht, *Pelagic*.

RIO de JANEIRO STOPOVER

'If conditions are severe when we approach Cape Horn,' said Jeffes, 'we will simply hole up in one of the numerous anchorages nearby and wait until it moderates. Anyone attempting to go west against storm-force winds in the 200-mile danger zone, where waves roll off the continental shelf, will simply wear out boat and crew and, at best, end up a long way south, if not south-east.'

Jeffes hoped things sounded less daunting when he pointed out that the chart of the area looked similar to the wilder parts of the West Coast of Scotland. It was on a similar latitude. Some of the crew were reassured (despite Jeffes' omission of large, uncharted white lumps floating about down there). The Scottish analogy entered the annals of *InterSpray* myth and came back to haunt him.

Crew preparations for the long haul ahead came in different ways. Ricky, the only *InterSpray* crewman who had been down to the Southern Ocean, on cargo ships in the Merchant Navy, knew about the extreme cold. Realising that one of the worst jobs aboard would be working in the yacht's bows, in icy storm-force winds, he made a 'hank puller', to extract frozen piston hanks on foresails frozen to the forestay. It could be used wearing mittens.

Duggie shipped out to Rio a special Gore-Tex bladder for his bagpipes. It would replace the normal sheepskin one, which might deteriorate in the damp Southern Ocean conditions.

Silk underwear, which stayed warm when wet and dried easily, was the first layer for Southern Ocean Michelin Man. It was followed by polypropylene long johns, a fleece-lined body suit, thermal socks, leather-lined boots and a dog otter one-piece dry suit. Ski-goggles and balaclavas were all part of the kit for facing icebergs, sleet, freezing fog and enduring numbing cold.

Safety in the galley was paramount and pressure cookers were purchased in Rio to minimise the risk of scalds, together with Thermos flasks. With the prospect of 60 days-plus at sea on leg two, it wasn't surprising that the purser's trip to the Cash and Carry for extra provisions took eight hours. Each yacht a budget of almost 18 million Brazilian cruzados to supplement the dried food.

But as Julian reported: 'The main preparation has been within ourselves. We know the boat is strong and well-equipped, but none of us has ever experienced the forces of nature that we'll find as we turn the corner at Cape Horn.'

Chay Blyth's crew briefing on the Friday night before the race re-start was in Rio Yacht Club's gymnasium. Blyth, who has battled around Cape Horn four times, was well versed in the dangers. He once spent 19 hours in the waters of the Horn when his trimaran *Beefeater II* capsized during an attempt on New York to San Francisco record.

His Christmas present from the Southern Ocean in 1970, as he rounded the Horn in *British Steel*, had been a huge sea that smashed his self-steering beyond repair and badly gashed his forehead. He still bore the scar.

His Challenge crews had lost some of their innocence during the rites of passage to Rio. Their ultimate baptism awaited.

Leg two

InterSpray's Whispering Forties

Start Sunday, November 15, Rio de Janeiro to Hobart, Tasmania, 8,800 miles

With Force 5 winds and brilliant sunshine, spectators thronged Copacabana beach, as well as taking to the skies in helicopters and microlight planes from Rio Aero Club, for the spectacular start of leg two. *InterSpray* was the first boat to leave Rio yacht club, piped out by Duggie in full Highland regalia with kilt and sporran.

Jeffes drilled the crew with three timed runs up to the start line, powering down at 8-9 knots under genoa and full main, with John Davis on the bow calling the distance.

Trying to arrest the momentum of 40 tons without brakes was not easy, but Jeffes rounded up twice, letting the sails flog, to stall the yacht before assuming pole position. The starter's gun fired at 1400 local time and *InterSpray* was first across the line, with *Hofbrau* a whisker away and *British Steel II* a boat-length away.

In their enthusiasm to get into the most favourable position, three yachts and 120 tons of steel had converged on starboard tack on the weather end of the start line. The windward boat was *Group 4*, with *Nuclear Electric* to leeward. Both

advanced either side of *Heath Insured*. Adrian Donovan's correct course (as the Protest Committee later decreed) was to keep clear of *Nuclear Electric*, which had right of way. *Group 4* was forced to tack and clear the mark on the wrong side. Mike Golding gybed and crossed the line. Donovan, trying to get the right side of the buoy, sailed too close to *Nuclear Electric*, and called for water.

Both skippers took avoiding action, but *Heath*'s quarter smashed into *Nuclear*

Above: highland high-jinx before the Rio re-start. Piper Duggie leads Jeff and Carlton in a deck dance. Below: one second early over the start line? 'Nonsense!' says Julian, consulting his watch

Electric's topsides. At a subsequent Protest Committee hearing, *Heath* was penalised by two hours. Donovan had not been entitled to request room. After the Southampton snarl-up he was getting a reputation with the buoys.

'This is amazing,' said Blyth. 'They have 8,800 miles ahead of them and they are not giving an inch. These guys have lost their innocence since Southampton.'

InterSpray, meanwhile, was surprised to get a scrambled radio message from the Race Committee informing them that they had been one second early over the start line. There had been no sound signal from Rio de Janeiro Yacht Club and Flag X-RAY had not been flown from Fort Copacabana's flag staff. By now it was too late to turn back. Jeffes would appeal if there was an attempt to add a two-hour time penalty.

'If we get a penalty it will have been worth while,' he reflected. 'It was good for morale to lead *Hofbrau* and *British Steel II* right along Copacabana Beach.'

Commercial Union, starting six days behind the fleet on elapsed time, had their own morale booster when the jury halved their four-time penalty imposed for the premature start by Sutherland in the Solent. *Group 4* also had their penalty from the Solent start reduced to a half-hour.

Once round the Fairway buoy off Copacabana Beach, the last mark the yachts had to round before leaving Cape Horn to starboard, the fleet tacked out to sea, still led by *InterSpray*, now flying her new asymmetric spinnaker,

The first hazard they all faced was a giant iceberg reported to be the size of the Isle of Wight, which had drifted north from the Antarctic on the Falklands Current and grounded off Montevideo, at the mouth of the River Plate. Blyth warned skippers it had begun to break up and 12 mini-bergs, some the size of the Albert Hall, were floating around north of the Falkland Islands – 'two of them are right in your path,' he added comfortingly.

Alison's broken toe meant that for the first couple of weeks she would be running the galley, doing the cooking, with assistance, and standing short watches in the early hours. Otherwise it would be fixed watches all the way to Cape Horn. Julian's watch comprised Ricky, Duggie and Jeff. John had Dominic, Paul Buchanan and Barry, while Carlton had Juliet, Patrick and Brian.

The system of six-hour watches during the day and four at night remained in place. When the weather got cold and nasty the four on watch split into two on deck and two in the doghouse, swapping over every half-hour.

Before leaving Rio, Jeffes had spent two evenings getting weather routing advice from Martin Akery, at Noble Denton, in London, and spent a morning discussing strategy with Pete Goss and his first mate, Jack Gordon-Smith, on *Hofbrau*. The two boats were sharing weather information and outside assistance was allowed up to the five-minute gun.

Akery advised sticking close to the shore for the first 36 hours. But it wasn't clear whether to go directly south or further west. For the first two days the yachts were so close together it was difficult to plot positions on the charts. By day two, as the yachts worked their way down the South American coast, they had split into two sections, with *Hofbrau*, *InterSpray*, *Commercial Union* and *Rhone-Poulenc* all within sight of one another inshore and leading the fleet, hoping for some further advantage from the south-going Brazil current.

Further offshore, the rest of the fleet headed east in search of more wind.

By day three the fleet had seen four different leaders since leaving Rio, and *InterSpray* had slipped to tenth place, though still only 17 miles behind leader *Nuclear Electric*. Life was becoming less comfortable, beating into 20-25 knots of breeze with 30 degrees of heel and slamming. With so many sail changes, the standby watch were cold, wet and exhausted and there was sea sickness among some crew. Several hairy chins started to develop as shaving at an acute angle became dangerous.

On *British Steel II* Richard Tudor's crew were madly eating bananas and apples which had started to rot.

With strong winds and a lumpy sea there was chaos down below in the saloon when the galley bench seat – used for storing fresh foods – broke away from its floor mountings at breakfast time. Ricky and Julian were halfway through their porridge on the high side, bracing their feet against the seat which gave way. The skipper was left holding the stainless steel backrest bar. Carrots, onions, oranges and potatoes scattered every-where. It looked like Covent Garden market. Ricky and Julian ended up on the floor with 20 fingers and their chins visible above the table's edge.

The helmsman, naturally, was to blame and a notice was pinned in the galley: 'The management would like to apologise for any inconvenience. Normal service will be resumed as soon as possible.'

At the same time, the staysail sheet broke, necessitating a tack, as potatoes and onions rolled in sympathy to the other side of the saloon.

John, ship's carpenter, spent eight hours repairing the seat with bolts though the floors and bearers, which made it stronger than the original.

News came over the radio during the early hours of the morning of day four that *Group 4*'s 22mm stainless steel fore-stay bottlescrew, with a breaking strain of 16.5 tons, had broken while she was beating in a wind of 26-32 knots. While Mike Golding diverted to Florianopolis, in southern Brazil, to make emergency repairs, *InterSpray*'s deck watch checked all stay and shroud attachments. Group 4 Securicor's worldwide express delivery service were working round the clock to get a replacement bottlescrew flown out

from the manufacturers in Southampton. 'We may be down, but we're not out,' reported Golding. *Group 4* crewman Martin Hall was having a birthday he wouldn't forget.

Leading the fleet for her second day was *Nuclear Electric*. Her switch from tenth place the previous day showed the rapidly changing fortunes in the race.

By mid-day on the fourth day, *InterSpray* had covered 561 miles in 72 hours, but next day the wind had blown itself out and the yacht wallowed in light air and a swell left over from three days and nights of 20-30ft waves. Duggie checked the mast and minor running repairs were carried out.

By day five *Nuclear Electric* had gone further east than the rest of the yachts and had a substantial lead of 100 miles on the last boat. *InterSpray*, facing light, variable winds, was lying in fourth place. The fleet were spread over a 180-mile area, east of Rio Grande and north of the Brazilian border with Uruguay. If anyone had told the crew they would have to wait another 85 days, until the Hobart start of the third leg, before they could improve their position they wouldn't have believed it. Taking the most westerly inshore track was to prove a tactical error which put them on the wrong side of the wind changes and would cost them dearly. Meanwhile, there was Carlton's birthday to celebrate with cake for tea.

Group 4 was back in the race on day six with a new rigging screw, less than 48 hours after her forestay drama. Her No 2 Yankee had been repaired by North Sails' loft at Sao Paulo and flown back by chartered Lear jet, courtesy of one of their sponsor's companies.

Obligingly, the fleet had run into calms while *Group 4* was making her pit-stop. But she was still 150 miles behind the leaders. *InterSpray*'s 24-hour run for the day was down to just 115 miles and showed little improvement with the following day's run of 126 miles. The

crew, including Jeffes, were starting to feel pretty demoralised.

Within the space of five days from day seven, *InterSpray* lost 525 miles to *Nuclear Electric*. It was starting to get colder and the four or five whales blowing and swimming 300 yards to port created only a temporary distraction from the yacht's troubles.

In the early hours of day eight, Dominic and Barry were taking down the No 1 Yankee in high winds, after the one inch diameter sheet had broken. It was, said fellow watchman Buchanan, a rollercoaster in some of the biggest seas he had yet seen. One minute the bows were 20ft up in the air, the next 2ft under water.

'As the wind caught the sail, Dominic was being pulled up the forestay like Mary Poppins,' said Barry. Then a breaking wave swamped the foredeck and Dom disappeared over Barry's head, bending a stanchion beyond recognition as he went over the side of the yacht. Barry, too, was washed overboard. Their safety harnesses checked them. Helping Dominic back on board, Barry admitted: 'I was more shaken than he was.'

Watchleader John Davis made a mental note that it would be important in the days ahead to keep weight off the foredeck during sail changes in such conditions. The bows had a tendency to plough through the waves. It would also be important to think ahead and keep sail changes to a minimum, to avoid a wet, cold, and exhausted foredeck team.

Over the next four days, distances run every 12 hours varied from a disappointing 59 miles, to a depressing 41 miles, a woeful 21 miles and a wretched 12 miles.

InterSpray fought her own Battle of the River Plate between the Monday evening of day nine and the Friday morning of day 13. And she lost. *Rhone-Poulenc* and

A seagull's-eye view of **InterSpray** *at the start of leg two from Rio*

Hofbrau were both in sight before *InterSpray* fell into her big, private black hole. *Hofbrau* struggled with them for a while and then headed due west towards the shore and escaped.

It was frustrating with boats less than 50 miles away on either side finding wind, while *InterSpray* was fated to wallow helplessly in the middle. At one point the yacht was surrounded by seals languishing in the calm water and waving a lazy flipper, while seabirds glided in light winds. *Nuclear Electric*, meanwhile, was tearing along at 9 knots opening up a formidable lead.

Jeffes and his crew were facing the doldrums they had missed at the Equator, though the scenery was different. On day ten, east of the River Plate, the top of an Albert Hall-sized iceberg, with several growlers, was sighted on the horizon. Sea temperature had plummeted from 74°F to 50°F and thermal socks, leather-lined wellies, long johns, and ocean suits, even Dog Otter drysuits, were *de rigueur.* Yet some crew still remained cold. There was another 1,000 miles southing still to go.

Nuclear Electric reported an iceberg 250ft high and half a mile long and there were radar checks for growlers at night. The sea had turned icy green and the wind from the South Pole was bone-chilling.

'We have arrived in the Southern Ocean,' announced Julian, who was using his sleeping bag for the first time since Portugal, two months before.

While *InterSpray* had been covering 15 miles in a 12-hour period between radio round-ups, other yachts been doing 70, 80 and 90 miles. Worse than that, the boats further ahead were likely to extend their lead as they found more wind. 'We now understand something of what *Commercial Union* went through,' reflected Julian.

There was drama when *InterSpray*'s man overboard alarm sounded. John Davis did a rapid head count on the foredeck before discovering that Julian's EPIRB had automatically triggered when his oilskins filled up with a wave.

On the evening of day 11 decent weatherfaxes started to come through for the first time. There were good maps from Valpairiso and maps of varying quality from Buenos Aires, but nothing had yet been picked up from the Russian Antarctic Station of Molodezhnaya.

The maps offered no respite for *InterSpray*, though, as the navigator stared impotently at chart table instrument gauges, showing six knots of breeze. The boat was moving at 1.5 knots over the ground with 0.7 knots of current against it. On Julian's watch the crew stood helplessly while they drifted backwards four miles.

'This may all seem grim,' mused Barry. 'But night watches are beautiful with Orion and the Southern Cross clearly visible. Shooting stars abound. The sky is vast. Sunsets and sunrises breathtaking.'

At night, when freezing mist encircled the yacht, Rene's Cafe was overrun by bearded SAS men in balaclavas. Role Playing at Sea is a phenomenon well-chronicled in a book called *The Psychology of Sailing*. Boredom and stress can unlock stowaway characters aboard ships.

On *InterSpray* it unlocked a Hereford-based regiment of gentlemen all answering to the name of Smith. Sergeant Major Plummer-Smith, dressed in the traditional style of a public convenience cleaner, was Training Officer and recruited Cpl Duggie-Smith for covert operations.

Ghost-like shapes departed stealthily from the cockpit on dangerous missions, often unarmed, except for a bowl of McDougalls dumplings. There was insubordination in the ranks when the yacht's newest recruit, Barry F, plainly in a state of post traumatic shock, secretly scribbled in his log: 'We are all turning completely apeshit. Jeff raided the galley last night and shot us all with his cap gun.'

(A firearm, incidentally, on loan to the yacht from Monsieur Rene-Gelder on a previous mission to South America.)

Julian optimistically noted that a telex from Race HQ suggested that the weather might change before Christmas.

'Don't cancel flight to Hobart just yet,' he telexed Trisha.

However, the plan to stay inshore, where favourable weather systems should have been found, had gone disastrously wrong. The same tactic of looking for land and sea breezes which brought success on leg one now brought failure.

The River Plate was where the south-going Brazil current met the northerly Falklands current, which was pushing *InterSpray* backwards, at two knots in places. The River Plate added its own off-shore push while *InterSpray* tried to stay inshore of the 200m contour line to avoid losing more ground. The navigator had switched to the South Atlantic Chart – from Rio de la Plata to Cabo de Hornos.

It was supremely ironic that *InterSpray* entered the Roaring Forties when they were barely whispering. It was a flat calm as she drifted over the 40°S line in the early hours of day 12. The familiar sound of the mainsail slatting and the boom clanking was an inescapable torture.

InterSpray had, in the words of the skipper, reached the nadir of her fortunes. *Group 4*, which had 160 miles to catch up after their unscheduled stopover, over-hauled them during the night on an inshore course.

'We are trapped it seems, doomed forever to sit in this bloody high pressure area south-west of the River Plate,' cursed Jeffes.

Desperately frustrated, he watched *InterSpray's* respectable lead from the first leg being eaten away. Things were at their lowest ebb. Keeping up morale while the fleet steamed away was difficult.

'They must be tearing their hair out at home watching *Group 4* go by. I'm not sure who must be suffering more. The people back home or the crew. It will be interesting to see whether we, as a team, have got the backbone to recover our position over the next 7,500 miles and put this leg of the race back together again,' Jeffes reflected.

By the evening of day 12, *Nuclear Electric* was leading tenth-placed *InterSpray* by 525 miles and was ahead of the rest of the fleet by 252 miles.

After nearly five days caught in the high pressure area a decision had to be made, even if it proved a failure. Julian, John and Carlton discussed with Jeffes the option of heading west into shallower water where, hopefully, they would encounter less current and be in a better position to take advantage of forecast winds from the north-west.

Reluctantly, Paul agreed. But they monitored the current closely. For the first six hours it was adverse, but after a time they were able to detect changes resulting from eddies and swirls. The period of 'slack' water began to increase and as the wind swung to the north they could bear away south-west.

Jeffes had been up all night, In his own words 'pestering about wondering what to do to make the boat go faster.'

He was bitter that the weather gods had dealt *InterSpray* such a devastating blow at the early stages of a crucial leg of the race. The crew felt cheated that the yacht had lost so much ground.

From Chay's point view, however, the three boats that hadn't shone in first leg were now making up for it. *Nuclear Electric* (seventh into Rio) was first, *Coopers & Lybrand* (9th in Rio) was second, and *Commercial Union* was romping along in third place.

'It becomes increasingly difficult to sound convincing when you say "Never mind guys, things are going to change soon," and things just don't,' lamented Jeffes.

'I guess everybody is thoroughly demoralised, but different people have different ways of coping with it. Most people are a bit thoughtful about it and everyone is clearly hacked off. We've just got to put it behind us and make sure we don't let it affect boat speed any more than necessary.'

On the morning of day 13 *InterSpray*'s luck changed. After five days of watching the fleet steam away, with Chittenden now 680 miles ahead, *InterSpray* had her best 12-hour run for three days, with 50.2 miles. True, *Hofbrau* managed 110 miles, but *InterSpray* followed up with 104 miles and 123 miles,

'Finally we seem to coming to the end of the dreadful period in this small, intense high pressure area which every one else managed to miss,' said Jeffes.

The yacht was heading south-west at 7 knots-plus, under lightweight spinnaker and main. She crossed the thin blue line of the 200m depth contour, so that any effect of being on the continental shelf, in terms of reducing the Falklands Current, should be felt in full measure. They were 200 miles off the coast of Argentina.

It was a tremendous morale booster for the crew. Jeffes, who had been under a lot of pressure and had taken *InterSpray*'s poor performance very much to heart, was rejuvenated.

Dominic, Paul Buchanan and Barry were revelling in the conditions, surfing under spinnaker, and setting up helming competitions. Top speed by Ricky was 16.1 knots after changing to the tri-radial kite.

Before darkness, with 35 knots of apparent wind over the deck, the decision was made to change to the heavier asymmetric spinnaker. John Davis, whose watch had just taken over, was by the mast with Barry and Dominic lowering the spinnaker pole when, under huge compression, the pole shot down the mast track like a pile driver. John, standing underneath, was pole-axed.

He collapsed on a sailbag, blood oozing from a gash in his forehead by the right eye. As Jeffes arrived on deck, John looked up and said: 'I don't think I'm concussed. I think I'm okay.'

He was helped below to his bunk by Julian, suffering from shock and concussion. The force of the blow had strained his neck muscles, chipped his front teeth and also damaged his knee. His right eye closed up. Fortunately, he had been looking up when the pole knocked him sideways striking his forehead. 'If it had hit him square on the top of his head it would have killed him for sure,' said Jeffes.

The injury Julian most dreaded was a nasty bang on the head. But the fact that John could speak without slurring his words and could walk was reassuring. John was to remain in his bunk for two or three days. He emerged looking like an extra from a horror film, with a swollen, bloodied eye, like an overripe tomato, and a lump the size of a tennis ball on his forehead.

The treatment prescribed was to bandage the wound, provide mild pain relief and let the patient lie in his bunk 'where, with difficulty, we kept him for 48 hours,' reported Julian. John was on light duties for a week.

In Hobart, he was later to have a brain scan which revealed bruising of the soft tissue around the back of the eye some 40 days after the impact.

With his convict haircut and black eye, the accident had visibly aged John. 'He almost looked 40 for a while,' jested Julian of *InterSpray*'s Dorian Grey. After a decent interval the yacht's photographer took a picture of John holding a number in front of his chest, like a hoodlum from police files.

'John is a very fit guy and leads from the front,' said Jeffes. 'But he may have to be talked into letting someone else take the risks from now on.' Back in the cockpit John played an important role as helmsman and sail trimmer. His accident meant that his additional duties as rigger, frequently ascending the 86ft mast, would have to be curtailed.

As *InterSpray* charged along at 13 knots in the early hours of day 14, news filtered through on the radio that *Rhone-Poulenc* had suffered a knockdown while surfing at 18 knots. She had been hit by a 38-knot gust that snapped her spinnaker pole and pinned her down as the wind continued to fill the asymmetric spinnaker. Their GPS aerial had been damaged, which suggested they had been laid flat on the water. Skipper Peter Phillips later reported they were navigating by sextant and dead reckoning and motoring to Port Stanley in the Falklands to check damage to mast and rigging.

InterSpray had her best noon-to-noon run of the leg, with 263.4 miles. This prompted a vintage sample of Jeffes optimism. 'I've calculated that we made 50 miles back on *Nuclear Electric*, so we've only got to do that 12 times and we're right back up with her!'

By the Saturday afternoon of day 14 the wind had dropped, and with it the good progress south, as frustrating calms came and went. On day 15, *Nuclear Electric* was rounding Cape Horn in sunshine and unexpectedly gentle conditions, with *Commercial Union* in second place some 130 miles behind her.

Chittenden had 598 weather observations for the Horn on his chart and just two of them indicated calms. 'It's very frustrating,' he said.

The Commander of a Chilean naval vessel told him: 'It's never like this here. You are very lucky to see the Horn in these conditions.' Chittenden and his crew begged to differ after the anticipation of a Southern Ocean skirmish.

As *InterSpray* approached the Horn, news was coming through from the Vendee Globe Challenge singlehanded round-the-world race, in which 14 boats had set off from Les Sables d'Olonne and been decimated by gales in Biscay. British sailor Nigel Burgess had been found dead in the water after abandoning his yacht and American yachtsman Mike Plant, on his way to the race, was missing after his yacht was sighted capsized. Others had been dismasted or were turning back for hull repairs. It didn't help the crew's apprehensions, but the strength of steel around them felt more secure than high-tech carbon fibre and bulb keels.

A constant breeze was still eluding *InterSpray*, lying last, some 500 miles behind Chittenden, but the wind had returned. On Monday, day 16, *InterSpray* outran everybody by some 20 miles with a 12-hour run of 94.9 miles. *Rhone-Poulenc* had reached Port Stanley to check their rig and were temporarily out of the race as *InterSpray* moved up a place.

Around this time Paul Buchanan noticed the label on the tub of Julian's high-fibre bran supplement, which he had been sprinkling on his breakfast cereal: '4 level measures daily for large dogs.' If he wasn't barking mad now, he soon would be.

On the last night of November, Barry, Dominic and Paul Buchanan formed the Secret Society of the Green Flash, having watched the sunset and claimed to witness the elusive phenomenon as the last vestige of the sun turned green as it dipped below the horizon. By now *InterSpray* was so far south that nights lasted only a few hours, with long periods of twilight.

John was on early morning watch and carrying out half-hour radar sweeps for growlers after more icebergs had been reported by the fleet. He did a 24-mile sweep, a 12-mile sweep and then a 6-mile sweep, for greater detail.

By evening someone scribbled in the log: 'Brilliant sailing Force 4-5 wind, white tops, sun and blue sky, 9.5 knots, dolphins and seabirds. Where else do you want to be in the world?'

On Day 17 promised NNW winds arrived as *InterSpray* sped south into the Furious Fifties, surfing at up to 14 knots with her asymmetric spinnaker poled out. With 30 knots-plus of wind the decision was made to change down to a headsail. The spinnaker was on a fixed strop to prevent chafe, so someone had to go out to the pole end to remove it. It was blowing too hard to let the pole right forward with the sail driving. The pole would simply have collapsed.

Duggie was asked to go.

'In those conditions I wouldn't have blamed him if he had refused,' said Jeffes.

Duggie thought: 'This could be pretty hair-raising.' But it was a question of 'just get up there and do it quickly.'

He told Ricky and Pat tailing the halyard attached to his climbing harness: 'Get me up and down quick, lads.'

Duggie got the strop off, but as he started to come back down the pole downhaul, a gust of wind and a big wave caught *InterSpray* and she broached badly, slewing up into the wind.

'I turned around and sensed something wasn't right,' said Duggie. 'An extra large wave picked the yacht up and spun it round. Instead of being horizontal, the pole was vertical, with me hanging from the end of it. In a split second I looked back to the cockpit and saw anxious faces as everyone shouted: "Hold on!"'

'Get him down quickly,' shouted Jeffes, worried that if the pole snapped he'd be smashed into the side of the yacht or rigging.

In the few seconds that the yacht rounded up, the asymmetric split across the middle to the luff tapes. The spinnaker pole was bending like a banana.

Julian, on the helm, bore away and Ricky grabbed Duggie, hauling him down the deck, still attached to the spinnaker halyard, back to the safety of the mast. He, too, was worried the pole might snap at any moment. The sheer force of the wind on the spinnaker halyard outside the sail had been lifting Duggie off the deck before he could release his harness line.

By now the asymmetric kite was horribly knotted around the inner forestay.

'We were trapped over on our side for just enough time for the wind to backfill the spinnaker and completely destroy it,' said Julian, who had been on the wheel for two hours before it ripped. He remained for a few more while the skipper, No 1 foredeck man Patrick, plus Brian, Paul Buchanan, Barry and Carlton worked in shifts to untangle the mass of wet sail cloth as solid water swept the foredeck regularly.

'That's ocean racing,' thought Julian. 'Very sad, because the asymmetric has been a wonderful sail.'

Part of the sail was wrapped around the inner forestay and some was in long ribbons. Jeffes was balanced on the spinnaker pole, 10ft above the foredeck, trying to get the sail down as the yacht was bowling along at 10-12 knots under mainsail alone in a steady 40 knots of wind. After five hours they had to abandon the attempt. It was too dangerous. 'If anyone had gone overboard we'd never had recovered them,' said Jeffes.

Julian tried later again in the afternoon, cutting away the tatters, and eventually the asymmetric was recovered, by cutting the torn leach tape to free it. Repairs would be a sail loft job. The sail was put away. It proved to be no great loss on this leg, with precious few occasions when they'd be able to use it between the Horn and Hobart.

That evening Carlton gained the helming record with 18.1 knots. The skipper was standing beside him while on the foredeck they worked on the spinnaker snarl-up.

'I was transfixed,' said Jeffes. '18.1 knots was the fastest we'd ever been.' White water was flying either side of the yacht. The foam was level with the top amidships stanchions. The front of the yacht, from the mast forward, was out of the water.

When the yacht hit the bottom of the trough and roared into the back of the next wave, the bow wave towered above the heads of the guys clinging to the foredeck. There were whoops of delight (or was it terror) at the spectacle.

'Very large bow wave. Very sharp intake of breath,' was the terse entry in the log.

Julian achieved 18.6 knots (the GPS registered it as 20.7 knots) in the middle of the night, riding down the face of a wave. He was enjoying the strongest winds and roughest seas he'd encountered. 'You accelerate down the face of a wave and it's a terrific relief when the yacht lifts its bow up. You almost feel it's a pitchpole situation – except it's difficult to imagine 40 tons being pitchpoled.'

Two days later *Group 4* issued its own Challenge, announcing they would award a trophy to any of the other nine yachts which beat their speed record of 21 knots, which they set in winds of 35-45 knots after rounding the Horn. Julian was close Golding's fast runs were helping him make up lost ground after their unscheduled stop.

That evening, *Pride of Teesside* became the eighth yacht to round the Horn, after a close duel with *Heath Insured* in 35-knot winds. They reported hitting a heavy object. 'Could it have been Chay Blyth's wallet?!' asked skipper MacGillivray.

Twelve of MacGillivray's crew had opted to have their ears pierced with a sailmaker's needle in the tradition of old Cape Horners who wore a gold earring in their right lobe.

On day 18 *InterSpray* was off the Straits of Magellan, getting ready for her charge down the perilous passage through Le Maire Strait, a tidal sluice-gate between Tierra del Fuego (Land of Fire) and Isla de los Estados (Staten Island). The pilot book warned of treacherous tidal overfalls, capable of breaking up big ships, with 8-10 knot currents in the mountain-lined gateway which linked the Atlantic and Pacific. Old sailing ship masters feared the 20-mile wide strait more than Cape Horn itself and one national newspaper sailing correspondent had described it as 'a deathtrap.'

With pressures from some sponsors to make this leg of the race safer, the RORC had suggested at one point adding a waypoint east of Staten Island, effectively keeping the fleet out of the strait. In Rio, Chay announced the waypoint, but dropped the idea after discussion with skippers, who didn't want the decision taken out of their hands. In the end, it was left to the skippers' individual judgements. To go round the longer way meant adding 70-80 miles to the passage time.

A move later to add a new, safer waypoint between Hobart and Cape Town, to avoid ice, would meet with the same response from skippers and crews – 'not to soften up the world's toughest yacht race'.

InterSpray had sailed 400 miles in 48 hours, including a record noon-to-noon run of 269 miles. 'It's unlikely that any other boat will be driven totally out of control for as long as 24 hours,' thought Julian.

But it looked as if *InterSpray* had arrived at Le Maire Strait too early. The tide, which peaked at six knots, was against them (though fortunately it was neap tides) and there was a strong northwesterly wind. The waves were so steep initially that the crew's first glimpse of land for 18 days revealed only the sharp peaks of Staten Island and the light of Cabo St Diego.

Julian woke the skipper at 0500 to make the difficult decision of whether to go through the Strait or not.

They had arrived at the worst possible time, with wind over tide. The conditions the pilot books warned against.

InterSpray altered course, sailing east towards Staten Island, for an hour, while the crew battened down for heavy weather. The rig was snugged down with two reefs in the main, No 2 yankee and staysail. All superfluous rigging was taken below.

These waters were notorious for quick changes of weather. Going for the strait in 35 knots of wind, with more expected, the yacht would stand a better chance of beating back out under shortened sail if conditions became too much.

All the other boats, with the exception of *Rhone-Poulenc* in Port Stanley, had gone through the strait. *InterSpray* was so far behind the fleet that the decision was made for them.

The passage took more than three hours on a bright moonlit night with a huge swell running and the yacht rising and falling through seas as tall as a three-storey house. It was like going up and down in an elevator. 'Yacht performed faultlessly and very good helming by Carlton,' (whose watch it was) wrote John in his log. It was 'knife-edge stuff,' thought Juliet, with cavernous craters opening up behind the yacht.

Cape Horn, the silence of the cemetery

As *InterSpray* emerged from Le Maire Strait conditions became more favourable. The genoa was hoisted and poled out and the yacht sailed into the sunset against a spectacular backdrop of the saw-toothed, snow-capped mountains of Tierra del Fuego. Alison spotted her first albatross, with a wingspan of nine feet.

Jeffes was on the radio to Cape Horn when John spotted a black squall coming and gave the order to drop the genoa and hoist the No 2 Yankee.

Jeffes stuck his head through the hatch: 'What the hell's going on! There's no wind between here and the Horn. I've just been on the radio to them.'

Before he could finish the sentence... Bang! The wind gusted in an instant from nine knots to 35 knots and the heavens opened as the yacht shot off at an alarming angle.

'Good call John!' said Jeffes as he went back to the radio.

Sudden changes like this would be the pattern for the next 6,000 miles across the Southern Ocean. But after Le Maire Strait it was a light run to the Cape, with blue skies.

Rhone-Poulenc had left Port Stanley at 0200, rejoining the race 237 miles behind *InterSpray*. New cap shrouds, a masthead bolt and rigging wire, and replacement spreaders, had been flown out from the UK on a routine RAF flight and the yacht's spinnaker pole repaired locally.

On John's midnight watch he spotted the lighthouse on the eastern end of the island, of which Cape Horn is the southernmost point. 'Crocodile', by now recovering rapidly from his pole-axing, should really have been nicknamed 'Hawkeye'.

The watch system disintegrated and nobody went to their bunks. It was as if they were arriving in port as everyone stayed up for their first sight of Cape Horn in the dawn of day 19 (Thursday December 3). It was, after all, the most legendary and feared nautical landmark on the globe and, at 56°S, the literal peak of their sailing ambitions. The dream, or nightmare, of every yachtsman.

The large-scale GPS display was switched on at the chart table to show the moment when *InterSpray* rounded the Horn and crossed from the grey-green waters of the South Atlantic into the dark blue Pacific. It was 0815 GMT. Fourteen more had joined the exclusive Society of Cape Horners, the ninth amateur crew to round the great Cape from east to west.

Rounding the brooding Horn in warm sunlight on a calm blue sea was like visiting a peaceful battleground. It was if they had crept round a sleeping giant. There was a mixture of relief and disappointment at finding themselves becalmed in the windiest place in world. It was an anti-climax for those who had read all the horror stories and watched the videos. While others were thankful as they contemplated all the sailors who had perished in these lonely waters. It was a place haunted by life and death struggles against storms which were capable of tearing the masts out of tall ships as well as small ships.

'The silence of the sea was like the silence of the cemetery', was the description from French singlehander Olivier de Kersauson, when he rounded the Horn in similar conditions three years earlier.

Plainly, Skip Novak's advice on safe anchorages would not be needed.

There was a champagne toast and fruitcake for breakfast. Dominic put bells around his Musto oilskin trousers and performed his ritual morris dance, waving two handkerchiefs as though he was back on the village green in Kent. Paul Jeffes got out two big cigars he had been saving from his Christmas supplies, gave one to Barry, and lit up. Glasgow may be on a similar latitude to the Horn, but things looked different down here, he thought. Julian had a solitary slug of Scotch on the foredeck and contemplated that only 19 days had passed and at least another five weeks lay ahead before he would see Trish. Paul Buchanan performed a juggling act, while nature provided her own acrobatic display as a school of a dozen dolphins performed amazing leaps and aerial barrel rolls out of the water, staying with the yacht for several hours. John Davis was filmed declaring: 'I claim this land in the name of Paul Keating' – Australia's Prime Minister.

Behind *InterSpray* lay the magnificent, wind-swept scenery at the tip of

LEG TWO

South America, with its 13,000ft jagged, snow-capped mountain ranges.

The yacht more or less ground to a halt at the Horn. On the radio, *The Times* yachting correspondent, Barry Pickthall, had told Jeffes he couldn't get a helicopter to the Horn in time for their ETA. But *InterSpray* was still becalmed in front of the Cape, bobbing up and down under full main and genoa, when Pickthall's chartered helicopter arrived to take photographs. They remained there, grinding their teeth for the next 16 hours, while the rest of the fleet charged off westwards, gaining another 100 miles. *Rhone-Poulenc* was catching up, too, just 146 miles behind.

Some of Jeffes' crew were claiming to have rounded Cape Horn twice, as current swept the yacht back. 'There was always a swell. I'm sure it's never a flat calm,' said Jeffes. 'We were lucky we didn't get swept back into the Atlantic. Each time the current caught us, the wind puffed up to give us steerage way and maintain a knot or so.' *InterSpray* may have been the only yacht to pass the Horn in both directions on the same day. But their position in the fleet was more important than an extended opportunity for sightseeing.

As they waited for the wind, group photographs were taken and some of the crew did their washing as the world's southernmost Chinese-style laundry floated south-west. Far from being at the bottom of the world, *InterSpray* could have been anchored off the Isle of Wight on a spring day. Ironically, though, 50-knot winds were reported in the English Channel at that moment.

Paul Buchanan telexed home that his bronzed sea god-looks from the tropics had been ousted by a salty, bearded sea dog. 'Cape Horner's earring and tattoo in Hobart!' he threatened. 'Wooden leg and eye patch in Cape Town?'

Barry went to bed for two hours and was surprised to find the yacht *still* at the Horn when he awoke. He went up the mast to replace the wind instruments, taking his camera to get a shot of the Cape from the masthead. 'How many people have done that?' he wondered.

The crew heard that there was a gathering of old Cape Horners that day at a memorial service at the Cape. They were told that the chance of calms at the Horn was just one per cent.

By evening a breeze kicked in and the Cape disappeared, as *InterSpray* hastened away from the danger zone, hoisting her spinnaker. A small tear appeared and it was taken down to be patched, by which time there was wind enough for a headsail.

Although the Horn was, in Blyth's words, 'only the starting gate of the worst to come', Jeffes and his crew felt the psychological barrier had been lifted, even if the wind gods had cheated them once again.

Apprehension remained about being close to the continental shelf, where the sea floor climbs dramatically from two miles deep to 600ft, like a 4-in-one hill. The 500-mile wide Drake's Channel, between Antarctica and South America, has the effect of funnelling the Southern Ocean rollers and winds, which sweep around the globe unchecked for thousands of miles.

InterSpray passed the Islas Diego Ramirez in darkness next morning and crossed the continental shelf out of the danger zone. It was a relief to be back in deep water. 'It was as though we'd crept past while the sentinels of Cape Horn slept,' said Jeffes.

Later, on the radio to Peter Goss, he remarked how lucky the fleet had been to escape the wrath of the cape.

'There's going to be an invoice in the post. There's a price to be paid for it somewhere,' said Goss, who was later to go searching for the postman in the high latitudes of 61°S, the so-called Screaming Sixties.

From Staten Island until they were 100 miles west of the Horn, *InterSpray* experienced light winds in one of the most dangerous stretches of sea in the world. 'Dangerous by what criteria?' asked neophyte Paul Buchanan.

'Any, just pick one,' was the reply.

At least Jeffes and his crew had Toni Knights' oil painting of *InterSpray* to remind them what it could be like at the Horn.

There would be nights now when it never really became dark. The sun dipped below the horizon, but night-time was a permanent dusk, which made helming and sail trim easier. Sunset and dawn merged, and only the seabirds knew that day was over and seemed to disappear. In daytime there would be petrels, prions, shearwaters and the occasional Albatross. Below 67°S it was the land of the midnight sun. At *InterSpray's* furthest point south, in four days time, one degree of longitude equalled just 36 miles and they were having to alter their clocks by an hour every few days.

When the fresh butter had run out the pursers turned to the six tins of butter bought in Rio. Despite the promising shape of a cow on the tin, it turned out to be caramel butterscotch – for spreading on cakes. It looked like winch grease and tasted very sweet. The skipper's breakfast toast would never be the same.

On day 20, with the Advent calendar up in galley, it was time to blow up the inflatable cake for Duggie's 26th birthday. It was hardly worth deflating, with Jeff's 45th birthday next day.

On deck in the afternoon, Paul Jeffes noticed a sag in the cap shrouds – the rigging wires that support the mast from the masthead. He speculated on whether it might be a similar problem to that which Peter Phillips had suffered on *Rhone-Poulenc*, when the masthead bolt for the cap shrouds had bent. With all the strain on the rig at that one bolt as 40 tons of yacht heeled over and was thrown off the tops of waves, it certainly concentrated the mind.

Jeffes, not wanting to raise unnecessary anxieties amongst the crew, sent a coded telex to Challenge Project Director Andrew Roberts at Race HQ asking for advice. But he kept his fears to himself.

By day 22 *InterSpray* had plunged south into high latitudes, looking for stronger winds and shortening the distance to the waypoint. Chasing the leaders hard, she was the furthest south in the fleet, at 59°S and was achieving faster day's runs than the other yachts. She'd clawed 100 miles back on *Nuclear Electric,* who were still 500 miles ahead, in four days.

Then came alarming news over the radio chat show that *Coopers & Lybrand's* forestay bottlescrew had failed. Within hours *Group 4's* new bottlescrew, replaced 16 days ago in Florianopolis, had broken, shredding their foresail. Overnight *Hofbrau* was to suffer the same fate.

Within the space of a few hours seven yachts found themselves sailing into a hostile wilderness, the greatest desert on earth, with an unexploded time bomb on the bow, while three yachts were counting the cost of the blast.

'We started to feel like the 10 little Indians,' said Jeffes. 'Wondering who was next. . . '

A broken forestay on some yachts inevitably leads to a dismasting, but the Challenge yachts had inner forestays, baby stays and had been built to rugged specifications.

Nevertheless, telexes from Race HQ to all yachts were coming in thick and fast. Yachts were advised to change the suspect forestay bottlescrew for an aft lower screw, as soon as conditions allowed. Metal fatigue was thought to be a contributory factor in the failures, with huge loads on the rigging from driving so hard to windward.

Roberts pointed out: '*British Steel Challenge* did 28,000 miles with the same pattern forks. An altercation with a certain bridge broke the wire (BS at least 25 tons) without bottlescrew damage. The only apparent differences are greater rig tension and possibly the asymmetric spinnaker.'

InterSpray meanwhile, with a suspect cap shroud bolt, no longer had the option of being able to make a pit stop *en route*, like *Rhone-Poulenc*, in the Falklands. Jeffes and his crew were past the point of no return. Turning back would mean abandoning the race. But setting off across 6,000 miles of savage ocean with three bottlescrews in the fleet snapped and doubts over the integrity of the cap shroud bolt was one of the hardest decisions of the race for Jeffes. It was a decision only he could make. The loneliness of command struck home as he kept things to himself whilst contemplating the likely consequences of his decision. Eventually, after consultation with Race HQ, he confided in Julian and John that they may have the same problem as *Rhone-Poulenc*.

The problem was reduced when the top section of rigging was tightened, lessening sag in the top span of the cap shrouds.

'Of course, what we don't know is whether the bolt at the top really is taking the strain,' said an uneasy Jeffes.

Another telex from Roberts to all yachts reported that the reason for the bottlescrew failure was still not clear, but analysis of *Group 4*'s first failed bottlescrew, now back in the UK, might help.

Roberts suggested 18mm rope strops should be tied around the rigging screw and stem roller to back up the suspect screw. 'Lashing should not be too tight,' he added.

Back in England the midnight oil was burning. Roberts issued a 12-part questionnaire to affected yachts requesting one word answers and signing off wearily 'Good night – again.'

Jeffes, keen by now to avoid high anxiety and control the flow of information about rig damage on other boats, banned his crew from reading incoming telex messages until he had vetted them.

Preventative measures were carried out on *InterSpray*'s rig with an 'arrester', comprising two spinnaker halyards and another halyard lashed through the bow roller from the masthead. '. . . so we'll just keep bashing on . . . only 4,000 miles to go,' estimated Jeffes. With no shelter in sight.

Despite her rigging screw failure 1,000 miles from land, Vivien Cherry and *Coopers & Lybrand* maintained third place, having exchanged the broken bottlescrew with one from the leeward shroud. *Hofbrau* replaced theirs from the aft lower shroud. The consequences would be discovered later.

Jeffes was still frustrated to be 500 miles behind the fleet leaders, with the chances of catching them getting thinner every day. 'We need these guys to run out of wind in a big way, but the prospects of that happening, I fear, are nothing like as good here as they were off the South American coast.

'It's a big uphill task. All we can really do is to contain that damage until we get into some less predictable weather. The continuous stream of low pressure zones as we get closer to the waypoint give us less scope for making changes in the course or for running south and playing with the latitude. At the moment we're a bit of a procession going across the Southern Ocean.

'All I ask is to have a fair chance of getting back up with the leaders so we can make a fight of this again. We really haven't had a fair chance from the weather gods at all,' he concluded.

The yachts sailed a lot further south than expected after Cape Horn – so much so that half the fleet sailed off the edge of charts supplied by the Challenge Business for two thirds of their passage west of the Horn. The charts supplied went only as far south as 51°S, whereas on the Great Circle route between the Horn and the 52°S 120°W waypoint the maximum southing was 57° 18'S. Between the waypoint and Hobart it dropped to 58° 15'S. Going further south added to the distance, but could mean finding more wind.

InterSpray went down to 58°S, navigating on the equivalent of a school atlas, using large-scale route-planning charts. 'We were going to use the inflatable globe but thought the dividers might puncture it,' said Dominic.

Life below decks was an incessant round of bilge and radar inspections. The ship's log was a litany of such checks, so that watchleaders knew they had been done. The forward collision bulkhead also had to be periodically drained of water which leaked through the pulpit fittings.

Barry, meanwhile, deeply engrossed in a book on the history of circumnavigators, frequently entertained the crew with tales of people dying of scurvy. He quoted: 'December 12, 1740, Mr. Robert Weldon, our purser, being quite worn out departed this life.' Barry's latter day version was: 'Dominic Mathews, our purser, being knackered f*** died.' For days to come, Barry on meeting Dominic in any state of tiredness would lose no opportunity to exclaim: 'Oh! Dom, you look quite worn out.'

By now damp had got in everywhere. Anything with salt water on it soaked up moisture like a sponge. With the water temperature at 05°C and air temperature at zero, every breath inside the boat created more surface water and all the bulkheads were running and ceilings dripping, especially cabins with air vents that had been sealed due to water over the deck

Some crew were using Gore-Tex bivi bags over their sleeping bags to keep dry. The survival suits became very wet inside and cold after long periods of work.

'The gear we have is performing well and mentally we are all prepared for much worse,' said Buchanan on day 24. 'As the boat slams around it sometimes goes oddly silent and still. At first you relax and can move in superhuman weightless conditions. Now we have learned to react very differently. You tense up, ensure your tongue is clear of your teeth, and hope you are wedged in somewhere tight, because any second you know your legs are going to buckle as the floor comes up to meet you.'

Paul ended this observation with the afterthought: 'Have you ever considered Chile as a holiday destination? You can fly out to Santiago then transfer by light aircraft to a holiday centre I haven't built yet on Robinson Crusoe Island. . . '

Later Buchanan displayed more of his imperishable brand of humour when he learned that Bracknell Weather Centre in England, who were short of information from these latitudes, had asked the fleet for daily weather bulletins.

'I thought they were supposed to be telling us!'

He also impudently observed that it took Chay Blyth 14 days to sail from Cape Horn to 100°W, while *InterSpray* managed it in just seven.

'But then Chay did go several hundred miles further north,' was his parting shot.

Someone must have been watching over Buchanan on Day 23 when his lifeline harness shackle fell apart. Other crew members were quick to check theirs.

Barry felt equally unlucky when girlfriend Kerry telexed him from 14,000 miles away: 'You are definitely in the best place. your car got stolen this week and I managed to get caught up in an IRA bomb attack in Manchester!'

Trisha, meanwhile, passed on the news that Buckingham Palace had announced the forthcoming wedding of Princess Anne to Commander Tim Laurence.

As *InterSpray* blasted through the night, Julian was in his bunk contemplating that the ocean could be an awesome, un-friendly sight. All you could see by day for 12 miles around was grey sea, grey sky, a few seabirds, and enough white horses for an appaloosa ranch. Safe, warm beds seemed a distant prospect – there would be another 6,000 miles on the ship's log before he reached Hobart. There were no ships and no planes. It was too far south for shipping lanes or flight corri dors. At these latitudes humans were intruders, trespassers observed only by the albatrosses.

The Furious Fifties may have been at the same latitude as Britain, but summer temperatures in the Southern Ocean were the same as February in Europe. How of-ten did it snow in Shropshire in August? And there were no icebergs in the Solent. On day 25 *InterSpray* had the fleet's second fastest run of the day, one mile less than *Rhone-Poulenc* and 15-20 miles more than the rest of the yachts. The GPS was giving a Hobart ETA as varied as Boxing Day and next June.

Everything was now becoming a su-preme effort. Moving around the boat was an act of faith. You burned up calories just trying to stand upright. Down below it was easier to move around by sliding along bulkheads at an angle of 40 degrees.

Going to the heads was a delicate balancing act. Sitting on the heads, less delicate. As the boat drove over the top of a big wave, hovered for a split second and then dropped 30ft feet with a loud, reso-nant bang from the steel hull, what was being sat upon rose alarmingly towards the sitter. 'It puts a whole new meaning on getting your own back,' said Barry.

Paul Buchanan had a disaster of Mr. Bean proportions when the pump valves jammed in the heads as he was pumping. 'I could barely hold the lid down against the back pressure as the yacht fell off the waves. The head was six inches deep in sewage and the walls and ceiling splattered. I had one last go before re-sorting to dismantling the whole thing.

Mercifully it cleared, leaving me with the mess to clear up.'

Beating to windward was like beating your brains out, covering half an inch on the chart in six hours (perhaps 30 or 40 miles) knowing there were thousands more to come. 'Everyone is wet, be-draggled and a bit smelly. The oilskins absolutely stink,' protested one dog otter. The grinding exhaustion of slogging along to the waypoint, nearly 1,000 miles away at 52°S 120°W, was taking its toll.

'It was a feeling of ugh! and yet again elation,' said Julian, who had never felt so acutely that he was missing his family, and all the little things, 'like going down to the pub, waking up in the morning and finding frost on the car. . .'

Thankfully, his medical services had not been called upon, other than for liberal supplies of udder cream for sore noses from strong UV light, salt water and wind burn.

Ship's doctors in the Challenge fleet didn't have the queue of patients that you see in many a doctor's surgery on Monday morning. Perhaps it has something to do with the fact that they had names like Dr Death or the Witchdoctor. On *Heath Insured*, which had suffered a plague of boils since Rio, their first-aider, Arthur Haynes, was variously known as the Carbuncle King of the Southern Ocean and the Driller Killer – the latter because ever since he attended a crash course in trauma surgery at the Haslar Royal Naval Hospital, he had perfected, as a machine toolmaker, a specially angled bit for drilling into the skull to relieve pressure in cases of severe head injury.

He had been practising on a dog's skull and got it down to 10 seconds. How did he know when to stop? 'When the blood spurts out!' was his reply.

In his starboard quarter bunk Paul Jeffes had decided that when he designed a Whitbread boat he would add a tumble dryer. 'I don't care what it weighs, we need it. And a generator to power it.

Another thing we need is a good old-fashioned mangle, to squeeze the water out of all this high-tech clothing to dry it quickly.'

The skipper's one consolation in the cold of the deep Southern Ocean was his Dennis the Menace hot water bottle. He didn't know other crew members had stowaway water bottles, too. 'But after everyone saw mine, the others all came out of the woodwork. They felt a bit sheepish, but having warm feet in your sleeping bag and some softness in this damp, cold, grey, hard world is very pleasant,' recorded the skipper as he snuggled down with Dennis.

Two weeks away from Christmas, on day 28, InterSpray again recorded the longest day's run of the fleet, storming along all night beating hard into gale. On occasions the cockpit would be filled up like a bath.

They received a promising forecast from the Antarctic Survey Ship James Clark Ross, showing light winds around the waypoint, which the fleet leaders had just reached. Was this their chance to catch up from ninth place, they wondered. So far, every time the crew had got a break, the wind gods snatched back their good fortune.

Rhone-Poulenc, 200 miles astern, had reported a two foot rip in her mainsail and were sailing under trysail. The sewing circle would be back in action for the next 37 hours before the sail was re-hoisted.

Taking advantage of a lull in the wind, InterSpray's crew dropped the mainsail to repair a batten pocket and replace a batten. Was this the calm before the storm? They also double-checked the forestay bottlescrew.

Alison, who was back in the watch system, having recovered from her foot injury, was preparing an estate agent's blurb for her accommodation: 'Windward aft bunk. Nice length. Comfy lee cloth. No sick stains. Good view. Next to the skipper. . .'

The wind hole awaiting the fleet leaders never materialised and on day 29 InterSpray's wind continued to build, unexpectedly from the east. The heavy spinnaker had been up for five hours, but by late afternoon, with occasional gusts of 37 knots true, the watch had changed down to a poled out No 1 yankee.

Ripping yarns and a missing mast

Calamity at sea is often caused by failure of the smallest, seemingly most insignificant component, as the elements expose the weakest link. InterSpray's disastrous chain reaction began that night with the failure of a snapshackle as the yacht charged downwind in darkness in a full gale.

Paul Buchanan was on the helm when the yacht rolled in rough seas and a snapshackle holding the boom preventer broke open. Buchanan was powerless to prevent the involuntary crash gybe that followed. Watchleader John, down below, making a plot on the chart, rushed on deck as the boom gybed back. At that moment the spinnaker pole guy snap-shackle broke open, too, sending the foresail flying forward to wrap itself around the forestay. It was later discovered that both snapshackles were undamaged and had simply released under pressure.

In no time at all, the yankee sheets had knotted themselves together and the clew of the sail was trapped between the forestay and two spinnaker halyards, rigged to support the mast in the event of forestay failure. To complicate matters, the wire genoa halyard had been shackled to the toe rail as an extra mast support. The wrap of sheets prevented the spinnaker pole being lowered.

Julian's watch woke to the sound of flogging sails and got ready to go on deck and help untangle the unholy mess. The wind was increasing in ferocity.

For Jeffes and the others, climbing into their oilskins and one-piece drysuits, it was to be the beginning of their longest, wettest, and coldest night of the voyage so far.

John had taken over the helm and fought to keep the boat in a straight line as *InterSpray* tore off downwind into the pitch black with up to three crew working on the exposed bow in the eerie glare of the deck floodlight. The roar of the wind snatched speech into nothingness. Shouts were drowned in the deafening noise of the flogging sail.

The violent pitching of the bow threatened to catapult overboard anyone not clipped on. Staring through the guardrails there wasn't time to be conscious of the white-capped cliffs of water ahead, or the bottomless black valleys rising up in a mad smother of foam. Every now and then the foredeck team were engulfed in icy water.

On the helm, John couldn't tell whether they were running by the lee or not, since the wind instruments had failed and the masthead light, illuminating the Windex, had also gone out. For him there was 90 minutes of agonising suspense ahead, wondering if he was going to have a disaster on the front end. His biggest fear was that if *InterSpray* broached, he might lose someone off the foredeck, whether they were clipped on or not, such were the forces of waves, wind and boatspeed. With no way to tell the wind direction, Julian was in the cockpit interpreting what instrument readings they had for the helmsman.

If the next hour felt like a lifetime to John, it went like a flash for Jeffes and Patrick Brockman, by now struggling on

the foredeck in torrents of freezing water. Paul Buchanan was hauling out lines at the mast. Numb fingers wrenched at rope and cloth to try to untangle the giant Gordian knot. It had a wrap at the top and at the clew, with the mid-section flogging out of control. Jeffes was ten feet up the forestay balanced on the spinnaker pole trying to pull the sail down. After 20 minutes the first rip began to appear and soon the mid section had several bad tears.

The nightmare battle went on for 90 minutes and then, with winds gusting to 55 knots, Julian sent someone up to the foredeck to say that they had to reef the main. The safety of the yacht and crew had become paramount, before misfortune led inexorably to disaster and the mast was torn out.

'Just give me five more minutes!' said Jeffes, who realised that rounding up in 55 knots to reef would probably destroy the yankee.

InterSpray seemed to be trapped in her own private vortex as the time bomb of a suspect bottlescrew ticked away at the back of each crew member's mind.

Finally forced to abandon all hope of saving the sail, Jeffes returned aft to take the helm from John, by now in a bad way, suffering from wind chill and fatigue. After driving the boat on the brink of disaster, John reported he'd had no feeling in his hands for the past 30 minutes. Paralysed with cold, he went below. His hands had to be held in warm water under the galley tap and as the circulation returned, the pain was excruciating. Alison rubbed his hands between hers to get them warm.

On deck Julian was organising two reefs in the main. As Jeffes rounded up the yacht, the yankee, already split, caught the full force of wind and shredded itself in seconds into a line of rags. It looked like dirty washing streaming from the forestay. The wind had come round 180 degrees in two hours.

To get back on course, it was decided

to tack the yacht, rather than risk a gybe. But the seas were so enormous that she wouldn't go round. The boat staggered on the top of a wave and slid backwards. The wheel was wrenched from Jeffes' hands, spinning from lock to lock. It was only later, in Hobart, that one of the rudder stops for the steering quadrant (a 6in square, 3ins thick teak block) was discovered smashed in two.

The slack staysail sheets, meanwhile, had flailed about and twisted into such a mass of knots that the foresail had to come down to untangle them. With the wind still howling at 50-plus knots and the yacht blasting into the night at 12 knots under two reefs and bareheaded, they could see they would have to go for a third reef.

This time they decided that instead of tacking the yacht they would gybe the main inside the runners and put the staysail back up afterwards.

But when the wind suddenly changed octaves and began shrieking at hurricane force, the idea of hoisting the staysail was abandoned. *InterSpray* was now ploughing through the Southern Ocean maelstrom at 10 knots under triple-reefed main and nothing else.

Pieces of the No 1 yankee, torn to ribbons, flew over the heads of the cockpit crew and disappeared into the blackness astern. The streaming tatters flogged with a noise like a volley of pistol shots.

'I'll never forget the bangs and cracks from that sail flogging itself to bits above my head like a fusillade of rifle shots,' said Jeffes, whose feet had gone totally numb. It wasn't until he went below that he realised that for the last five hours he'd been wearing his trainers instead of leather-lined boots, such was the rush to get on deck when the troubles began.

The yacht continued to shudder as the backstay vibrated with the thrashing of the foresail remnants. Not only was it irreparable, but for the time being irretrievable. It was out of the question to send anyone up the forestay to cut away the rags of sail. Conditions remained so wild that it would be 12 hours before Julian could venture halfway up the forestay with a Stanley knife, scissors ('and a prayer book, if I'd had one') to cut away as much as he could. 'Just half an hour up there was totally, physically exhausting,' he reported.

Someone wrote in the log: 'Hove-to, cut ⅓ of yankee from forestay. Attempt to be made now to pull it down. Julian is our hero.'

'Oh no he's not!' scribbled Julian.

Despite the enormous vibrations straining the rig, conditions did not allow clearing the forestay until 24 hours later, on day 30, when a line was put around the highest piston hank on the remains of the sail, and it was winched down to deck level.

Painstakingly, inch by inch, using the primary cockpit winch, they dragged it down until, after three hours, there was a sorry heap of tattered sailcloth lying in the sail forepeak.

Everyone had kept their nerve in the violent storm, despite confronting very real fears as the yacht pitched and rolled on the edge of control. Any remaining tensions were defused by Dominic, observing later with a mischievous grin: 'At least we don't have to change the No 1 yankee all the way to Hobart!'

While *InterSpray* suffered a bad night and continued to face the fury of the Southern Ocean with storm-force winds for the next 48 hours, the rest of the fleet had their own dramas.

Heath Insured had became the fourth yacht to suffer a forestay bottlescrew failure. They also had a suspected broken ankle on the foredeck. On *Hofbrau*, Tristan Lewis, coming off watch, dislocated his right shoulder doing nothing more dangerous than getting undressed as the yacht took a violent lurch. *Pride of Teesside* had a radar failure and were heading north out of iceberg territory.

LEG TWO

Above: we made it! Fourteen more sailors join the exclusive society of Cape Horners. It was as if InterSpray's crew had crept around a sleeping a giant, as they found themselves at the windiest place in the world in an almost flat calm. Below: Cape Horn as it should have been – in Toni Knights' dramatic painting of InterSpray

Vivien Cherry came on the radio asking Julian for advice on painkillers; someone on *Coopers & Lybrand* had cracked a rib. *Rhone-Poulenc* had two crewmen bruised from battling with a flailing sheet who looked 'very similar to a number of the Friday night customers I used to deal with as a copper,' reported skipper Peter Phillips.

Despite broken bones, and broken rigging screws, the crews' morale was holding up with a sense of humour and their mettle, though dented, had not fatigued.

Jeffes and John Davis, in the outer bunks at the aft end of *InterSpray*, were having difficulty sleeping with the violent motion whenever the yacht corkscrewed off a wave.

'I nearly stove in the planking beside my bunk,' said Jeffes, while John got a nasty bump on his head. The berths amidships, nearer the centre of gyration, seemed a lot more civilised.

To add to the problems, there were numerous reports coming over the radio of icebergs and growlers around the waypoint. One of the few consolations of being at the back of the fleet was the comforting thought that other yachts acted as pathfinders. But it was still a game of Russian roulette. There were radar checks every 15 minutes and bilge checks every half-hour.

On the radar screen a tiny green blip an eighth of inch long was in reality an iceberg a mile long, 300ft high, and weighing millions of tons. And if the yacht was heeled over, the blip vanished from the screen. Spurious echoes and radar 'clutter' from wavetops made the deadly growlers, mini-bergs, invisible to radar.

Jeffes had an iceberg drill with every watch at least once a day: Watches were given 30 seconds to avoid a hypothetical berg. Heave-to, tack, gybe? They sat and talked it through. There was also a forestay failure drill.

Meanwhile, they continued to chip away slowly at the leaders, but it was painfully slow progress. 'At the moment it's a toss up whether we run out of sails before we catch up or not,' said Jeffes, who had been pushing the boat to its limits to make up lost ground.

On the evening of day 31 at 2149 GMT *InterSpray* rounded the waypoint at 52°S 120°W. 'Only 3,539 miles to Hobart,' said the log.

Julian was now getting weatherfax pictures from Hawaii. On the Chat Show it was learned that *Commercial Union* had stolen the lead from *Nuclear Electric*, while *Hofbrau* were limping north after problems with their jury-rigged aft lower shroud. Geraint Lewis had broken his collarbone when his bunk lee cloth gave way aboard *Coopers & Lybrand*. From home came news by telex of Prince Charles and Princess Diana's official separation.

More chilling was news of the concentration of icebergs, around the waypoint, designed, ironically, to stop yachts straying too far south into iceberg territory.

The descriptions of icebergs which came over the radio from other yachts varied from 'Dome-shaped', to 'Twin Peaks', 'Sydney Opera House' and 'Polar bear on top of glacier mint'.

With headwinds of around 30 knots for the last 60 hours, *InterSpray*'s crew were now experiencing the biggest seas they had yet seen, with the yacht frequently semi-submerged as she was swept by 60ft waves. The stainless steel cages for both lifebuoys had been bent by wave action, even though they were on the inside of the pulpit. Driving through a wavecrest, the yacht would emerge on the other side into a vacuum, dropping down with an horrendous crash before surging on to the next wave. There was no horizon beyond the wall of angry waves at the bow.

At one point, with triple-reefed main and storm staysail only, the boat was going so fast to windward that Jeffes, fearful of the pounding that *InterSpray* was taking, shouted through the hatch to the helmsman: 'For Christ's sake try and slow it down a bit guys!'

A spontaneous cheer of relief and approval was heard from the off-watch in the saloon. 'It was the only time I ever told them to slow it down,' said Jeffes. 'Though I'd told them to speed it up on innumerable occasions.'

On these occasions the forced humour down below could not always disguise people's apprehensions. Deep down some knew they didn't want to be here. And there would be *no* way some of them would ever be coming back. But for others, it was the masochistic promise of moments like this that had made them join the Challenge; to face ultimate danger and see how they would react. 'I couldn't possibly say I'm enjoying this. It's real survival stuff,' Julian spoke into his tape recorder to his family one grim night.

Sleep deprivation, exhaustion and occasional low morale, meant that mood swings on *InterSpray* went from resignation and trepidation to exhilaration (for the helmsmen) and even a kind of Southern Ocean rapture where, on the worst days, the splendour of their isolation and the desolate beauty of this inhospitable region held a fateful fascination.

Nuclear Electric's John Chittenden found the slamming of the yacht going to windward almost soporific compared to a Whitbread maxi flat out under spinnaker. 'To some extent we are racing Morris Minors compared to the Whitbread Ferraris,' he said, adding that the yachts were a credit to designer David Thomas. 'Speeds near 20 knots have been reported, but a Morris Minor will do 100 mph if driven over Beachy Head,' he added dryly.

One afternoon of day 32, Dominic was on the helm, with Julian riding shotgun, with his back to the bow to shield the helmsman from sleet and hail. Suddenly Dominic looked up at the sky and uttered an expletive as *InterSpray* climbed a towering wavecrest. A wall of green water rushed down the sidedeck, past the chart table window, where Jeffes sat plotting.

The next moment Dominic was gripping the rim of the wheel as his body streamed horizontally, his legs floating over the pushpit guardrail. He had been lifted bodily out of the helmsman's well. Julian, meanwhile, had been swept off his feet and was up to his arms in frothing water, pushed through the stainless steel crash guard into the wheel. Both were clipped on.

Monster waves like this one had been rare up to now, but in the uphill struggle to Hobart the deck was beginning to look more like a surfacing submarine than a sailing yacht. Barry and Jeff had a similar experience and emerged from the white water rapids in hysterics. 'Incredible, spectacular, frightening,' wrote Barry, his expletives-deleted.

Down below it had been dubbed 'The Pots and Pans Gale'. In the galley, Alison and Jeff were preparing the evening meal. First the cheese mix went all over the floor and saloon seats. Next, as Dominic's Big Wave struck the yacht, the big cooking pots went into orbit from the stove on the high side.

Alison went in one direction and a two-gallon pan of spaghetti bolognaise sauce (deflected by Jeff's head) disappeared through the doorway into the skipper's cabin, its lid conveniently coming off as it smeared its contents over the aft bulkhead, floor and ceiling, decorating any boots and clothing that were hanging up to dry in its path.

In Jeff's inimitable graphic commentary: 'It was as if a giant had spewed up all over the saloon and passageway.'

Fortunately, the pan of boiling water ended up over the sink and missed scalding anyone. Brian and the skipper scooped up the spaghetti with spatulas and supper began for a third time. Paul Buchanan had taken to closing his cabin door. 'If I'm thrown out of bed, I have less distance to fall.' He had earlier been

thrown out of the port head, across the companionway and into the starboard head in mid-flow. Fortunately it had been empty at the time.

An ocean racer needed to be a cross between a ballerina and a cat and while upper body strength developed from all the winching and hanging on and tensing yourself above and below decks, leg muscles wasted away. By the time they got to Hobart some crew reported leg muscles had just 'shrivelled up'.

After the Pots and Pans Gale, the diesel-fired Eberspacher heater was pressed into service in the increasing cold. The sea temperature hovered just above zero degrees centigrade and with icy Antarctic winds the helmsman soon got very cold. Brian rigged a length of hose from the cabin heater out to the cockpit and down the helmsman's oilskins. Soon after this, over-enthusiastic Carlton set fire to his own underpants.

A smell of burning was noticed by Brian who spotted Carlton's smouldering pants on the heater's exhaust pipe. Carlton was accused by the safety officer of setting the boat on fire. This was the cue for an underpants competition with marks out of 10. Ricky came top, because of the sheer acreage of his underpants. Carlton was second, and Jeffes third, for artistic impression. He lost on technical merit. The hot exhaust pipe was declared out of bounds for drying clothes.

After the three-day gale had abated, the hanks on the staysail were seen to have worn through with constant abrading on the inner forestay. It was as if a bronze termite had taken bite-sized chunks out of them. Spare hanks were scavenged from the luff of the destroyed yankee to replace them. Sail repairs were carried out in the narrow confines of the companion-way, often at night and in the gloom of emergency lighting.

InterSpray *was becalmed at the sailors' Everest of Cape Horn for 16 hours*

After the continual pounding of the yacht, Jeffes and John inspected the keel bolts and the mast step, wondering how much the rig could withstand.

In the early hours of day 32, at 0510 Jeffes was sitting at the chart table listening to the radio when he overheard news being relayed to *Commercial Union* that *British Steel II* had been dismasted mid-way in the Pacific. Richard Tudor reported in a calm voice that no one had been injured and the mast had sheared off at the gooseneck, toppling over the side into the sea.

A crewman on deck watching for icebergs had stared in horror as the bottlescrew broke with a gunshot report. A second later the preventer stay snapped. He turned to yell at the helmsman. When he turned back the mast was gone. Crewman Patrick Quinn (53) was sitting below deck. There were two bangs. And then a deathly silence. The roar of the wind in the rigging had suddenly, stopped. There was uncanny silence.

Hofbrau was one of the closest yachts and Goss was immediately on the radio offering assistance. *InterSpray*, though two days sailing away, also offered fuel for motoring.

Back in London, with a five hour time difference, Andrew Roberts was at a RORC meeting in St James's Place on Wednesday morning when he heard, via a telex from duty yacht *Group 4*, the news he must have dreaded. The dismasting had happened at the remotest point from land on the globe, but Roberts knew about it within 12 minutes of it happening, thanks to state of the art satellite communications.

It was the sixth rigging screw to have failed, this time with a vengeance. The odds were shortening every day on who would be next.

Tudor, like others, had exchanged his forestay rigging screw with that of the aft lower shroud, and it had been the latter that failed, causing the dismasting. Jeffes had deliberately ignored Race HQ advice to make the switch of bottlescrews. The lower aft is a highly loaded shroud carrying significant thrust from the boom vang.

Roberts had received a telex from Tudor the day before the dismasting: 'Taking a hell of a pounding. This is what we paid for and it really hurts. Tempers are becoming frayed. . .' The telex had made Roberts 'go weak at the knees', with the yacht reportedly going to windward at 10 knots in gale-force conditions. Injuries on board were already a slipped disc and a sprained arm. Fortunately none of the crew were hurt when the dismasting happened.

Jeffes and John Davis spent several hours on *InterSpray's* foredeck the next day, on the advice of Race HQ, reinforcing the jury rigged forestay with an 18mm Spectra preventer (13,000 kilo breaking strain), running from above the rigging screw down to the anchor roller and tack eye. If the screw broke they had an arrester by-passing it. It wouldn't hold the tension, but it would stop damage to a sail. Meanwhile, Tudor, who had been leading the fleet on combined times, was out of the race and faced the daunting task of getting to New Zealand, 2,400 miles away, under jury rig, with just a boom and two spinnaker poles to work with.

'Attempting to sail upwind with such a rig is like walking up the down escalator in roller skates,' thought Tim Jeffery, sailing correspondent of *The Telegraph*. The fleet had just one spare mast.

In better spirits later, Tudor reported 'I've always wanted to cruise the South Pacific in a motorboat.'

Group 4 and *Heath Insured*, meanwhile, were diverting to rendezvous with Tudor's stricken yacht in the middle of the loneliest place in the world for a precision operation to exchange 105 gallons of diesel by heaving line. Amidst huge Southern Ocean rollers, flares were fired into the night sky as the yachts lined up alongside each other.

British Steel II looked 'like a bird without wings', said Lisa-Marie Wood, radio operator on *Heath Insured*, whose crew were moved to tears. Tudor's crew hadn't lost their sense of humour. They thanked them by passing over a compact disc of *South Pacific*.

On day 33 Chay sent a telex to all yachts: 'No doubt you are all worried after the dismasting of *BS II* and the rigging screw failures. Everyone at Race HQ and the sponsors, who met last night, expressed their support and concern.

'To win this leg, and indeed the race, you have to sail over the finishing line. With this bottlescrew problem I strongly suggest you "nurse" your boats. There is nothing we can do from here to help you, other than verbal advice! It is down to your initiative. You may wish, for example, to rig extra preventer lines where the bottle screws have been changed and be a little gentler when the dicky bottlescrew is under pressure. What ever happens from now on please, (as I've always said) stay upwind of the rig for obvious reasons.

Good Luck, everybody is rooting for you all. This is some trip you're doing. Best Wishes, Chay.'

To conserve fuel, in the event of *InterSpray*'s dismasting, and until she was past the mid-ocean point of no return, Jeffes ordered engine running hours cut to three hours a day. There would be less hot water for showers.

InterSpray had seen five icebergs. One was quite small, about the size of a large tower block. Two large ones rose from the sea vertically to 500ft, with sheer faces and flat tops. One was a mile long. You could hear the faint echo of waves breaking against the sides and see ice caves in the side.

'We were all admiring it when we saw some breaking water 50 yards away – we'd missed a growler. It was our only

close encounter,' said Jeffes. 'It felt eerie to be so close to icebergs. It's hard to believe they are real when they look like lumps of icing sugar. So beautiful, but so deadly.'

On the evening of day 33, during a period of light winds after the storm, Barry went up the mast to put a new bulb in the navigation light, which illuminated the Windex. With malfunctioning instruments it was difficult to sail the boat to windward at night without the Windex.

The Lewmar 56 mast deck winches had also begun slipping and on stripping them it was discovered that the pawls were sticking open. It was only a matter of time before one failed with a spinnaker halyard under load and Jeffes banned their use for taking a man up the mast.

It meant that when winching Barry up the mast, a line had to be led through a snatchblock on the toe rail and back to the primary winches.

As Barry ascended, Alison was helming the yacht at eight knots through moderate seas. They didn't seem so moderate from Barry's bird's-eye view. 'I was thrown about all over the place and thought I was going to die.'

The crew had now been at sea for 34 days and, amazingly, the biggest source of friction on board was Mars Bars. They had been going mysteriously missing and were now rationed only to crew on late night watches.

The Great Mars Bar Robbery began when Mr. Angry (Jeff) came on nightwatch, taunting the skipper with his Mars Bar. Jeffes, twisting Plummer's balaclava back to front, confiscated his ration and promptly found himself accused by Plummer of being in illegal possession of said chocolate bar. A date was set for trial in the galley

Dominic was elected judge, because he looked suitably judicial in his red Musto hard hat, with earflaps, and Plummer elected for trial by jury.

The only way to get an impartial jury on *InterSpray* was to select the ship's

mascots and hot water bottle characters. The skipper's Dennis the Menace bottle was foreman, on account of being the most life-like. Miss Piggy, Leo the Lion, Gordon the Gopher and Hearty Bear were also voted on to the jury. Julian was Counsel for the Defence and Carlton Prosecutor.

Alas, the case never came to trial. Jeff decided not to proceed because he felt the jury might 'bottle out'. British justice was dead on *InterSpray*, he claimed and he had no witnesses to the robbery.

On the radio chat show ex-policeman Peter Phillips offered to 'come aboard with my truncheon and handcuffs if there's a bit of crime going on.' Tail-end Charlie *Rhone-Poulenc* was 200 miles behind eighth-placed *InterSpray* at the time.

Joker Phillips, the third skipper of *Rhone-Poulenc*, was reported to have played a practical joke on his old mate Chay Blyth when he telexed Race HQ to say that he had fallen out with his crew and they were all getting off in Hobart.

'I'm carrying on and need 13 replacement crew,' was the message sent home. Rumour had it that RHQ had a list of replacements drawn up before they realised it was a joke.

On *Coopers & Lybrand* they had so many injuries aboard that Vivien had re-christened her boat *Cripples & Liedown*. This could be added to other fleet nicknames, *Rhone-Plonkers* and *Nuclear Dyslexic*. InterSpray had been called *InterSun*, after sticking so close to South America at the start of the leg.

The Great Circle route to Hobart was known to Vivien's crew as 'the Piccadilly Line' after naming all the waypoints on the electronic navigation system after the London Underground stations between Holborn and Earls Court, the Aussie end of the line. It made the ocean seem a friendlier place.

She reported her crew getting tired of the wet, the same food and the endless

Above: ten hours behind GMT, Christmas celebrations began early on InterSpray *and went on for 34 hours, to keep in touch with UK time and local time.*
Below: up on deck it was a different story from the snug saloon, as Juliet looks apprehensively at another advancing wave. Facing page, top: Dominic morris dancing at Cape Horn. Below: the skipper celebrates while a surreptitious slurper hovers in the background

sail changes. 'It's some of the best sailing in the world for the purists, but a long way to come for it.'

Santa's Southern Ocean survival course

By day 37 Paul Buchanan recorded alarmingly: 'I don't recognise parts of my body, particularly my legs. They are very thin. Also my arms and face are thinner.'

Barry wrote: 'This leg has become a survival course rather than a race, but we're still trying to catch up.'

Rhone-Poulenc were said to be operating ship's time on GMT. Very British this, since the yachts had passed through seven time zones since Rio and were now nine hours behind GMT. This meant that in the Southern Ocean Phillips and his crew had breakfast at 4 pm, lunch at 10 pm and dinner at dawn!

Some 500 miles nearer Hobart, the youngest skipper in the fleet, 27-year-old Richard Merriweather, and his crew on *Commercial Union*, were giving *Nuclear Electric*'s master mariner John Chittenden a good run for his money, changing places regularly.

The Southern Ocean was at its softest on the evening of day 37 when the deck watch were singing Christmas carols to the accompaniment of Jeff's harmonica under a sunset of red, purple and orange, climaxed by the famous Green Flash. Down below a gambling syndicate was in play.

By the following night, with 45 knot squalls, *InterSpray* passed the 2,500 mile mark to Hobart and soon Christmas Eve was a day away. Juliet decorated the saloon with balloons and streamers and a miniature plastic Christmas tree was suspended upside down from a light fitting, in recognition of the fact that they

were at the bottom of the world. An inflatable Santa Claus presided.

Nobody on *InterSpray* had spent Christmas on a yacht before, including the skipper and, despite the festive decorations, there was an underlying sense that everybody wished they were somewhere else. It was even suggested that Christmas should be treated like any other day, since celebrations would merely heighten the sense of isolation and add to the emotions of being away from families. But Jeffes and the watchleaders felt it important to make the most of what was potentially a miserable time,

Jeff was pretending to be Mr Scrooge but Julian wasn't so sure and telexed home: 'Entertainments Officer Jeff, on whose shoulders all Xmas arrangements fall, is to Xmas what Margaret Thatcher is to Communism. Nightly we hear him tramping the deck, dressed only in a nightgown, dragging the anchor chain behind him. Jeff has announced that we will have a pure Xmas devoid of western trappings during which we will think only of those less fortunate than ourselves.'

Hofbrau, sailing down in the Screaming Sixties, was one such deserving case. They had ice on the decks, with sheets and halyards frozen solid like sticks. Goss ventured down to 61°S and *Commercial Union* and *Coopers & Lybrand* both dipped below 60°S.

InterSpray, being 10 hours behind GMT, began celebrations for Christmas early, to keep in step with the UK, and then continued in local time for the full 34 hours. A Christmas Eve carol concert had to be postponed with storm-force winds and a radar alert for icebergs. Barry was helming 'in disguise' as Santa.

While *InterSpray* crashed through the night, the skipper had made a mincemeat tart, which varied in thickness, depending on the heel of the yacht. At midnight the crew munched tarts and sipped cheap white wine which, after six weeks' abstinence, tasted like champagne as they bounced through 20ft waves in 40-knot winds.

The Southern Ocean was an uncompromising host for a party, thought Julian, as he took the helm in his Christmas party hat, enjoying an hour's solitude in the cockpit. His miniature Father Christmas was firmly pinned to his lifejacket as the icy cold southwesterly wind swept off the Antarctic. The regular squalls, seen on radar by standby watch in the warmth of the doghouse, were full of hail that hit bare flesh like sharp needles.

Like everyone on board that morning, Julian was in sombre mood, thinking of his family and feeling a pang of guilt that his girls would be spending Christmas without him.

Back home, though, Trisha had prepared a life-size cardboard cut-out of Julian, dressed in real oilskins and Musto hat, which was already propped up at the Christmas dinner table.

Down below in *InterSpray*'s snug saloon, the awkward atmosphere was relaxing as the wine flowed and Patrick got out a litre bottle of whisky given to him by his father. Later Julian came below and produced one of Mrs Shortland's famous cakes, preserved by its alcohol content.

This helped to explain the note in someone's log: 'Skip later fell over in cockpit and bruised ribs. Coincidence? We think not!'

Propagation that morning was good enough to allow radio telephone links home, via Portishead, as crew wished wives, girl friends, children and (in Juliet's case) husband, a happy day.

Julian got through to Shrewsbury. 'It was lovely to hear Emma's voice squeaking with delight when she answered the phone and realised it was me. That was one of the most precious memories of Christmas. It just somehow brought everything that much closer,' he confided.

The skipper and watch leaders took over the running of the galley and yacht on Christmas Day, while crew had a day off. Carolyn had provided festive hats and crackers. Paul and Carlton cooked Christmas dinner. There would be no turkey with trimmings. The only bird likely to be sighted in these latitudes was an albatross. Instead, the menu was lentil soup, fresh bread, chicken curry and rice. To follow there was Christmas fruit cake, with rum and chocolate sauce, or custard and whisky, all washed down with liberal quantities of Southern Ocean-chilled Muscadet.

Christmas presents were opened. John had a musical kangaroo (what else?) with a toy sack that, when squeezed, played a medley of Christmas tunes. Jocelyn, his wife, had packed it five months ago, wondering if the batteries would last 14,000 miles, and all the way back to Australia. The skipper had a pair of musical socks which played *Jingle Bells*. Dominic, who seemed to get a present most days, was inundated. 'Where does he store them all?' crew asked themselves.

Julian had made a rash promise to friends in Shrewsbury that at midday GMT he would toast them from the top of the mast. But with the 10-hour time difference and 30-plus knots across the deck on it suddenly didn't seem such a good idea on this black night.

British Steel II, wishing Santa would drop a mast through the hole in their deck, sang at the end of the radio chat show their own rendition of *The Twelve Days of Christmas*, '. . . on the second day of Christmas my true love sent to me, five bottle-screws. . . and a mast as a Christmas tree. . . '

Chay and his team sent a telex: 'A very Merry Christmas to all of you down there in the Roaring Forties. We had a wee staff party and raised our glasses to drink your health. You were well and truly on our minds.'

Christmas hadn't materialised in quite the way the skipper or anybody else had intended. But everybody had made a great effort to enjoy themselves. 'It was,'

Above: the champagne flows for Barry.
Right: Julian enjoys an hours' solitude
on the helm on Christmas Day

said Jeffes 'a British stiff upper-lip affair. Everybody wished they were somewhere else. It was quite strange. . .' It was certainly a Christmas unlikely to be forgotten, or repeated.

On Boxing Day the only bottle unscrewed was the one on the foredeck, as *InterSpray* became the sixth victim of a broken forestay.

The wind and sea had kept up its angry onslaught all day and into the night. At 0315 local time, Patrick was on the wheel driving the yacht hard and discussing *InterSpray*'s arrival time in Hobart with Julian. '10-14 days,' reckoned Julian.

'Providing something doesn't break,' cautioned Patrick.

'You mustn't get spooked about breakages and be pessimistic, we've got to behave as if isn't going to happen and keep sailing the boat as fast as we can,' said Julian.

INTERSPRAY'S RACE AROUND THE WORLD

As he finished the sentence they heard a loud bang. At first it sounded like a wave smacking against the hull, but then the No 2 yankee started luffing and the curve of the slack forestay could be seen in the gloom. They looked at one another and both thought: 'Forestay!'

Julian rushed on deck. Sure enough, the bottlescrew had sheared, at exactly the same place as the other five, but the Spectra arrester line had saved the sail.

Paul Jeffes, in his bunk, had noticed the change in the yacht's motion as she came upright. At first he thought the main was being reefed, until Barry, on standby watch, burst into his cabin to say the bottlescrew had gone.

Julian, now joined on the waveswept foredeck by Paul Buchanan and Duggie, grappled in the near gale to get the sail down as quickly as possible. By the time the skipper and John Davis had got into their oilies and on deck they had the headsail down and were taking it off the broken forestay. The mast was supported by the Spectra spinnaker halyards.

There was much amusement among the rest of the crew as a drenched Buchanan came off the foredeck, his boots full of water and his dry Christmas clothes saturated, protesting: 'If this was a job, I'd leave.' Another one for *InterSpray's* Book of Quotes.

There had been no real emergency. The fact that so many forestays had already broken had made it seem almost routine. Jeffes and John spent the next few hours of twilight on the foredeck making up a forestay to enable them to fly the No 2 yankee again. It was a relatively simple job, but trying to do it on a bouncing bow digging itself in water five degrees above freezing was not so easy. They had to hold on with one hand while trying to do the job with the other.

The jury rig involved doubling a piece of the Spectra spinnaker guy around the remains of the bottlescrew, through shackles fixed at the tack-eye. The whole thing was then winched up tight with the staysail sheet led back to the primary winch.

To get the jury rig tight enough to fly a headsail, the 86ft mast had to be tilted forward a foot or so while still sailing to windward at seven knots in 25-30 knots. Jeffes wasn't about to heave-to and risk losing more miles to the fleet leaders, 700 miles away.

He conducted the operation from the shrouds. The backstay and runners were eased and the mast canted forward by taking up on the jury-rigged stays. These were winched up as tightly as possible to support the front and mid-section of the mast. The serious tension could then be applied by cranking up the backstay. By 0930, with little visible sag in the forestay, the No 2 yankee went back up and *InterSpray* was back in the chase with 1,800 miles to go. The remarkable fact that the boat speed never once dropped below six knots throughout this tricky operation was due entirely to the advance preparations made for a forestay failure.

Other Challenge yachts had been moving quickly in the northerly airstream, *Hofbrau* covering 115 miles in 12 hours. But *InterSpray* was not the slowest boat, despite several hours' slow progress while sorting out the forestay.

The forestay was checked at half-hour intervals. Brian later made up a string of shackles as an additional back-up. With a suspect forestay there would be no more trips up the mast.

British Steel II, meanwhile, had rendezvoused on Boxing Day with the container ship *NZ Pacific*, which transferred 100 jerry cans containing 1,000 litres of diesel fuel on a pulley in less than an hour. 'The best Christmas present we could have hoped for,' reported crewman Kevin Dufficy, as they motored to Chatham Island 1,000 miles away for another refuelling. They were also given strawberries and cream, wine, whisky and a Christmas tree.

As *InterSpray*'s misfortunes started to make some crew grouchy, a Politeness Society was formed. Jeff said he'd try, but threatened to form a splinter group, The Grumpy Society.

By day 44, *Heath Insured* and second-placed *Commercial Union* reported problems with damaged steering cables. 'Our steering wheel has assumed a slightly different shape after Sue Tight landed on it,' said Merriweather.

On *Heath Insured*, lying seventh, their steering cable broke and they rigged the emergency tiller and managed to continue making 9 knots on a good course while mechanic Ken Pearson had a two-hour repair session. The cable broke again and repairs took a further three hours.

InterSpray's steering had taken some huge knocks, too, and underwent maintenance by the Brothers Grimsby (Ricky and Brian). 'Temporarily turned to rat shit the course,' said a succinct log entry by someone who had not yet joined the Politeness Society. Two killer whales escorted the yacht for a half-hour, maintaining station just three feet away.

On day 45, with winds of 40 knots, occasionally building to 50, *InterSpray* was hurtling through huge seas in a blinding welter of spray on one of her longest, fastest runs. The boom occasionally dipped in the water and the spray on the face of the helmsman was painful. For 36 hours the yacht roared along at 11-12 knots, catching the fleet leaders under triple-reefed main and storm headsail. 'We're screaming along like a bat out of hell, but totally under control. No one can sleep for the noise,' complained Buchanan.

During such a storm Julian recorded an interview down below on video which was to appear in the BBC documentary. Looking suitably gaunt and fatigued, he said: 'I thought I'd just see if I could borrow a 10p and nip out to the phone box and tell Mr Blyth he was obviously completely crazy to do this on his own.

It's okay in company, but I think on your own it would be hard work. . .'

The day was also a nautical milestone as *InterSpray*'s Time Travellers crossed the International Date Line at 1930, going instantly from 12 hours behind the UK to 12 hours ahead.

'We lost Wednesday the 30th entirely,' noted an incredulous log entry. On *Nuclear Electric* Martin Barker, who was off watch, went to bed on Christmas Eve and woke up to find it was Boxing Day. He missed Christmas altogether

There will always be some doubt over who was helming *InterSpray* at this historic moment in her circumnavigation, since Dominic and Paul Buchanan were grappling on the wheel for line honours, as Carlton refereed, though the entry in the log asserted: 'Dominic at the wheel'.

Perhaps it was best summed up by the crew member who thought: 'It's like New Year really; a bit of an anticlimax when it happens, because nothing actually changes.'

Passing the 180° line of longitude did mean that *InterSpray* was close to Chatham Island and New Zealand.

The crew's main concern was that they might have lost New Year's day entirely. Instead, they clocked up the longest run of the fleet: 119 miles, with just 1,337 miles to Hobart.

Quote of the day was from the skipper: 'There's no kudos for me sitting at the chart table, they think I'm just keeping out of the wet.'

A telex from Chay on December 30 acknowledged that the yachts had gone further south than was ever envisaged when crossing the Pacific – 'driving the yachts almost to breaking point in making 5,500 miles against the worst weather the world has to offer.' It was a feat unlikely to be repeated for years, if at all, he said, and 'an achievement of which you all can be rightly proud.'

But while leg two had shown how well the yachts performed to windward in bad

weather, Blyth feared that leg three could be worse, with the ice limit further north this year. He was anxious about reports from competitors in the Globe Challenge sighting as many as 20 icebergs a day as far north as 48°S. The Race Committee meeting at the RORC had recommended a change from the Kerguelen Island waypoint at 50°S to one nearly 800 miles north, at Amsterdam Island, 37°S.

'My object in this race has been to provide you all with a tough challenge, but also some enjoyment. I would like you to have more enjoyment this time,' said Blyth. Some crew must have wondered if it was a practical joke.

Skippers were invited to discuss the new waypoint option with crews. They had a choice of either battling against the wind along the Great Circle route or taking a longer route in the north-east trades. An answer was wanted within 48 hours.

'Amsterdam or Kerguelen? No explanations needed, Regards Chay.' the telex ended.

The vote was not in doubt for most. Jeffes reported back to Race HQ overnight that *InterSpray's* crew were unanimous in rejecting the Amsterdam diversion.

Softening up 'the world's toughest yacht race' was not an option. The decision wouldn't be made until mid-way in the Hobart stopover, but Kerguelen it would be.

By now the yachts were making such good progress that the Challenge support team were having to advance their flights to Hobart to meet them in time.

Around this time Jeffes and other skippers received a confidential coded telex from Chay requesting them to: 'Please reconfirm your Centurion status.'

'Centurion' was Chay's code word for any potential drop-outs from the

Previous pages: all hands on deck: dropping the damaged mainsail for essential repair work

Challenge. It was part of a contingency plan to enable Race HQ to bring a reserve crew list into play to replace anyone jumping ship at stopovers. It was felt that by Hobart there might be some crew who would think they'd done the hardest part of the circumnavigation and want to get off.

'Why call them Centurions?' Paul had asked Chay at a skippers' meeting in Rio, 'Are you expecting legions of them?'

For his part Jeffes was able to confirm: 'Centurion status zero.'

New Year's Eve came between watches, during Barry's four-hour sleep period. But Dominic got him out of bed at midnight to join the celebrations, letting off party poppers and drinking champagne and whisky. Hip flasks appeared, and on deck they got a wind shift and were laying the course with less than 1,000 miles to Hobart.

'Had a cigar and quite a glow when I went back to bed for an hour. The 0200 to 0600 watch was hell, but we made it,' said Barry.

With little more than a Fastnet Race equivalent left between *InterSpray* and Hobart, Julian had a sense of the anti-hero as he reflected that the Southern Oceans had may have roughed them up, but they had escaped comparatively lightly.

'Every one of us will remember how we felt on the really bad nights. And we all know that we were frightened and the adrenalin was flowing, but generally speaking we have been very lucky.'

A New Year message telexed from Roger Peek said:

'I have been thinking more about your alleged early start in Rio by one second and think I have an argument for you: Race starts when the gun goes. First sign of gun going off is the puff of smoke. The sound of the gun is heard after the puff of smoke is seen, as speed of sound is less than speed of light. Being blessed with a skipper with razor-sharp reflexes, you were clearly across the start line at the first sign of the puff of smoke. At the speed of sound it would take one second to hear the gun from a distance of approximately 340 yards, if you were 350 yards or more from the gun then you would have crossed the start line a fraction after the actual gun, but a second before the sound of the gun. Understand International Jury is due to sit in Hobart on 14th January.

Happy New Year, Roger.'

From Andrew Roberts came the message: 'The support team wish all of you a very happy New Year. May it be safe, successful, satisfying and not too sober. You have earned our great respect for your enormous efforts, determination and achievements in recent weeks and months. We are sure the next 14,000 miles will continue to be a great race. Good luck and we'll see you in Tasmania.'

A big high pressure was now developing over Hobart and with it the hopes that it might slow down the front runners and give *InterSpray* a chance to close the gap. If they didn't get a shift in weather fortunes soon they would run out of distance to do it.

Food rationing was now in operation as everything except McDougalls dry foods and pasta was running out. Crew morale was high, despite the leg position, with all aggression targeted at the Wind Gods.

On day 46, *Group 4* and *Pride of Teesside* were placed equal fourth when, after 7,000 miles racing, Mike Golding had his first sighting of another yacht since breaking away from the fleet towards Florianopolis to repair their forestay.

For some reason Race HQ had requested pictures of *InterSpray*'s crew shaving. For race sponsor Gillette, probably. Julian's reply: 'Sorry no pics of crew shaving. Whole operation considered too dangerous by most crew and we are going easy on water supplies. Only two girls without beards so far.'

At 0200 GMT on day 48, *InterSpray* sighted land for the first time since Cape Horn on December 3, when they passed Campbell Island, visible under cloud 18 miles away on the port beam.

All the way from the Horn to Campbell Island there had been only one or two days when the hatches could be opened, it had been so cold. Thermals and mid-layers had been worn all the way. Since leaving Rio de Janeiro's tropical beaches they had experienced sub zero temperatures, fog, hail, sleet, icebergs, storm-force winds and constantly wet bedding and clothes. The end of the ordeal was in sight.

The dog otter drysuits had proved a literal headache for some. The reluctance to take off layers of clothing to go to the toilet meant people were not drinking enough and on a diet of freeze-dried food the lack of rehydration bought on a crop of headaches which exhausted the ship's entire stock of paracetamol. Julian was convinced the hangover-type headaches were caused through dehydration.

InterSpray was some 300 miles south of New Zealand and as she sailed further north nights became distinctly darker. On the morning of New Year's Day (the 49th day) there was seaweed floating past and Auckland Island was sighted to port at breakfast. Forty miles long, it was an uninhabited pinprick on the chart.

British Steel II had reached the end of her marathon motor-sail, arriving in Chatham Island to refuel, after some 2,200 miles across the Pacific. She left the island with a new schooner rig (a mast dug up from a farmer's field) bound for Wellington, New Zealand, 500 miles away.

A telex from race HQ said that *Hofbrau* had discovered a large horizontal crease and crack in their mast at deck level. It was possible this had been caused by whiplash during the forestay failure and it was recommended that the area be examined for signs of cracking by other yachts with damaged bottlescrews. When Vivien Cherry checked she found

LEG TWO

Left: after 9,760 miles, the end is in sight. Ricky, Julian and Dominic on the sharp end in the River Derwent. Above: a homecoming smile that says it all from John Davis, the only Australian in the race

similar cracks. The radio chat show crackled with news of mast damage. *InterSpray*'s mast was A1.

Nuclear Electric, meanwhile, struggling against calms to complete the final 200 miles to Hobart, was having her lead almost halved by *Commercial Union* as Merriweather closed the gap.

Pete Goss had stripped away the gaiter where *Hofbrau*'s mast came through the deck aperture and found a crack that ominously snaked around three-quarters of the mast. The jagged aluminium split, which you could put a finger in, opened and closed like a demented grin with the rhythm of the waves. Goss drilled a hole at one end of the crack in an attempt to stop it completing its deadly circuit. So worried was Goss that they were close to disaster, that the boom had been removed, the main-sail stowed below and bolt cutters stored on deck, in case the mast toppled over. 'Everyone on the crew has a mental picture of where to take cover,' said

Michael Calvin. 'Mine is a sunken corner of the cockpit.'

Spencer Drummond telexed: 'You should be very, repeat very, careful. There are no spare masts.'

Aboard *Hofbrau*, Rebecca Slater was just emerging from 34 days working below decks on 100,000 separate hand stitches to repair their 5,800sq ft spinnaker, which had been shredded off Argentina. *Hofbrau* had chosen to keep the sail damage from their rivals. Rebecca had started work setting herself a target of finishing before 1993 arrived.

To some of *InterSpray*'s crew it was unthinkable that one crew member on a yacht should endure such solitary confinement and miss out on the sailing adventure. And with their damaged mast, Rebecca was even to be robbed of the reward of flying the spinnaker into Hobart.

Finally on day 49 *Nuclear Electric*, which had led for all but four days of the seven weeks from Rio, slipped into

Hobart under cover of darkness at 0126 local time. Their time was 48 days 22 hours 26 minutes, some 13 days ahead of the original estimated arrival time. Chittenden said his crew 'had given 100 per cent in effort, had 50 per cent of the ability and 20 per cent of the knowledge of Whitbread crews, but the latter percentages were increasing.'

Commercial Union was second into Hobart, some ten hours behind Chittenden, a remarkable change in fortunes under their new skipper after their disastrous first leg to Rio .

Hofbrau crossed the finish line in third place at 1229 local time next day, followed six hours later by *Coopers & Lybrand*, flying their spinnaker and racing at 9.5 knots, despite their badly cracked mast. Perhaps Vivien was hoping to get a new one.

Group 4 and *Pride of Teesside* were the next boats to finish, within three hours of each other, followed by seventh-placed *Heath Insured*.

Mike Golding arrived with a crew rendition of *Waltzing Matilda* and was congratulated on recouping so much time after his pit-stop in Brazil with the fleet's first bottlescrew failure.

In preparation for *InterSpray*'s return to civilisation, Julian shaved off his beard and Dom, sitting opposite him at breakfast, didn't even notice. As the yacht closed on Australia, John Davis's smile got wider and wider and peeling him away from radio contact with all and sundry was a major feat, even at chat show times.

Duggie was servicing his bagpipes by day 52, a sure sign of imminent arrival in port. His spare Gore-Tex bag had not yet been used and he applied a mixture of whisky and honey to lubricate the pigskin inner bag. Was this the cause of the unique Duggie Drone?

With Tasmania in sight, and Duggie practising his pipes, Barry lay back in his bunk for the last time, looking at his photos of Kerry and Matthew pinned on the bulkhead. It was with mixed feelings that he finished this leg.

The race was nearly over for him and work and normality awaited. The rest of the crew expressed their sympathies. Barry's reward next day was to helm the yacht for three hours of a six-hour watch in big seas and 35 knot winds – 'and to put a reef in the main without slowing the boat down, so that I'd be under water most of the time!'

By the early hours of day 53, Jeffes and his crew had been pounding the boat mercilessly as it became a race against time to cross the finish line before they lost their overall second place on combined times to *Hofbrau*. Jeffes telexed back to International Paints: 'It looks as though we may make it into Hobart second in the fleet overall by the skin of our teeth.'

For John, the only Australian in the fleet, it was an emotionally charged homecoming, after the loneliness of the Southern Ocean, as *InterSpray* spent a final night beating down towards Tasman Island. An obliging wind shift sped them across Storm Bay.

On the helm John savoured the magic moment as they reached Iron Pot, with the sun rising over the mountains and the broad river spread out before him. You could smell the eucalyptus from miles away. It was quite overpowering.

It was an esoteric experience to find himself helming *InterSpray* into home waters as dawn broke at the lower reaches of the River Derwent, without a spectator boat in sight. They seemed to have it all to themselves.

With a light breeze springing up, the crew raised the spinnaker and then found themselves frustratingly becalmed for a brief period halfway up-river. It was a first chance to take in the Tasmanian scenery of Hobart's beautiful deep water harbour nestling at the foot of Mount Wellington. Hobart was an amphitheatre with its surrounding thickly forested green, rolling hills. And, though the crew didn't realise it at the time, the yacht was being silently observed by early morning Taswegians breakfasting on their balconies.

'The smell of pine, instead of the crew is wonderful,' Buchanan remarked. Julian had already telexed ahead that the yacht had suffered water-maker problems and water rationing. 'Deodorant stocks low. Hobart will smell us coming,' he warned.

As *InterSpray*, having now dropped her spinnaker, ghosted up river under genoa, several boats came out to meet them. John's great motivation in racing across 14,000 miles of ocean had been to see his wife Jocelyn and family in Hobart.

The welcoming boats included yachts from the Royal Yacht Club of Tasmania, the Derwent Sailing Squadron, who would adopt *InterSpray*, and International Paint's Doug Gandy, plus the Challenge boat, with Chay, photographer Mark Pepper and others shouting encouragement. Duggie took up the bagpipes and played his solitary, stirring dawn chorus.

They crossed the finish line off Battery Point at 0743 local time, champagne corks popping, John helming with a broad, relaxed grin, and Jeffes dispensing champagne as they moored alongside the city's Elizabeth Street Pier.

After racing halfway around the globe, Jeffes and his crew, placed eighth on the leg, had kept Hofbrau out of second place in the fleet on combined times, by just 82 minutes (barring protests and redress). They had completed the longest leg of the longest one-design endurance race, notching up the fleet's fastest time from Cape Horn to Hobart. They had gone the distance, despite a forestay failure, without motoring to port for assistance and without damaging their rig.

They had crashed to windward for what was judged to be the equivalent of three Whitbread Round the World Races, or 20 seasons of average sailing.

They had sailed 9,760 miles from Copacabana Beach in 52 days 4 hours 44 minutes at an average speed of 7.79 knots.

The final telex transmitted back to Southampton was terse, but it said everything that needed to be said: 'JUST TO INFORM YOU THAT COURTAULDS INTERSPRAY CROSSED FINISH LINE AT 20.44.30 GMT WEDNESDAY 6TH JANUARY 1993. THANK GOD WE'VE FINISHED.'

Race Leg 2 Rio de Janeiro to Hobart

Placing	Yacht Name	Arrival	GMT	Leg Time			
				Days	Hrs	Mins	Secs
1st	Nuclear Electric	03 Jan	14:26:03	048	22	26	03
2nd	Commercial Union	04 Jan	00:20:21	049	08	20	21
3rd	Hofbrau Lager	05 Jan	02:29:55	050	10	29	55
4th	Coopers & Lybrand	05 Jan	08:43:19	050	16	43	19
5th	Group 4	05 Jan	20:47:11	050	16	47	11
6th	Heath Insured	06 Jan	05:59:06	050	23	59	06
7th	Pride of Teesside	05 Jan	23:58:20	050	01	58	20
8th	InterSpray	06 Jan	20:44:30	052	04	44	30
9th	Rhone-Poulenc	09 Jan	22:58:40	055	06	58	40
10th	British Steel II	16 Jan	06:15:00	061	14	15	00

INTERSPRAY'S RACE AROUND THE WORLD

Leg Results: Combined Times (Legs 1 & 2)

Placing	Yacht Name	Combined Time			
		Days	Hrs	Mins	Secs
1st	Nuclear Electric	080	20	06	29
2nd	Heath Insured*	081	09	53	26
3rd	InterSpray	081	17	11	55
4th	Hofbrau Lager	081	18	33	50
5th	Group 4*	082	01	19	14
6th	Pride of Teesside*	082	09	59	24
7th	Coopers & Lybrand	082	14	44	14
8th	Commercial Union	087	04	14	06
9th	Rhone-Poulenc	087	04	50	43
10th	British Steel II	090	16	53	26

*These times were adjusted by the Protest Committee.

The redress for yachts assisting *British Steel II* was as follows:

Heath Insured -	16 hours
	(net 14, allowing for two-hour penalty at Rio start).
Group 4 -	12 hours.
Pride of Teesside -	6 hours.

Hospitality
Hobart-style

If race stopovers were characterised by some yotties as pleasure between legs, Hobart, famous for the annual Boxing Day Sydney to Hobart Yacht Race, provided contentment in full measure. The Challenge yachts received their warmest welcome of the race. Everyone in Tasmania, Australia's smallest, most southerly state, seemed to know all about the British Steel Challenge; where it came from, where it was going and when it should get there. The hospitality was

All the yachts were lifted out of the water and had their masts removed in Hobart

overwhelming in this most English and seafaring of Australian towns. It was difficult for crews to buy their own beer in some bars. Each yacht had generous shore hosts in the charming city.

Paul Jeffes had only encountered goodwill like this once before – in Lerwick, in the Shetland Islands, where they are renowned for taking yachtsmen home for hot baths and meals during the Round Britain and Ireland Yacht Race. Hobart was, said many, like England back in the 1960s.

InterSpray was adopted by the Derwent Sailing Squadron and the crew invited to dinner at the squadron's clubhouse on their second night in town. Richard Johnson, liaison officer, also organised a champagne breakfast before the start of the third leg.

Trisha and John Davis contacted North Hobart Rotary Club, whose president, Murray Yaxley, organised accommodation for crew with various Rotary hosts, mostly from his own club, but also through Bob Wilson, President of Hobart Rotary Club. Generous John Roberts had four crew members sleeping in his home.

John Davis, meanwhile, had the distinction of staying in the same apartment where Pope John Paul stayed during a visit to Hobart when he was a cardinal. Juliet had flown to Adelaide to resume her honeymoon, interrupted after two days six months earlier when she'd joined *InterSpray*. Carlton's girlfriend, Cherie Brain, made a surprise visit to Hobart after winning a free trip in a competition on Ed Stewart's Radio 2 show.

In between a comprehensive yacht maintenance programme, crews enjoyed tours around the island, to Cradle Mountain and the rainforest and wilderness areas, as well as the mainland and New Zealand. They joined in the Hobart Regatta, drinks with the Governor of Tasmania, trips to Salamanca's Saturday street market, prizegivings and, naturally, lots of barbies. The art of the Oz barbie was soon

learned: 'Get your meat portion, slap it on the grill, and steal someone else's that's already cooked!' said the Commodore of the Royal Yacht Club of Tasmania.

Chay Blyth and Peter Phillips, meanwhile, old buddies on the ocean racing circuit, were engaging in some high jinx of their own; a 'British Steel Challenge' with a pair of stainless steel steak knives, which they stabbed with increasing bravado and velocity between one another's fingers spread on a table. It was, said someone, an old Parachute Regiment game. Rigger's tape found other uses that afternoon.

Nine days after *InterSpray* docked in Hobart she was motoring out from Elizabeth Street Pier to join a strange but moving spectacle: nine unmasted yachts meeting one dismasted yacht. *British Steel II* motored up to the finish line and sailed across on January 16, one month to the day and hour from her dismasting.

As well as flying his jury rig under a spider's web of ropes, skipper Richard Tudor was flying a protest flag. The Race Committee may have 'retired' him from leg two, but it didn't seem he was giving up. He had motor-sailed further than any other dismasted yacht – more than 3,500 miles, the equivalent of a New York to Southampton crossing and then some.

Some crews would be questioning a different kind of 'jury rig' after the quixotic decision by the Race Committee several days later to reinstate *British Steel II* in the race and allow her finish time to stand. Tudor's request for redress for time lost because of the dismasting was denied, however. On combined times Tudor would start the next leg only three days behind last-placed *Rhone-Poulenc*.

The Challenge yachts had been designed to be bullet proof. It was the amateur crews whom the sceptics expected to crack up after their Southern Ocean ordeal. Cracked ribs there may have been, but the Hobart travel agency which the jeremiahs predicted would get rich quick selling one-way tickets back to Britain was facing a recession.

The crews were not quitting. What, for them, had started as an epic adventure, with a yacht race thrown in, had turned into a cut-throat contest – with some spectacular misadventures.

John Chittenden said he'd 'never before bashed to windward for so long, or for so far.' His yacht, *Nuclear Electric*, was one of the first of the fleet to be slipped in Hobart.

As she was winched up the slipway, someone noticed a jagged rust-stained line running vertically down the centre of the keel. It was cracked from top to bottom, down its thickest 17-inch-wide mid-section, through 12 tons of ballast. Metallurgists in Hobart confirmed that it was a casting defect, with the damage caused by internal stresses in the keel not affecting the keel bolts. It would have taken a week for the keel to cool after casting. Paul Jeffes had seen a similar split in a 35ft Jeanneau that had hit a rock. Experts agreed that *Nuclear Electric*'s crack had happened in Rio and heat may have been the catalyst. Chittenden recalled relaxing aboard the yacht at anchor there when a tremendous noise like a cannon shot reverberated around the hull. He had to wait 10,000 miles before solving the mystery in Hobart. Steel splint straps were put on his keel for race home.

InterSpray and *Pride of Teesside* had non-structural cracks between the side of the skeg and hull shell, which were ground down and rewelded.

For the first time the effects of the relentless pounding to windward across the Southern Ocean were visible the on 4mm steel hull plates. They were no longer smooth and rounded, but had a corrugated effect where they had been hammered against the longitudinal stringers. The boats that went further south, like *InterSpray*, were worst affected. Richard Jerram from International Paint was delighted, though, with the pristine condition of the hulls below the waterline and above.

A new mast was flown into Hobart for Richard Tudor and Dave Freemantle, the 'Proctor Doctor', was kept busy fitting internal sleeves at deck level on the other nine masts, for extra strength. *Nuclear Electric* needed a new topmast section, while *Hofbrau* and *Coopers & Lybrand* had new sections to replace their badly cracked masts.

For the people responsible for the day to day running of the world's most complicated charter fleet, Hobart was a massive logistical exercise in refitting the ten yachts on time. Some 200,000sq ft of sails were inspected and 400 litres of antifouling bottom paint applied to hulls. Below decks, the yachts were stripped out and washed down. Andrew Roberts, Alistair Hackett, Gara Hampton and Chris Winzar had their work cut out. Peter Vroon arrived from Hood Sails and Steve Moor from Autohelm.

The failure of the six Norseman Gibb screws was due not to any defect or to being incorrectly specified, as had been asserted by some experts. The solution to the enigma was almost too simple. Full articulation of the bottlescrew had been prevented because the foresail tack fitting was too close to the screw.

The fitting was re-located, but not before 10 costly, custom-built screws, with Nitronic 50 steel threads, and upgraded wire had been fitted to the fleet in Hobart.

The major damage toll, though dramatic, was no worse than on many long-distance ocean races. The fleet had come halfway round the world and all the boats had arrived safely in Hobart. No one had been seriously injured. For an 'amateur' race it was a considerable feat.

Others argued that the Challenge had escaped a public relations disaster, or worse, by the slenderest of margins. There was only one spare mast, and Peter Goss and Viv Cherry had only saved their masts by a cat's cradle of ropes and stays.

Paul Jeffes, Andrew Roberts and Richard Jerram inspect **Nuclear Electric's split keel**

Peter Phillips pointed out: 'In transatlantic races like the OSTAR it's not unusual for a third of the fleet never to get to the other side. Yachts sink, hit whales, tree trunks, suffer storm damage. Keels drop off, masts fall down.'

On the plus-side, the toll in human damage caused only two crew to drop out in Hobart: John Kirk (49) on *Coopers & Lybrand*, who had broken his back 15 years ago and suffered problems from the start, and *Hofbrau*'s Michael Kay (44), Sales Director of the Challenge Business, who returned to Britain to supervise sponsorship for Blyth's next yacht race. A one-legger on *Nuclear Electric*, who failed to fly out from America to sail the third leg to Cape Town, was replaced by 36-year-old Hobart firefighter Bill St Leger, after a last-minute Tassie TV appeal by Chay Blyth.

The most serious injury on leg two was to *Heath Insured*'s Steve Stamp (37), a one-legger in every sense of the word. Swept along the deck by a wave he had torn tendons, a crushed cartilage and a broken bone in his leg. Phil Jones on

Coopers & Lybrand lost two stone in weight, suffering seasickness for 43 of the 50 days aboard. There were cracked ribs for Jack Gordon-Smith on *Hofbrau* and Eric Gustavson on *Commercial Union*.

On *InterSpray* there were no serious injuries, apart from John's concussion, from which he had recovered. But Jeff's girlfriend, Carol, having survived the paranha-infested Amazon River and the muggers of Rio, fell off a molehill while sightseeing in Tasmania, and broke her leg in two places.

As the time grew nearer for the race to begin again it was Phillips who declared: 'The party isn't over yet. The longest leg is over, but we still have some of the worst seas in the world to cross, including those around the Cape of Good Hope, also known as the Cape of Storms. Leg three has the potential to be much worse. On the Whitbread and BOC races there is more damage in the equivalent of leg three than on the run around Cape Horn.'

He was right.

Everybody seemed to think that the fleet would encounter its worst conditions

HOBART STOPOVER

The unmasted meet the dismasted: **British Steel II** *arrives in Hobart*

en route to Cape Town. It was partly psychological, because the yachts had escaped relatively lightly so far.

Julian and Duggie met Hobart harbour pilot Dick Williams, a master mariner and experienced offshore racer, who warned that ice around the French Kerguelen Island waypoint would be more dangerous because it was late in the season and would be compacted glacial ice. At this stage, the option of a waypoint at Amsterdam Island, some 700 miles north, was still being considered by Chay.

Julian arranged for *InterSpray*'s crew to visit Australia's Antarctic Survey Centre, in Kingston, south of Hobart, where more advice was forthcoming. Hobart had been the stepping off point for a host of adventurers, including Roald Amundsen.

'A voyage we all dread is from McQuarie Island to Heard Island, on a latitude of 53°S they said. 'In these latitudes you can expect 10 seasons in an hour,' they told the crew. 'If you want to know the forecast you have to look out of the window.'

They didn't know it then, because options for a northern route were also being evaluated, but *InterSpray* would be going even further south than the Antarctic folk's dreaded 53°S. There was more reason to feel apprehensive when Alan Wynne Thomas, the only British entrant in the singlehanded Vendée Globe Challenge, limped into Hobart at the end of January. His yacht *Cardiff Discovery* had suffered several knockdowns at 52°S – between Kerguelen Island and Heard Island.

He was towed in darkness the last few miles up Derwent River to the Royal Tasmania Yacht Club, where several crew members from *InterSpray*, helped him tie up. Exhausted after sailing 13,588 miles in 68 days and still in considerable pain from several cracked ribs, Thomas (51), described how the knockdown smashed his rudder, snapped the tiller and hurled him out of his bunk, 10ft across the cabin.

'I couldn't breathe at all for five minutes and took to my bunk for eight hours while mayhem went on all round,' he said. A Hobart doctor diagnosed several broken and one splintered rib. He had a partially collapsed lung. He was lucky to be alive.

'The statistical chance of the big wave in that part of the Southern Ocean is quite high,' he said. 'I was half knocked down two or three times a day when the yacht was simply picked up out of the water by large waves.'

Meanwhile, the news from the Challenge Protest Committee was good and bad. Jeffes was summoned to appear and told that, although the committee had decided *InterSpray* was over the line at Rio, no further action could be taken because Rio Yacht Club had used the flag INDIA, instead of the correct signal X-RAY, to inform him of his error.

'Don't think *we* will make the same mistake at the Hobart start line,' he was cautioned. 'Because we won't.'

Time allowances for yachts that went to the assistance of dismasted *British Steel II*, however, put *InterSpray* back to third place as *Heath Insured* moved up from fourth to second. Most skippers felt the time allowances being claimed were excessive.

Heath Insured claimed and received 16 hours (reduced to 14 after their own two-hour penalty at the Rio start), *Group 4* 12 hours and *Pride of Teesside* six hours, although her services in diverting had not been needed in the end.

Local help before the restart came from Peter Rees, a Hobart veterinary surgeon, who provided surgical soap for *InterSpray* and a fishing lure to catch tuna and squid, while his son, a catering lecturer, provided home-made sauces for the galley.

Two days before the start of the third leg, Jeffes received a letter from Chay: 'As you have been provided with a new headsail you will be penalised in accordance with General Sailing Instructions. After passing Iron Pot to port, proceed eastward to pass through a penalty position which you will be given on the morning on the race.'

The course would not be decided until the conditions for the race start were known – before casting off for the start line.

Another course that *had* been decided for the fleet was the controversial waypoint in the iceberg belt at Kerguelen. Crews had overwhelmingly rejected Blyth's offer to move the race out of the Roaring Forties and into the more benevolent Thirties. Eighty-two per cent voted against the soft option. 'It was,' said Michael Calvin aboard *Hofbrau*, 'as if turkeys had voted for the retention of Christmas.'

Blyth responded with a 'no guts, no glory' crew briefing.

Leg three

The penalty kick

Start Saturday February 13, Hobart to Cape Town – 6,800 miles

It seemed as though the whole of Hobart had turned out to see the British Steel Challenge fleet set sail for Cape Town. The city had not seen such a waterborne spectacle on the River Derwent since the Tall Ships race during Australia's 1988 Bicentennial.

InterSpray's penalty for replacing the destroyed No 1 yankee was to sail around an extra mark of the course. But the details of the course had not been released until the 11th hour. 'Quite deliberately, it seemed, we were being kept in the dark,' thought Julian. 'It seemed underhand to some of us not to be told how the penalty would be constructed.'

In the cockpit Paul Jeffes briefed the crew on the details he had just been given. Rounding the extra mark at 43°18'S 147°58'E represented an extra 30 miles on the chart. In light winds it would take four to six hours. *British Steel II* had a 17-mile penalty for their new No 3 yankee.

Everyone knew from the hardships of the last leg, that the story of the race so far was that yachts at the back of the fleet lost touch and failed to get back in the race. But it was too late for recriminations or an

appeal. They hadn't been given time. Jeffes rallied his crew. There was a job to be done and, as always, they would give it their best shot.

Carlton was standing down as watchleader, after an insect bite had become severely infected with a danger of septicaemia. He was replaced by Dominic.

As the yachts cast off from Elizabeth Street Pier, crowds were standing ten deep, For once, *InterSpray* was not the

127

Duggie in Aussie hat and highland kilt, pipes InterSpray *out for start of leg three*

first yacht to leave. While Duggie played his bagpipes for the spectators, *Commercial Union* slipped away. On *Group 4* a crewman's trumpet sounded out with *When the Saints Go Marching In*! As *InterSpray* followed *Hofbrau* out of the dock, crews gave three cheers for the people of Hobart.

For one-legger Roger Peek the answer to the question people had been asking, 'Are you looking forward to it?', was 'Yes, with some trepidation, but I'm probably looking forward to reaching Cape Town even more.'

When the early morning cloud lifted, it was a beautiful, clear sunny day with a good breeze as *InterSpray* practised tacking through the spectator boats for the start line. Paul Jeffes had already had the chance to do some sailing on the river and thought 'it's not unlike the Clyde.' It was the West Highlands versus the Southern Ocean again.

The International Paint supporters' boat was close enough to talk across the gap. Among those on board were the four prizewinners for guessing *InterSpray*'s time into Rio: Steven and Roberta Sharpe, from Rio, and Don Smith, export manager of Courtaulds' Epiglass, in New Zealand, with his wife Barbara. Also there were Courtaulds' Colin Ravenhall and his wife, Lynn; Doug Gandy, of International Paint, in Melbourne, and Ken Pearce from Courtaulds' Taubmans paint company, Brisbane.

When the gun fired at 1300, off Battery Point, *InterSpray* stormed across the line, second behind *Commercial Union*, and into a stiff southeasterly breeze, forcing *Nuclear Electric* to tack away on to port. As Jeffes overhauled *Commercial Union*, Richard Merriweather tacked behind *InterSpray*, and went for the western side of the river.

InterSpray, the only yacht on starboard tack, stuck to the eastern shore as the rest of the fleet took off for the right hand side of the course, heading downriver past Mount Wellington, and taking with them most of the spectator boats.

The few that stuck close to *InterSpray* reassured the crew that they had chosen the right side of the river. They were soon proved right as Jeffes stole a lead.

InterSpray, sailing alone for 30 minutes, was beginning to feel left out of things until the spectator fleet trailing the other Challenge yachts realised who was in the lead and swarmed across. At one point Jeffes' elated crew lost sight of the fleet behind the mass of spectator craft encircling them.

By the time the yachts reached Taroona, an hour from the start, *InterSpray* had established a firm lead and when she reached Iron Pot, at the mouth of the River Derwent, 12 miles from the start, Jeffes and his crew were more than a mile and half ahead of the fleet.

Chay, Greg, Andrew and Helen on the Challenge support boat, and families and friends on International Paint's boat, as well as yachts from the Derwent Sailing Squadron, waved their goodbyes.

But as *InterSpray* headed into Storm Bay, the mood of euphoria gave way to one of frustration and anger as she was forced to turn her back on the fleet and tack away east, beating upwind to the penalty mark, and going instantly from first place to last. The Challenge fleet, sailing free, off the wind, peeled off southwest under spinnakers for Cape Town.

Defeat was not a word in *InterSpray*'s vocabulary, but this was a bitter pill for Jeffes and his crew to swallow.

The order of the fleet out of Derwent River had been *InterSpray*, *Nuclear Electric*, *Group 4*, *Hofbrau*, *Rhone-Poulenc*, *Pride of Teesside*, *British Steel II*, *Commercial Union*, *Coopers & Lybrand* and *Heath Insured*. The first three yachts behind *InterSpray* were the first three yachts into Cape Town, confirming Jeffes' belief that in an upwind race the boats at the front had a disproportionate advantage.

It was to take five hours from leaving the course before *InterSpray* rounded the penalty mark at dusk, having sighted a new landmark on the chart, named 'Rogius Peekus' in honour of the ship's latest recruit.

As the sun dipped below the horizon, the big kite was hoisted and *InterSpray* set off in hot pursuit, determined not to play tail-end Charlie. The best racing strategy is to win the start and cover the pack and Jeffes had cause already to regret that *InterSpray* hadn't covered from Rio.

Dinner that night, courtesy of International Paint, was Atlantic smoked salmon, king tiger prawns, trevalli, and salad. The standby watch had no cooking to do.

'Dominic has taken over!!' recorded the ship's log-keeper. 'Look out Cape Town here we come.'

Four hours later there was an anonymous entry: 'That's it, I'm off!'

The morning chat show on St Valentine's Day, with the fleet's first reported positions at 1900 GMT, held no romance for *InterSpray*. Not surprisingly, the yachts to the west had caught the wind first and *Nuclear Electric* was 59 miles ahead. The distance had increased 24 hours after the start to 76 miles. This equated to a time penalty of ten hours at the race average speed of 7.5 knots. The penalty had condemned Jeffes and his crew to their own private weather pattern.

Chay's one-design race had been turned into a handicap race. The Race Committee's penalty had proved totally inappropriate and the views of *InterSpray*'s crew were forthright: The boat resounded to protests of 'Outrageous!' 'Totally unfair.' 'A Major setback' and, from Paul Buchanan, 'It's enough to make you seasick!' It did, and he was.

Jeffes, infuriated that the race committee had made no effort to inquire into the circumstances of the loss of the No 1

InterSpray leads the fleet out of the Derwent River

yankee, nor given him any opportunity for explanation, telexed his strongest objections to David Hodgson at International Paint, in Southampton, asking for an opportunity to re-evaluate the penalty and present his case in Cape Town.

The draconian punishment had been applied for the loss of a sail, he said, which had been partially caused by the wrap round *InterSpray*'s jury rig, three extra preventer stays rigged as additional mast support in the event of bottlescrew failure.

While Challenge race rules had been framed to encourage good seamanship, the loss of *InterSpray*'s No 1 yankee could be attributed to these seamanlike precautions which had saved the mast and prevented any other damage when the bottlescrew snapped. Other yachts had been less successful in avoiding severe damage to rigs and sails when their bottlescrews failed. But they had incurred no extra penalties.

To Jeffes, his crew and their supporters back home, *InterSpray* had already paid the price of several hours hove-to, trying to save the No 1 yankee, and had sailed more than 5,000 miles without it.

She was now being punished with a 30-mile extra course, which had resulted in almost 80 miles and 10 places lost to the fleet leader, as well as the psychological disadvantage of sailing at the back of the fleet.

In retrospect, some crew felt *InterSpray* should have refused to leave the dock at Hobart. 'We should have said we were not prepared to sail under these circumstances. That ultimatum would have enabled us to do something about it. But we weren't to know how much it would cost us until the wind changed,' said Julian.

Twenty-twenty hindsight is a wonderful gift.

After their long fight back across the Southern Ocean, to retain second place in leg two, *InterSpray*'s crew now steeled themselves for another test of their resolve across a further 6,000 miles of the world's worst seas. The momentum of their brilliant start helped to keep morale up as they began their fight-back.

Day three found the yacht reaching in sunny skies and relatively calm seas. The sea temperature had dropped from 18°C to 13°C and it was noticeably colder as thermals and mid-layers were worn. The chat show revealed a new fleet leader. *Commercial Union*, who were to swap the lead with *Nuclear Electric* over the next couple of days, were some 50 miles ahead. Fourth-placed *Coopers & Lybrand* had ripped their spinnaker right down one leach and across the foot in a forestay wrap.

InterSpray had clocked up two consecutive 12-hour runs each topping 100 miles. The distance run may have topped the other yachts, but if they were going to recover distance lost in the penalty, the northerly course looked short of wind, with high pressure in the Great Australian Bight. The entire fleet was less than 70 miles apart in distance to the finish, but spread over a 120 mile front.

A composite Great Circle route from Hobart to Kerguelen Island would take them as far down as 53°S. Jeffes' strategy was to plunge further south, as deep as 56°S, in the hope of finding stronger winds. The distance was marginally longer and could mean losing ground to the leaders in the initial stage, but it might pay dividends later. The Antarctic Circle lay at 66.5°S.

On the food front, things were greatly improved with fresh fish, bread, water melons, and stir fries. Sirloin steak was on that night's menu. 'How would you like your steak, Sir?' Chef Plummer inquired. For breakfast there was bacon and scrambled eggs. The pursers planned to avoid dehydrated food for at least two weeks. Shining the searchlight on the sea, hundreds of squid could be seen. *Calamari a la InterSpray* for supper?

LEG THREE

The Southern Ocean had decided to wake up by day five with winds of 40 knots. Life was back at a 25 degree angle and Hobart was a warm and distant memory as *InterSpray* dipped back down into the Furious Fifties.

Roger had his first baptism in the Southern Ocean, most of it inside his oil-skins. He took some ribbing when he came on deck remarking on the mountainous seas, which, to the deck watch, veterans of miles of ocean alps, were mere molehills.

The Ryme of the Apprentice Mariner appeared in the logbook:

A young sailor by the name of Roger
Hesitated as he stood by the dodger
A wave came by and aimed at his eye
and Roger, poor chap, failed to dodge 'er

Peek, for once, was crestfallen.

Later, dressed appropriately for the Antarctic blast, including *de rigueur* ski goggles, Roger picked himself up from the back of the cockpit during a particularly vicious squall one night as 60 knots of wind lifted razor-sharp spray into the air around and remarked 'doesn't the moon on the water look romantic?'

The magnetic South Pole was only 900 miles away and the Aurora Australis, the Southern Lights, provided a spectacular light show for night watches, with shafts of iridescent green light fanned out across the sky to form a shimmering organ pipe effect. It sometimes appeared to arc right over the yacht.

A suggestion made by Brian Warr in Hobart was adopted for each crew member to have a free 24-hour period every 10 days, 'to catch up on sleep, write personal logs, or visit the pub', instead of doubling up on a second day's standby watch.

Dominic, following his appointment as watchleader, was heard singing: 'The working class may kiss my arse, I've got the foreman's job at last.'

February 17 was also Dominic's birthday. A cake made by Jocelyn was decorated with candles. Son Giles had given his non-drinking father two bottles of beer. There was toffee from Thomasina and a Huon pine pen from the mysterious Elizabeth, a (very) distant relative, claimed Dom. 'A strange collection of presents, each one more inappropriate and useless than the last!' someone remarked.

The noon to noon run on day six was 218 miles, with *InterSpray* 65 miles behind the leaders. Two days and nights of winds of 30 knots-plus had given her a big push and by evening she was only 18 miles behind ninth-placed *Pride of Teesside*. Every minute of every watch was taken up with trying to find ways of making the boat go faster.

Roger, sharing the portside three-berth cabin, had trodden on Jeff's prized Akubra cattleman's Stetson, bought in Hobart, whilst climbing into his bunk. He was now reduced to calling Jeff 'O Great One', averting his eyes to his feet when speaking to him. The cabin became known as The Swamp ('Authorised personnel only, chemical warfare suits to be worn by order') as conditions became damp.

By driving the yacht hard, concentrating on the wheel and not letting up 24 hours a day, *InterSpray* was gaining a few miles every 12 hours. The sea temperature was down to 7°C.

The Aurora Australis was more spectacular each time it appeared, the sky aflame with arcs of yellow and green and beams of blue piercing the heavens. A trip to the London Planetarium would never be the same.

Day seven found Brian in a smoke-filled engine room gasping for air, eyes streaming. The shaft brake pin had sheared and the tufnol brake pad created acrid smoke. He soon had things under control, replacing the original brass pin. 'Bilge Rat triumphs again! said the log. 'Smoked bilge rat for supper? inquired someone in the galley.

The radio chat show revealed positions

Above: enjoying the fresh fruits of Hobart. Right: 'Gone fishing,' says Dominic

changing constantly by very small distances at the front end of the fleet. *Group 4* took the lead for the second time on day seven and *InterSpray* passed the 2,000 miles mark to Kerguelen Island.

A telex came through that one crewman's personal distress beacon on *Group 4* had activated when a breaking wave hit the foredeck during a sail change. The signal was picked up in Canberra, and relayed to Falmouth Coastguard. *Group 4* contacted Canberra direct to inform them that it was a false alarm. 'It must be comforting for all of you to know that there is an organisation out there listening out for you,' said Race HQ.

On day nine, after a wild night with 40-45 knots over the deck, *InterSpray*, flying along with three reefs and the No 2 yankee, had the second best run in the fleet. On the chat show the encouraging news came through that they had overhauled *Pride of Teesside* by nine miles and closed the gap on most of the fleet by an average of 12 miles. The clocks went back for the third time since Hobart as they flew westward.

Rhone-Poulenc crewman Jerry Walsingham had gone up the mast to replace a navigation light, and came down to say he felt he'd 'done a couple of rounds with Frank Bruno.'

Down below in the relative peace and quiet of *InterSpray's* galley Chef Buchanan's dish of the day was lamb steaks with honey and ginger sauce. Cooking for 14 in gale-force conditions is always an experience. At one point the sauce leapt from the tray and smoked out the galley, while the rest spread itself around the galley walls.

As if to prove that you couldn't please all the people all the time, Ricky led the protest that real food created too much cooking and washing up. One more day and then McDougalls would rule again. Ali and Dom's Fast Food Emporium ('lamb and three veg, no problem') would be closing down until leg four.

In the storm force winds a red plastic crate full of Pilot books, weighing about 50lb, flew off the doghouse shelf, smashing against the foot of the chart table, gouging grooves in the wood and leaving shards of plastic embedded in Buchanan's seaboots. He was wearing them at the time.

InterSpray was now 120 miles further south than the closest boat, and nearer the ice limit, with the barometer plummeting like a stone. They hadn't been able to get good weatherfaxes for three days now because of sun spot activity creating atmospheric interference on the HF radio.

The morning chat show on day ten listed *InterSpray* with the second best run of the fleet, 99 miles, taking three miles on average out of the rest of the yachts, except *Pride of Teesside* to the north. With the sea temperature dropping to 5°C, cold and damp began to seep everywhere.

'My oilskins are clammy and twice as heavy as when we left Hobart,' complained Buchanan.

'Everything I own is absolutely sopping wet and soaked in sea water,' said Julian to his pocket tape recorder while off-watch. 'I am lying in my bunk packed with sodden wet salt water clothing; my inner-layer, mid-layer and socks. I'm trying to get a bit of warmth in them before I put them back on in a few hours time.'

Crawling into the refuge of your bunk at the end of a night watch was an emotional experience of great relief. Up on deck it could be mind-numbing, with no instruments, pitch black, hailstones hitting you and 60mph squalls every ten minutes.

It became a major effort to undo zips and velcro to go to the toilet and dehydrated food seemed to make trips more frequent. The reluctance to strip off layers of foul weather gear was solved for the men by Doug Gandy and Ken Pearce, who had presented Paul Jeffes with a parcel in Hobart – three one-litre hospital bed bottles. The inevitable competition began with the skipper setting a ship's record of 100cl.

Hands froze in the wind chill, but gloves, which could get caught in blocks or winches, were worn only when the work was done. Cuts to hands healed slowly and could be incapacitating. For these extreme conditions there still wasn't a decent sailing glove on the market. You needed a rigger's glove for rope work and mittens to keep you warm when helming. Some even tried underwater welder's gloves.

On deck the sound of 30 knots of wind through the rigging and across the sail at night set up a roaring noise like a jumbo jet. With heavy cloud cover making the night pitch black the sound effect added to an acute sense of the savagery of the seas. Roger was riding shotgun for John on the 1800 to 2200 stagecoach, scanning the invisible horizon for bandits, redskins and icebergs.

Pride of Teesside, sharing the most southerly route with *InterSpray*, reported sighting two icebergs which, alarmingly, hadn't shown up on *InterSpray*'s radar. One was 'shaped like a recumbent teddy bear'.

InterSpray plotted their positions and realised they must have sailed fairly close by without realising. Back on deck the cloud cleared briefly to reveal the stars. Hawkeye Davis spotted the masthead light of *Pride of Teesside*, on the starboard quarter, eight miles away. They called MacGillivray up on the radio, but he couldn't sight them.

On MacGillivray's yacht the deck watch were straining their eyes into the blackness to work out where the next wave crest would come aboard, finding its way through every small gap in their protective clothing and soaking them to the skin.

The nights were now very dark with a constant radar ice watch every 15 minutes as the yacht ploughed on, maintaining her speed of nine knots fairly continuously, as she had for the past 72 hours.

The dark night also brought back phosphorescence so there were green 'fireworks' in the sea as well fireworks in the sky with the Southern Lights.

The crew were now experiencing the roughest conditions of the voyage so far. Gales in this part of the Southern Ocean were worse than anything experienced on the second leg, with abrupt changes in conditions as violent lows swept in from the west. But the crew's ability to cope was improved. They no longer felt they were in the most god-forsaken place in the world.

There were fickle winds at the centre of a low for several hours on day 11 before *InterSpray* finally got the south-west winds she had been expecting and shared the fleet's best run of 81 miles. They had taken seven miles out of *Group 4*, now 82 miles ahead and still leading for the fourth day. The fleet's ETA in Cape Town had been revised to March 18 (34 days), following its fast progress. Although the yachts had been close-hauled, little tacking had been required and their windward ability was proving excellent.

As duty yacht, *InterSpray* relayed that *Pride of Teesside*'s steering compass 'had ceased to function after last night's brilliant display of the Aurora Australis.' *InterSpray*'s barometer was also at its lowest ever, recording 980, with a sharp deterioration anticipated in the weather.

Rhone-Poulenc had been in touch with HMS *Discovery*, the ice patrol ship, which reported temperatures of -09°C, snow and sleet showers. Weather reports for the Challenge were also coming into *InterSpray* from the Australian Antarctic base at Casey, following Julian's contact in Hobart at their HQ.

Every day, when he could, Julian took a sun sight and did dead reckoning fixes. On the final few nights he would get star fixes, within a couple of miles of the GPS. Star sights proved incredibly accurate. It was difficult to discipline yourself to do sextant work with two functioning GPS sets, but the aerials could have been wiped out at any time.

The first chat show on day 12 had *InterSpray* sharing the day's best run of 76 miles with *British Steel II*. *Coopers* and *Heath* were only four miles ahead. All but the leading two boats were less than 40 miles ahead. The second results round-up was even better, placing *InterSpray* seventh – their best position since the River Plate, apart from the Hobart start. A real morale booster.

The wind had been building all day, averaging 35-40 knots, as the yacht crashed to windward under staysail with three reefs in the main in the first of a series of forecast gales. Occasionally she dropped off a wave with a bone-jarring metallic crash. By the time they got to Cape Town they would see that the percussive effect had turned the 4mm steel plate into something resembling the capsized bonnet of a giant Citroen 2CV.

Paul Buchanan was thrown across the saloon into a galley cupboard as the yacht bounced off one such wave, cutting his head over his left eye. No stitches were needed. The sideways G-forces down below caught people off their guard, whereas on deck they were forewarned and saw advancing waves. Most of the fleet's dislocations and cracked bones happened below decks where crew were not padded by oilskins, mid-layers and thermals.

The barometer, which had been as low as 980 and climbed to 1007, now plummeted back to 981 as the wind strength increased and sea conditions became very rough.

Frenchman Olivier de Kersauson, competing in the Jules Verne Challenge yacht race, had been forced to abandon his bid to sail round the world in 80 days in his trimaran, *Charal*, after hitting ice and smashing half a float off. He was limping into Cape Town. Race HQ were sending the Challenge fleet daily updates, on the end of weather bulletins, on the rapid progress of *ENZA New Zealand*, the 85ft catamaran skippered by Peter Blake and Robin Knox-Johnston, also racing round the world in the 80-day challenge with another Frenchman, Bruno Peyron skippering *Commodore Explorer*.

The night of the big wave

On deck in the early hours of the following morning the wind was deafening and the spray blinding as Paul Jeffes, Carlton and Dominic watched with fascination as the gale developed into a violent storm with 60 knot winds sweeping across a raging seascape.

Once the wind increased beyond 45 knots the yacht was running out of ballast, and with significant windage on the rig above 50 knots, the sailing was miserable.

Down below in the warm glow of the doghouse, Paul Buchanan was sitting at the chart table coming to the end of his stint on standby watch at 0400 and looking forward to some sleep. Jeff and Juliet, sharing the deck watch, were getting warmed up before going back on deck.

Buchanan was busy plotting positions from the radio chat show when shouts on deck signalled something was amiss. He switched on the deck floodlight as Jeff and Juliet struggled up the five wooden steps, slid back the storm boards and struggled out through the hatch into howling winds and a pitch black night. The pair crouched and half crawled into the cockpit, keeping to the high side, away from enormous dark seas which ran malevolently along the lee rail.

Deck work was not always a job for a submariner

The staysail sheet had broken. Jeffes had bought the flogging sail under control by winching in the lazy sheet. Now, with Jeff Plummer, he went on deck to re-attach the broken end of the working sheet. Dominic was helming the yacht through seas that were now mountainous.

Jeffes shouted back to Carlton to give him some slack, his words snatched away as soon as they left his throat. Carlton, misunderstanding, released instead the weather sheet and the sail began to flog violently.

Jeff was now trapped. His lifeline clipped on under a wildly flailing sheet capable of knocking a man overboard. He couldn't get close enough to unclip himself and lay flat on the deck keeping his head down.

Jeffes and Juliet, joined by Buchanan who'd climbed into his oilskins, tried to sheet the sail in, but the force of the wind was so enormous that even with three of them they couldn't pull in enough slack to get a turn around the winch. Jeff, somehow, managed to slide out from under the sheet without a thrashing.

They needed to get the sail down rapidly before it flogged itself to pieces. The nightmare scenario of the destroyed No 1 yankee had come back to haunt them.

With Juliet by the mast and ready on the halyard, Jeffes, Buchanan and Plummer fought to pull the sail down, sitting up to their waists in icy water as waves swept the deck. The tail of the halyard was caught, tied up in bungee. The sail flogged so violently that surely a split must appear any second. Jeffes cut the tail with his knife and, foot by foot, they dragged the sail down. It took the combined strength and weight of all three, as green and white water broke over them every few seconds.

By now the wind was a demented shriek as they finished lashing down the sail and a muffled cry came from the cockpit.

Carlton and Dominic had seen the crest of a towering wave advancing out of the blackness ahead of the yacht. There was barely a second's warning before it struck.

Jeffes had just unclipped his lifeline and was on his way back to the mast when he looked behind him and recoiled. There was nowhere to escape to.

'The last thing I remember is that I couldn't see the top of it and I thought there's no way we are going to go over this.'

The last thing he actually saw as he disappeared under the breaking water was the shrouds. Instinctively, as he was washed along the deck towards them, he curled himself around the rigging. Without this piece of luck he could have been lost overboard. It would seem an eternity before the water drained away and he wondered how long he could hold his breath.

Jeff, too, had turned to go back to the cockpit when Buchanan screamed: 'Hold on!' and at the same instant grabbed the inner forestay with both hands as a cliff-face of water engulfed the front half of *InterSpray*.

The top of the wave went through the lower spreaders. It was like being underwater in slow-motion. In the cockpit, Dominic had thrown himself to the deck behind the wheel. Carlton, beside him, was flattened against the pedestal by the force of water which filled the well.

As the 40 ton yacht rose sluggishly, like a surfacing submarine, a seething mass of water and foam cascaded off her decks, and Dominic and Carlton looked anxiously astern at the churning waters, utterly convinced that that all four crew mates on deck had been washed over the side by the force of water.

Juliet, more used to air turbulence as a former air stewardess, had been swept from the mast and dumped on the coachroof at the limit of her lifeline. She was out for the count. Jeffes shouted to Carlton: 'Get the medic!' Bruised and winded, and minus her contact lenses, Juliet was bundled below.

Jeff Plummer was groaning with pain and lying on his back. He had been swept along the deck, colliding with various fittings, including blunt-ended cleats and dorade vent cages.

'Stay put, you're alright,' Buchanan reassured him.'You're not going anywhere.'

Jeff was clutching his knee. His leg had totally demolished an industrial gutter pipe, used as anti-chafe protection around the baby stay.

'Sod this, I'm getting out of here!' he exclaimed, making a painful dash back to the cockpit.

Buchanan had been wrenched from his grip on the inner forestay, and hurtled backwards four feet above the deck, riding the surf feet first. His lifeline slid down the jackstay for 14 feet until he was stopped dead at the end of its limit. The force of the water had been so strong, he remembered, that he was suspended in mid-air for a split second before falling to the deck in a heap. It was like levitating.

The watch regrouped as the next watch arrived on deck in the aftermath to relieve them. Paul Jeffes had a deep dent in the muscle above his right shin after taking a hard knock against a dorade cage. It didn't seem a significant injury at the time.

Julian was off watch in his bunk when he was summoned for medical aid. In the doghouse he found Jeff, clasping his knee, and Juliet, who had cracked both her knees against the jam cleats at the foot of the mast. The treatment was anti-inflammatory pills and support dressings.

Back on deck the new watch were about to put the staysail back up when they realised the top two hanks had been ripped off. In 55 knots of wind, they made two trips to the foredeck to retrieve the staysail and hoist the storm staysail. The helmsman had to run off downwind while they sorted out the mess. The Big Wave had cost *InterSpray* 10 miles that night. But the cost had been cheap compared to what might have happened.

It was a common occurrence for people to be swept off their feet on the foredeck. What made the Big Wave an exception was that it caught both the deck crew as well as those in the cockpit.

To add to *InterSpray*'s problems the wind instruments had self-destructed at the top of the mast. The remains of the Windex spun uselessly, its tail snapped off. The electronic Autohelm wind direction indicator had also ceased working.

The yacht would now be sailing below its best, even in daylight, while in big seas at night, when the most experienced helmsman can quickly become disorientated without wind instruments, the danger would increase.

The wave had carried away two forward starboard dorades. This was day 13 of the leg. Coincidentally, it had been the 13th day of the month on leg two when John Davis had been felled by the spinnaker pole. Who said mariners were superstitious?

Down below it was some consolation that *InterSpray* had the joint second best run of the previous 12 hours. But *Heath Insured* had re-passed them and were now two miles ahead. So it was back to eighth place. Storm damage in the rest of the fleet revealed *Nuclear Electric* had broken all the hanks on her staysail, *Hofbrau* had lost her steering and was hove to for 40 minutes, putting a two-foot tear in her No 3 yankee, while *Pride of Teesside* had been forced to run before the storm. Less than 200 miles to the south-west the Arctic survey ship *Discovery* reported winds in excess 75 knots.

Roger was woken for his watch by Alison to learn that he'd slept through a hurricane. He was on the six-hour morning watch, with John, Ricky and Duggie sharing the helming in 45 knots of wind, sometimes gusting to 60.

By the afternoon when a snowstorm hit, it was decided to head north-west out of the 55°S zone. In these high latitudes,

changes in weather conditions and wind directions happened within minutes. A 20 knot breeze would suddenly veer to the north-west, gathering pace and whipping up a fury of white topped waves that were preceded by a menacing change in swell, height and direction. One moment the scene would be a magnificent alpine range, with mountains of blue water and white tops, turning suddenly to steel grey seas and a gunmetal sky as another squall came. An unnerving but amazing sight.

'Disney World hasn't produced a ride yet that compares to the bucking, rolling motion and breakneck speed that 40 tons of steel can be subjected to by howling 60 knot winds and enormous waves,' Julian telexed home.

There was, observed Roger, more nervous radio chat between the yachts during this day than any other day on the leg yet.

InterSpray's crew fully expected to hear they had lost a lot more hard won ground. But they had passed *British Steel II* and were back to seventh. *Heath Insured* were just three miles ahead, *Hofbrau* 16 miles ahead, and even *Group 4* were leading by only 57 miles. *Coopers & Lybrand* reported problems with the steering quadrant, as well as the wheel pulling out from its pedestal.

By the morning of day 15, *InterSpray* had moved up to sixth place and after 12 hours had picked up another place and was lying fifth in the fleet. Jeffes' strategy of diving into the watery wastes of the deep south seemed to be paying off. *InterSpray* was taking the fleet's most southerly route, while *Heath Insured* took the most northerly line.

Patrick and Paul Buchanan spent part of the rest of the day repairing the staysail ready for when the storm abated. Over the next few days telexes flew back and

Previous pages: Disney World hasn't produced a roller-coaster ride yet that compares to the Southern Ocean . . .

forth from the Southern Ocean to Hampshire in an attempt to trouble-shoot the failed Autohelm instruments.

Andrew Roberts sent a six-part check list for Jeffes to carry out on the electronics in the midst of the gales and added: 'I'm prepared to believe it's not so easy to check these things in your neck of the woods. Keep trying. Keep communicating. . .'

The frustration showed in Jeffes' urgent telex to Race HQ a few days later as the yacht slipped back in the fleet and the instruments were still not working: 'Please attend to my instrument problem immediately, or put me in touch with Autohelm direct. Lack of instrumentation visibly affecting boat performance.'

Trying to change sail combinations when they didn't have an accurate idea of the wind strength was a problem they couldn't overcome.

Sailing into the teeth of a Roaring Forties storm without wind instruments was graphically described by John.

'Imagine yourself hurtling down a mountain road in a coach. It's night and you've got no headlights. For some reason the windscreen has blown out and rain hits you in the face like bullets. You are tearing at full throttle down the wrong side of a road, full of potholes. Someone beside you is trying to point out the hazards. The throttle is jammed.'

A diversion from their own dramas came in a cryptic telex from Chay, who was planning the Southampton finish of the race and 'had one major suggestion', but wanted an undertaking of crew confidentiality before sharing his eight-part proposal for the crews' input. One yacht couldn't comply. The malicious rumour on *InterSpray* was that it must be *Hofbrau*, with Fleet Street's mole Michael Calvin aboard. There would be no leak, though.

Chay telexed that he was keen to have a stage-managed South Coast finish for all the yachts, a grand orchestrated arrival at

Southampton, instead of the staggered arrival of yachts at unpredictable and inconvenient times, which, up to now, had been the hallmark of every other round the world yacht race.

The plan was for the yachts to race to another port (to be decided) and await the arrival of the tenth yacht before setting sail en masse for a hero's welcome at Ocean Village.

Chay had, after all, delayed his own arrival home in *British Steel* by three days 22 years ago, to gain maximum coverage by Press and television. His impressive reception party included the Duke of Edinburgh, Prince Charles, Princess Anne and Prime Minister Edward Heath.

But after the bid to move the Southern Ocean waypoint north, from Kerguelen Island to Amsterdam Island, some crew felt this was another attempt to move the goal posts. It was not the race they had signed up to take part in.

The great debate began as telexes bounced up and down from satellites. *Hofbrau* were in favour of a stage-managed finish, which could be a major sporting and social event for supporters and crews. They voted for the Channel Islands as a holding port. One-leggers would join the yachts for a 'parade of sail' across the English Channel and up the Solent, in the order of the overall result.

A suggestion from *Rhone-Poulenc* of St Malo as a holding port was rejected on the grounds that this was a British event.

The argument was a cause of great controversy on *InterSpray*. 'Whatever you do, do it quick,' Jeffes telexed Chay. 'This is a can of worms you have opened.'

The vote on *InterSpray* was nine against, three for and two maybes. A few days later Chay was a gracious loser when he acknowledged the crews' majority vote of 'no' to his novel proposal.

'With so much else needing your attention in present weather, I appreciate all the work many of you have put into discussing and presenting your views on

"my suggestion". Many stressed the ethos of the Challenge and its importance to all crew members, which I respect and agree with. The "No Changes" have it by a substantial margin. The finish will remain at Southampton. Good luck and good sailing. Chay.'

Another telex that day contained the disappointing news that *ENZA New Zealand*, hundreds of miles to the west, had been forced to abort her attempt to win the Jules Verne Around the World in 80 Days race. The catamaran had collided with an unidentified object.

'There was quite a bang on the starboard hull,' reported co-skipper Peter Blake. 'The crew on watch thought nothing of it. But Don Wright thought something of it, for he was asleep in the starboard hull when 15 minutes later he started to float out of his bunk.'

ENZA had been 4.3 days ahead of schedule in her quest to climb the 80-day mountain. She shared the same sponsor with *InterSpray*: Courtaulds Coatings and International Paints.

When Knox-Johnston and Blake had entered the Southern Ocean, racing towards the Challenge fleet, Adrian Donovan, skipper of *Heath Insured*, warned them that 'a wall of steel is coming towards you.'

Knox-Johnston replied from his high-tech, carbon fibre catamaran, punching into the seas at 20-knots: 'A straw has been known to penetrate an oak. . .'

Their paths would no longer cross at the bottom of the globe. '*ENZA*, in no immediate danger, making emergency repairs and heading for South Africa,' was the message from Mike Millis, Duty OPs at Race HQ.

Down in *InterSpray*'s galley the day after the Big Wave, Jeff Plummer was hobbling about with a swollen knee, but he was not fit for deck work. Juliet was also improved after several hours' rest.

That night, after putting the third reef in the mainsail, a six inch tear was

'How do you like your bacon monsieur?' Jeff opens Rene's Cafe for breakfast

In the desolate wastes of the Southern Ocean storms rolled over relentlessly

discovered near the third reefing point close to the luff. At 1800, with the whole crew awake, the sail was removed from the boom and the trysail hoisted. Jeffes was worried whether the crew would manage it in a full gale with gusts of 40 knots, but there was no choice. It took 90 minutes to get the sail down below and everything went smoothly.

The mainsail was ready to re-hoist the following day after Julian and Patrick had worked all night while other watches kept the boat going at near maximum speed. Inevitably, ground was lost, not being able to point so high under trysail. With the continuing wind instrument problem they had dropped back to seventh place on day 16.

Light relief came in a telex from Barry and Kerry:

'How the ford are you? Bad news about the penalty. But they always handicap the fastest horses. Hear you have a new gaffer on board, Domineering Dom the Despicable Despot. Please note the change in personality and see if you can crowbar him off the helm, especially during sail changes.'

Heavy mettle

On the nightwatch of day 16 the waves were so high that they effectively wiped out 15-minute radar sweeps for ice. Paul Buchanan, on watch with Dominic, Juliet and Jeff, reported 'ice daggers for rain' in a sea temperature which was now 3°C. Buchanan frankly admitted: 'Taking the wheel was terrifying with no wind instruments as the boat veered off one way and then another.'

On *Coopers & Lybrand* they had taken to naming waves: there was the 'belly-flop', the 'bunk bouncer', the 'smoker soaker' and simply 'mountain'. On *Pride of Teesside* David Wallbank said: 'the boat can't decide whether it's an aeroplane or a submarine. We dream of the tropics.'

It was not entirely surprising that leg three was proving the most formidable of the race. In Chay's original westward circumnavigation, in spite of the ferocious reputation of Cape Horn, his worst storms had been in this part of the Southern Ocean. But he had been considerably further north and he was not racing.

By now most Challenge yachts had experienced gear failures in winds of 60 knots, but no one had stopped racing. Competition was intense with the whole fleet still bunched tightly together after 3,000 miles. *Pride of Teesside* to the north reported having a snow fight on deck.

On *InterSpray*'s deck the 'beachcombers' had found green pebbles. They had also seen them floating past. It was like a crumbly pumice stone. 'Radio active waste dumped by the Japanese,' was one wild suggestion. The Ocean Vigil experts discovered it was a product of the whale's digestive system, called ambergris, used in cosmetics as a fixer. It turned solid when it came into contact with air.

With a forecast for weather of Force 8-9 over the next 24-48 hours, mast man Duggie risked life and limb climbing the stick in a Force 5 to fit a spare transducer for the wind instruments. Now the compass seemed to be sticking. Due to their proximity to the South Pole, at 65°S and 140°E, many yachts had reported magnetic anomalies and sluggish compasses.

Despite the slog to windward and the discomfort, everyone remained in good humour. Alison's oilskins, she reported, 'smell really bad now. I keep noticing the aroma and presuming it's someone else – but now I know it's me!' Even with the heaters on all night it was still cold, damp and miserable down below. At least it had stopped snowing. The lack of instruments was by now really hurting progress and *InterSpray* had her worst run for two weeks, dropping back to ninth place on day 18.

As the boat did a wave jump there was a cry of pain from the galley. Alison scalded herself while stirring a pan of boiling water and pasta which slopped over, splashing across her thigh.

First on the scene were the skipper, Brian and Julian. They quickly pulled down her thermal long-johns and sloshed cold water over her thigh and groin.

Julian treated the scald with anti bacterial cream. Despite her painful injuries and blistering it was not long before Alison was back on watch. Julian, though, was angry that an unnecessary risk had been taken in heavy weather. In future, oilskin trousers were compulsory when cooking in bad weather.

Whilst the sea had its revenge on *InterSpray*, yachts ahead increased their lead, though *Pride of Teesside*'s decision to head north with leaks on either side of her skeg (the steel fin protecting the rudder) lost her 30 miles in 24 hours. She now trailed *InterSpray* by 115 miles.

With true winds of 30 and 40 knots, everyone was getting weary with the relentless battle with the sea. The so-called 'Foredeck Club' was becoming more exclusive with Patrick, Duggie, Paul Buchanan and Brian, plus honorary members Julian, Dominic and Carlton.

For a time on day 20, when the three race leaders rounded Kerguelen Island, *InterSpray* was forced to run almost due north in order to lay the course to round the waypoint. More than 120 miles south of the fleet, the survey ship *Discovery* was hove-to in storm-force winds. Jeffes had considered a short-cut around the waypoint, over shallows just to the north of Kerguelen, in hopes of improving the yacht's overall position in the fleet. He was eventually persuaded by Julian and John to leave a bigger margin of safety than he'd hoped. Race HQ answered a query on the waypoint: 'Kerguelen Island includes all outlying islets, including the black dot a little south of 165m sounding. You are strongly advised to keep outside 100m line as chart surveys are incomplete.

LEG THREE

Also shallow water rougher. Regarding Les Crozet, keep outside 200m line.'

French-owned Kerguelen Island, lying at the bottom of the Indian Ocean at 69°E, is inhabited only by a few research scientists and the climate is cold and windy all the year round. In a recent 68 day study there were 45 days of gales and only three without either rain or snow. Glaciers extend down to sea level even in summer.

Race HQ's advice held true, with vicious seas encountered as *InterSpray* passed close to the shallow waters around Kerguelen, experiencing some of the worst conditions so far in this leg. The motion of the boat was laboured and very awkward. The waves had been much bigger the previous week, but here the confused seas created steeper waves. It was here that the world's largest ever wave was recorded. And here that Alan Wynne Thomas and *Cardiff Discovery* had taken several knockdowns a few weeks before.

The call to change sails on the wave-swept foredeck in these conditions became, for some, a private nightmare, while delayed changes created extra work for a new watch and added to tension amongst the crew. Waves would sweep crew from their feet to land in a tangle of harness lines against rigging or mast.

When the fleet passed Kerguelen Island deep in the Roaring Forties, it was over halfway in what had already proved the toughest leg of 'the toughest yacht race ever.' They had made more sail changes and put in more reefs so far than in the entire 52 days of the last leg.

Blyth had called this part of his circumnavigation 'The Worst Ocean' and described 'a peculiar venom in the seas. A viciousness not experienced, even in the lonely wastes south of Cape Horn. Alone in a fierce sea you feel the ocean is making a determined effort to get you.'

The radio round-up reported *Pride of Teesside* pumping 30 gallons of water from her bilges every hour with the leak around her skeg. The hand pump, however, could cope with 30 gallons a minute. *Coopers & Lybrand* had found an estimated three tons of water inside their 'watertight' collision bulkhead. Vivien had been wondering why the yacht's performance was beginning to suffer. Water was coming through holes drilled in the pulpit for wires to the navigation lights.

Paul Buchanan, *InterSpray*'s video diarist, received encouragement from Chay, to get more good video shots after the screening back home on BBC television of the latest Challenge film: 'Now you've had a tough time, you ought to tell the world. You will only get this one shot; the next leg will be a lot easier,' telexed Chay to the fleet's cameramen. Ever-conscious of the sponsors' needs, he added: 'When taking pictures, if possible please make sure the crew are wearing your sponsor's branding!'

Intrepid Buchanan went out 'to film big waves, regardless of risk to cameras' The video camera (one of two) was swamped within minutes, and stopped working.

Jeffes' battle over the wind instruments continued. Autohelm and Race HQ had failed to solve the problem, although the telex was hot with an exchange of ideas. Onboard they had taken every connection apart and tried every spare instrument.

Without the instruments functioning, sail changes could not be effectively timed and in a one-class fleet, competitive upwind sailing was just not possible.

At one point, completely defeated by the lack of logic in their behaviour, they left the instruments switched on whilst having lunch. On return they found them working perfectly. Then they stopped. It was a complete puzzle.

When the yacht got to Cape Town and Autohelm's man checked the instruments, it was found that water had got into the cable where it entered the mast-head transducer. The man from Autohelm thought the yacht had suffered a

Below decks, life sometimes seemed normal as breakfast was served

knockdown. It showed the intensity of conditions encountered.

Storms continued to roll over with relentless aggression and the weatherfax chart was full of low pressure circles from which vicious whip-like cold fronts marched over *InterSpray's* sailing route, daily producing northwesterly, westerly and southwesterly gales.

Everyone was beginning to show occasional signs of irritability, the skipper because *InterSpray* was back down to ninth place. Julian had the additional aggravation that his bunk made a noise and he couldn't sleep. Paul Buchanan thought everyone was getting at him and Ricky was suffering a back injury. Jeff's bad knee still kept him below. 'Roll on Cape Town!' said Alison.

As tempers became frayed, morale was hard to bolster with the crew, battered both physically and emotionally, watching their uphill task made steeper. Limited sleep had drained some of energy and a few cracks were showing. John Cox on *Nuclear Electric* likened sleeping in the

berths aboard his yacht to being tossed around 'like a brick in a concrete mixer.'

But as Julian said: 'The team looks after its own, knowing that every storm will pass and the good humoured banter will return.'

It didn't do to dwell too long on their position in the race.

'We are here to enjoy it. It is a once in a lifetime experience and we must just get on and do the best we can,' he added.

But being at the back of the fleet didn't give the adrenalin buzz that helped to overcome such tiredness.

The skipper had decided Julian could issue no further sick notes. 'In future, death certificates only will qualify for time off watch.' At least humour was still alive.

On day 22, *InterSpray* was heading for the Crozet Islands, west of Kerguelen, and leaving them to port. The sea temperature was up to 8°C and the wind dropped as the sun emerged for the early hours of the day. Wind and sea built from mid-morning and by lunchtime they were back in gale-force winds for the next few days.

LEG THREE

Julian took sun sights on most days, to perfect his sextant capability

Below decks, although the sensation of speed was absent, normal life was impossible. Crew were flung around by the snatching and rolling. The corkscrew motion in the stern made sleep difficult and the galley was a disaster area, with pans clattering out of cupboards, cutlery jumping out of drawers and stores migrating from stowage areas.

Dominic was tossed from his bunk when the wooden leeboard burst out of its fitting. He landed on top of Juliet in the bunk opposite. As Juliet screamed in pain, or surprise, at this sudden, unwarranted intrusion, Dominic bit his lip, literally.

Often the crudest oaths were muttered from the heads, where even the most necessary of bodily functions was rudely interrupted. John described going to the toilet as 'like having a toilet strapped to you and riding a bucking bronco. . .'

On deck in a spume-blown seascape, the yacht climbed a series of waves like steps: 20ft, 40ft then 60ft. What lay behind them was anyone's guess. It could be a 20ft slide down, or a nosedive into a 60ft

trough. During a brief lull, Duggie once again ascended the mast to check the wind instruments.

Both *Nuclear Electric* and *Commercial Union* had their mainsails off with damage to batten pockets. Merriweather reported a blown-out storm jib and torn mainsail as his crew prepared for a marathon sewing session.

During the night Jeffes got up for the radio show, which had become a subdued and low-key affair as even the radio operators sounded fatigued. He was feeling unwell and complaining of a headache and aching leg. On his way back to his bunk he passed out in the galley. Julian put him in recovery position and as he came round he asked: 'What am I doing down here?' He was put in his bunk and when Julian went back to check him he was fast asleep. At the time there was no reason to connect his headache and general malaise to the leg injury from the Big Wave.

The following day, however, the leg was not only painful but swollen around the injury. Julian found the whole shin area enlarged and soft, indicating a possible abscess. He prescribed antibiotics and confined Jeffes to his bunk.

'It's a good job you're not a horse,' Plummer told him. 'You'd probably be shot!'

With a period of lighter winds the crew took the opportunity to get the mainsail down for the second time (leaving it on the boom) for more repairs. Patrick was concerned about the leech flogging. Seams were re-stitched and a few small holes patched, while Duggie fitted new telltales. It was re-hoisted within an hour. *InterSpray* had made 185 miles to Cape Town, eighth best, while *Hofbrau* managed 245. There were 1,887 miles still to go and the waypoint closing velocity, a computerised summary of the yacht's speed towards the Cape, was monitored constantly.

The wind continued to drop to the point where the genoa went up and they were making nine to 10 knots in sunshine and moonlight, with the night's run on day 26 clocking up 103 miles. Only one other yacht had topped 100 miles.

InterSpray was now in warmer waters and even the night watch didn't need wet weather gear and could enjoy the luxury of going straight on deck without spending half an hour struggling into clammy oilskins. It was the first quiet weather of the leg and they carried out maintenance, tightening the rig after weeks of the new forestays stretching, and anxiously listened to radio chat shows to check that other yachts were equally slow. Next day Dominic spotted the masthead light of a yacht ahead, thought to be *Heath Insured* off the starboard bow. 'We're coming to get you!' said the log.

Jeff Plummer, with a day off watch, decided to go fishing with the lure donated by an enthusiast in Hobart. (Rule 6.2.1 of the Challenge Race stated: 'Apart from fishing, a yacht shall not embark food, drink, or equipment,' though

rainwater collection was permitted.) With no sea life seen since Hobart, Jeff didn't catch anything.

The antibiotic treatment was doing its work on the skipper's leg, but the infection needed to be drained. *InterSpray's* saloon became an operating theatre and Alison administered a stiff whisky anaesthetic as Julian probed with needle and scalpel. Buchanan filmed the operation for the BBC. 'Skipper's abscess is being cut and drained, puss everywhere,' said the log. A plastic drain tube was inserted into Jeffes' leg, later replaced by a bandage wick to drain the infection.

After several days of continuing the antibiotic treatment and re-dressing the leg, it swelled up to twice normal size and Julian became concerned. Jeffes wasn't resting it enough and he was now told that if he didn't keep his leg up there might be a need for a medical evacuation from the yacht. The threat seemed to work. But episodes of sleep-talking increased as the skipper had long conversations about yachting and related topics without even waking up

In Cape Town the doctor's diagnosis of his leg was a poisoned haematoma. The 'horse doctor's' diagnosis and treatment had been spot on.

Meanwhile, the radio round-up listed damage reports from the fleet, including a small gas blow-out in *Group 4's* galley, an electrical fire in their watermaker control box, and 12mm deck cracks on *British Steel II* and *Coopers & Lybrand*, near the aft lower chain plate. *Coopers'* starboard head cubicle was also reported disintegrating after a 'crapper snapper' wave.

'*InterSpray* slowly falling apart: screws falling out of gooseneck fitting on boom. Galley stove gas pipe severed. Deck lifting near forehatch. Mainsheet car worked loose. Roll on Cape Town!' wrote Alison.

InterSpray's deck plates were lifting near the hatch. The under-deck tie bars had come adrift with the flexing of the babystay as the yacht fell off waves. It didn't compromise the structural integrity. Screws were also falling from the lower spreader root socket, where it had been discovered that half of them were loose. Jeffes reported, even more amazingly, that counter sunk machine screws in the spinnaker pole end fittings had worked loose after just sitting on the deck for 4,000 miles.

The steering pedestal had been lashed with a cat's cradle of ropes since before Kerguelen, to strengthen it against people being thrown into it. All this was in addition to routine wear and tear, with broken sheets and halyards and damaged sheet cars.

Disappointed still with their inability to get back up with the fleet, Julian and the crew received a rallying telex from Trisha: 'If good wishes from everyone could help, you would be in Cape Town already. It could be worse,' she reminded him. 'You could be squeezing anal glands. I hope you are not, however, for the crew's sake!'

With 1,000 miles to Cape Town, and lying due south of Madagascar, there were seven albatrosses following the yacht at one time.

At midnight on day 29 a note in the log recorded: 'Mr. Gillespie had a promising career in yachting ahead of him until one night he inadvertently opened the forepeak hatch and soaked the skipper and Mr Wells.'

Paul Buchanan was woken by the sound of rushing water outside his cabin, followed by loud and colourful language. Following Duggie's assurance that no water was breaking on deck, Julian had given the okay to open the forehatch. They were just passing a sail on deck when a wave came over the bow. The sea temperature was mercifully 20°C, but Julian had only just unzipped his foulie jacket and was given a thorough soaking.

The skipper was not wearing oilskins at all and had just put on his only dry mid-layer, while his spare was hanging up to dry in the forepeak. Thus, in one swell swoop, Duggie's wave soaked the clothes Jeffes was wearing and ones he was trying to dry, plus the rest of the crew's washing. Duggie was Mr Unpopular for a while.

As the welcome prospect of Cape Town loomed, the crew's top poll of what they were most looking forward to (a bath, real food, a beer and proper bed) was overshadowed by the need for dry clothes, rest from the incessant violent motion and toilets which didn't move.

By now, as *InterSpray* sailed further north out of the Roaring Forties, they were swapping sails between the asymmetric spinnaker and the genoa. Packing sails the size of a tennis court, and dragging them about on deck, was something they hadn't done for a long while. On day 32, with *Group 4* only 152 miles from Cape Agulhas, the winds came in gentle gusts followed by calms. While the first flying fish were seen since leg one, a covert fishing party in the cockpit were towing two lures behind the yacht, with a car inner tube on deck as a shock absorber.

Jeffes was in his bunk below resting his leg and could hear the commotion when they hooked something. The accidental 'catch' was an albatross caught in their line while they sailed at 7.5 knots. 'We heard some squawks and looked astern to see this big bird water skiing behind the yacht,' said Dominic, who tried to reel in the unfortunate creature to free it. For a moment he thought the bird was going to take off and turn into a kite.

Jeffes was not amused and gave the order to disentangle the bird quickly. 'Whoever started fishing has got a problem and had better sort it out quick.'

John took one look at the bird's considerable beak and went to get long gloves and a sail bag. He returned to pull in the line, but when the yacht accelerated in a puff of wind it suddenly snapped,

Golden moments Number Two: catching the sun during a lull between storms

leaving the doomed creature bobbing in *InterSpray's* wake. The skipper's refusal to turn back was not popular with Ocean Vigil enthusiasts on board.

In Cape Town, the incident entered into Challenge folklore, as *InterSpray's* crew were endlessly reminded of Coleridge's *Rime of The Ancient Mariner*, with its albatross, an omen of good luck, shot with a crossbow and a curse falling on the ship which was becalmed.

'It was a giant petrel,' insisted Jeffes, defusing the threat of terrible luck. 'A huge seagull,' said someone else.

Next day they sighted their first ship since Hobart, the *Hyundai*, a large iron ore bulk carrier, less than a mile to starboard, bound from Rio to South Korea. Later *British Steel II* were sighted ahead and then *Commercial Union*, which by nightfall was abeam with their deck floodlight illuminating the sails as they drew close enough alongside to see people on deck. Suddenly they bore off. The sheet on their No 2 yankee had broken. The radio round-up later showed *Commercial Union* two miles astern and

British Steel II one mile ahead, whereas 24 hours earlier they had been ahead by respectively 45 and 51 miles.

Group 4 crossed the finish line that evening at 2106 local time, after being stalled in the Cape 'Parking Lot', under Table Mountain's wind shadow. She had taken 33 days and 17 hours from Hobart. *Hofbrau* and *Nuclear Electric* would finish the following day after a pause in the Parking Lot, leaving *InterSpray* with 270 miles still to go. *Nuclear Electric's* overall lead had been reduced to 7hrs and 55min over Mike Golding.

After more than 6,000 miles and with two yachts in sight, it was proving a nail-biting race to the finish for *InterSpray*. A game of cat and mouse.

Nothing much changed until the evening radio round-up next day, when a wind shift had helped *InterSpray* to pull away from *British Steel II*, now 12 miles behind, and *Commercial Union*, 25 miles astern. But Jeffes and his crew faced a frustratingly hot day with little wind and the Agulhas current taking them south-west. Six hours seemed like 60 on

Above: 'Carol, I'm here!' says Jeff, arriving in Cape Town with open arms and damaged leg. Below: calm after the storms: safely berthed in Cape Town with Table Mountain behind

the afternoon watch with a split found in the foot of the mainsail, which Patrick repaired. Dominic had a rainwater shower and the evening brought dolphins playing around the yacht, making the most spectacular leaps seen on the voyage to date.

Heath Insured, Rhone-Poulenc British Steel II and *Commercial Union* were all further north as *InterSpray* switched to the first of her large-scale charts for the approaches to Cape Town.

Day 36 was Alison's birthday, but with the agonisingly slow progress she felt 'like an old woman instead of 25' The crew were disheartened when the radio show put Richard Tudor 16 miles ahead with Merriweather just eight miles behind. *Pride of Teesside* was rapidly catching up. Five days ago the gap had been 200 miles, now it was 40 miles. During the day several moths came aboard and the scent of land was in the dry air.

Alison's birthday party was celebrated with cake, wine, whisky and champagne, plus a six-pack of Tassie beer, the last drops of alcohol onboard. She had also won the sweepstake, coming closest to guessing the yacht's arrival time by putting down her birthday.

By day 37 *InterSpray* had at last found some wind and landfall was made in the early hours, with Cape Agulhas light. By dawn they were past Danger Point with a yacht astern which daylight revealed to be *Commercial Union*. By going inshore, Merriweather had forfeited ground to *British Steel II*, who would finish six hours ahead of them that afternoon to claim seventh place.

InterSpray and *Commercial Union* were locked in a close tacking duel which lasted several hours, taking them right across False Bay, around Cape Point and up the coast. Eventually Merriweather would tack away to gain clear air, sailing closer inshore where he found himself heading straight for a line of small buoys (fishermen's pots), off Cape Point. Tacking to avoid one dead ahead, the yacht

snagged a line around its propeller, which stopped it dead in the water. By the time Merriweather's crew had dropped the sails and put someone over the side to cut them free, *InterSpray* was five miles ahead, but had run into a hole. Every time *InterSpray* got a break, she seemed to get a kick in the teeth.

Merriweather's misfortune turned out to be his blessing in disguise. By the time he had disentangled the prop, a stronger breeze had come up from behind and he was able to sail right over the top of a becalmed *InterSpray*. It was a slender lead which *Commercial Union* maintained to the finish. It was the final blow to *InterSpray*'s pride, elbowing them back to ninth place yet again. The albatross's revenge?

Several small fishing boats came out to welcome the yachts to South Africa, but Jeffes declined the offer of crayfish as 'outside assistance'. 'We gave some wine to *Group 4* the other day!' said the pleasure boat captain.

When the wind dropped again, *InterSpray*'s crew knew their turn in the Parking Lot had come. On the horizon, astern in the late afternoon, loomed the spectre of *Pride of Teesside*, which had made a remarkable comeback. By evening there was a spectacular view of the coast, with the backdrop of Cape Town's floodlit Table Mountain casting a wind shadow across the sea. A tablecloth of layers of strata cloud was laid across. Ahead were the lights of Robben Island, where Nelson Mandela had been imprisoned for so many years.

Julian, who had once lived and worked in South Africa, was offered the helm to cross the finish line, but any sense of fulfilment was marred as the fickle wind gods teased *InterSpray* to the last. Four miles from the finish, the kite had to come down and the genoa went up to lay the mark.

Luke Werth, International Paint's Cape Town manager, was aboard the yacht

Lusty, with a group of *InterSpray's* supporters, including Lincoln Swann, who had given up his job to follow the yacht. *InterSpray* ghosted out of the darkness towards the elusive line, only to be becalmed again.

A motor launch with Chay and photographers aboard sped alongside.

'Why have you stopped?' joked Chay.

'What have you done with the wind?' asked Jeffes.

A tense silence hung between the two boats as *InterSpray's* crew waited for the breeze.

'I see you've lost your sense of humour,' observed Chay, impatiently speeding off to catch up with *Commercial Union* as she approached the finish line. A few minutes later, the shouts of jubilation and foghorns echoed across the water as Merriweather's crew crossed the invisible line somewhere a mile or so ahead in the darkness. The two yachts had never been more than two miles apart from sunrise to sunset.

It had been a long day, a long, exhausting 37 days, and the lighting arrangements for the finish line were proving inadequate.

InterSpray's's first indication that she had crossed the line was when the local lifeboat, *Rescue Three*, came on the radio and asked: 'Would you like your finishing time?' They had finished a minute ago at 2109 local time.

'Bear away, that green light is the end of the breakwater!' came Jeffes call from the doghouse. Several other yachts had experienced difficulty in finding the line after more than 6,000 miles of racing.

They had finished just 25 minutes after *Commercial Union*, in 36 days 17 hours and nine minutes, sailing a distance of 6,323 miles. It was an unsatisfactory end to an unsatisfactory leg, if measured exclusively on the leader board. Even the bagpipes were flat, said Duggie, as he piped the yacht along the breakwater.

The disappointment and fatigue showed on the face of Paul Jeffes. To have come in ninth again, after such a hard fought battle across the Southern Ocean, was a bitter personal blow.

But if success was measured outside the narrow ambitions of the timekeeper's clock and by the spirit of determination shown by *InterSpray's* crew, they could all share with pride a victory of another kind. They had survived conditions that would have tested ordinary yachts to destruction. Their Southern Ocean baptism was over.

As they came into the glare of the Victoria and Alfred Waterfront to moor alongside *Commercial Union*, the party was in full swing. Carol Preston was there, losing no time in coming aboard, despite her broken, bandaged leg. More cans of beer and champagne were passed across.

Chay came aboard and shook hands warmly with Jeffes, presenting him with a bottle of champagne: 'Never mind it's only a game,' he said, clapping him on the shoulder.

As the crew revelled in new company and old friends recriminations were put aside and they soon felt part of the whole fleet again. *Pride of Teesside* finished within the hour, so by 2200 the whole fleet was home. Congratulations and commiserations were exchanged. *InterSpray* had been adopted by the local waterfront Sports Cafe, and were invited for a celebration supper in the midst of an ear-blasting disco. It made the Southern Ocean seem peaceful. Almost.

Four days after the yacht's arrival in Cape Town, Jeffes found the opportunity to tell Chay of his deep misgivings about the penalty when they sat down on a bench on the waterfront looking across at Bertie's Landing.

'It's quite obvious to me you're not a happy boy,' Chay told Jeffes, who argued that the one-design race had been turned into a handicap race for *InterSpray*, with the way the penalty had worked out.

Chay gave one of his disarming smiles.

INTERSPRAY'S RACE AROUND THE WORLD

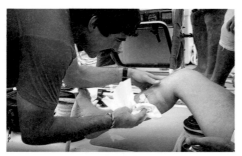

Julian attends to the skipper's abscess

'This whole thing is a great big learning curve. I can't disagree with you.'

He then dictated a note into his pocket tape recorder: 'To Capt Drummond. We have got to make the penalty a fixed time and let the yachts race together next time.'

Chay's admission was small consolation. The injustice remained and had cost *InterSpray* dearly. But there was still everything to play for in final race for home.

Race Results Leg 3 Hobart to Cape Town

Placing	Yacht Name	Arrival	GMT	Leg Time Days	Hrs	Mins	Secs
1st	Group 4	18 Mar	19:06:24	033	17	06	24
2nd	Hofbrau Lager	19 Mar	12:54:58	034	10	54	58
3rd	Nuclear Electric	19 Mar	16:23:02	034	14	23	02
4th	Coopers & Lybrand	20 Mar	19:06:58	035	17	06	58
5th	Rhone-Poulenc	20 Mar	23:34:48	035	21	34	48
6th	Heath Insured	21 Mar	02:46:40	036	00	46	40
7th	British Steel II	21 Mar	12:48:09	036	10	48	09
8th	Commercial Union	21 Mar	18:44:40	036	16	44	40
9th	InterSpray	21 Mar	19:09:12	036	17	09	12
10th	Pride of Teesside	21 Mar	19:53:54	036	17	53	54

Leg Results: Combined Times (Legs 1 to 3)

Placing	Yacht Name	Combined Time Days	Hrs	Mins	Secs
1st	Nuclear Electric	115	10	29	31
2nd	Group 4	115	18	25	38
3rd	Hofbrau Lager	116	05	28	48
4th	Heath Insured	117	10	40	06
5th	Coopers & Lybrand	118	07	51	12
6th	InterSpray	118	10	21	07
7th	Pride of Teesside	119	03	53	18
8th	Rhone-Poulenc	123	02	25	31
9th	Commercial Union	123	20	58	46
10th	British Steel II	127	03	41	35

In the Cape Doctor's Waiting Room

The Challenge fleet were the first to tie up alongside at the newly developed Victoria & Alfred Waterfront, now that Cape Town was back on the list of stopovers for major yacht races.

The third leg of the Challenge had witnessed the most unrelentingly atrocious conditions. Tales of crew from all yachts swept through guardrails and saved at the full stretch of their life lines were numerous. The catalogue of injuries was long. Paul Jeffes and Jeff Plummer

ENZA *and* InterSpray *crews line up on the giant, high-tech 85ft catamaran*

both consulted doctors in Cape Town.

One of the most serious injuries was to Simon Littlejohn on *Group 4*, who was forced to retire from the race after an operation on his leg in Cape Town. Littlejohn's left knee had twisted so badly as a wave struck him on deck, that it virtually 'exploded', to paraphrase the surgeon's two page report. It would take a year to mend. Littlejohn was in a high-tech leg brace for six weeks. His crew mate Rob Coles broke three ribs.

Carol Randall on *Heath Insured* sailed home with her right leg in a steel-supported canvas brace after more cartilage damage. and Gary Hopkins on *Coopers & Lybrand* dropped out after losing more weight through constant seasickness between Hobart and Cape Town.

Repairs also started on the yachts. Andrew Roberts had been on the receiving end of 112 telexes requiring his trouble-shooting skills during the third leg. (Many of them to were do with *InterSpray*'s wind instruments). The underwater cracks around the skeg on *Pride of Teesside* were welded again, but Ian MacGillivray had his request for a time allowance for taking a longer, less risky northerly course, rejected by the protest committee.

With *average* wind speeds on leg three of 35 knots, and days of 45 and 60 knots, sail repairs were still a fraction of what was expected.

Jeffes said: 'Once the sails were up that suited the conditions you could sail for hour after hour in gale force winds. The yacht was beautifully balanced in 30-35 knots of wind with three reefs in the main and the No 2 yankee and staysail. In 40-45 knots it was just staysail and three reefs. But she ran out of ballast after 45 knots and sailing was no pleasure.'

The fleet sails package for the Challenge cost close to half a million pounds – some £47,000 for each yacht. Hood were always confident that one set of mainsails would last around the world,

but the Challenge business played it safe and ordered 10 new mainsails. However, the yachts arrived in Cape Town with serviceable mainsails. Indeed, John Chittenden went as far as to say that the sails had another circumnavigation left in them. *Commercial Union*'s mainsail had split in two when the spare main wire halyard whipped through the leech of the sail, causing a tear that split it to the luff. The crew managed to stitch it back together.

With the skippers' agreement, the unused mainsails were shipped back to the UK. It was a tribute to the crews' seamanship as well as Hood sails.

With the Rothmans Cape to Rio Race recently finished and competing yachts back at the Royal Cape Yacht Club, Challenge crews were well entertained. *InterSpray* was adopted by the waterfront Sports Cafe, which entertained the crew to dinner the first night and offered open house thereafter. The Rotary Club of Tafelberg also adopted *InterSpray*.

The Tavern of the Seas lived up to its reputation and after confronting Cape Horn and Cape of Storms, *InterSpray*'s crew thought nothing of staring the odd lion in the face and went on safari to visit wildlife sanctuaries.

One of the highlights of the Cape Town stopover was a trip along the Cape Wine Route with some of the crew from *ENZA New Zealand*, who had been taking part in their own perilous adventure – attempting to sail around the world in 80 days – until they were forced to retire.

The wine tour, finishing at Stellenbosch, was arranged by Luke Werth, the local manager for Courtaulds International Paint, and his girlfriend Penny. Courtaulds had sponsored *ENZA* with their high-tech VC Systems antifouling.

Joining *InterSpray*'s crew were *ENZA*'s co-skipper Robin Knox-Johnston, David Alan-Williams, Ed Danby, Don (Jaws) Wright and Paul Standbridge. Peter Blake was in New Zealand pursuing new plans.

Above: casting off from the Victoria & Alfred Waterfront for the final 6,800 mile leg home to Southampton. Below: Robin Knox-Johnston swaps sea stories with (left to right) Brian Warr, Paul Jeffes, Ricky Scott, Dominic Mathews and Julian Wells

INTERSPRAY'S RACE AROUND THE WORLD

InterSpray had been 15 days out from Hobart when a telex came through from Race HQ that the giant catamaran had hit a submerged object and was limping to Cape Town with a hole in the starboard hull. Knox-Johnston was keeping his cards close to his chest about what happened next, having talked of 'unfinished business' in the Southern Ocean.

But his invitation to go aboard the 85ft *ENZA*, ashore at the Royal Cape Yacht Club, and awaiting shipment back to Britain, was enthusiastically accepted by *InterSpray's* crew. As *Formule TAG* the awesome multihull had held the 24-hour speed record of 518 miles in 23 hours 41 minutes in 1984.

As the first man to circumnavigate the world non-stop and singlehanded in 1969, Knox-Johnston's fame had started at a slower pace. He had taken ten and a half months, (313 days), at an average speed of 3.96 knots in his small teak ketch *Suhaili*. *InterSpray's* time at sea, the 'wrong way' round the world, had taken them a total of 118 days to Cape Town, at an estimated average speed of 7.4 knots.

The crew could have swapped yarns and statistics all afternoon.

In Cape Town some of *InterSpray's* crew were reunited with loved ones for the first time in six months. Julian saw daughters Jenny and Emma, accompanied by Trisha, while Ricky was reunited with wife Jane, daughters Julie and Joanna and son Philip. Other arrivals included Alison's parents, Juliet's mother, Mrs Grace Vincent, as well as Thomasina and Giles, Caroline Bird, Cherie Brain, Carolyn Elder and Paul Buchanan's sister, Ruth. John Davis flew back to Australia to spend some time with his family before returning to Cape Town a week before the restart. He took with him some wood smuggled from the bunkboards of *InterSpray*. The nature of his covert mission would be revealed in six weeks' time.

At Paul Jeffes' debriefing for *InterSpray's* crew two days, after arrival in Cape Town, he was careful to downplay the disappointment of the leg three position and emphasise that, win or lose, it was important the crew enjoyed the trip. 'What we don't want is people leaving the yacht in Southampton feeling bitter because we didn't win. Everybody who completes this race is a winner.'

To ensure that they had the best chance, the 24-hour 'holiday' below decks, adopted in leg 3, was abolished. With better conditions on leg 4 there would be a full watch on deck to increase teamwork.

The Cape Town stopover was also the occasion of Jeffes' 40th birthday on April 6, celebrated by the crew with a barbecue hosted by Luke and Penny at their home. Paul and Carolyn later sipped champagne on the heady heights of Table Mountain.

Shortly after the Challenge yachts berthed in Cape Town, the crews had heard an eloquent speech from Cape Town's Mayor at a welcoming reception. He didn't attempt to disguise the cracks in society and went straight to the heart of the country's racial inequalities, speaking of his high hopes for a better future now that sanctions had been lifted and sporting events like the Challenge were returning to the beleaguered country.

Tragically, a few days before the yachts set off from Cape Town on the homeward leg, South Africa's apartheid tensions erupted into riots across the country, sparked by the murder of black Communist Party leader Chris Hani.

During a national day of mourning millions of blacks stayed away from work and city centres were overrun by looting mobs. Cape Town's main shopping thoroughfare, Adderley Street, became a war zone as cars were overturned and burnt, and whites were assaulted. The only vehicles on the street were armoured cars as police opened fire, killing two rioters.

CAPE TOWN STOPOVER

The waterfront was an oasis from the city's ugly problems, but smoke from the riots still hung over the downtown area as *InterSpray*'s preparations continued for the race home. Dominic, returning from up country in a hire car with his family, nearly ran down one of the inhabitants of the notorious black settlement, Crossroads, beside the motorway. He was warned not to stop, because whites had been attacked. Families would need escorts to the airport after the yachts had left Cape Town.

While the Challenge fleet was in town it all seemed to happen. The smoke over the city was soon blown away when the Cape Doctor (the name given to strong south-east winds) blew so hard that the city experienced its worst storms for 20 years. A gust of 100 knots was recorded across the harbour. The roof of one waterfront property was blown clean off. Downtown, ropes were strung across the street so that pedestrians could cross safely. Australian single-handed yachtswoman Jill Knight, aboard *Cooee*, whom some of the *InterSpray* crew met at Hout Bay, was rescued by the local lifeboat when her 100-year-old wooden gaffer had its rudder smashed in huge seas. Not surprisingly, Chay was bustling around his fleet like a protective mother hen.

In the early hours of the morning of race start day, Paul Jeffes went with Luke Werth to International Paint's factory in Cape Town's docklands, to collect the latest weatherfaxes from the UK. He left it until after midnight so he could get the most up-to-date 24-hour forecast from Bracknell. Luke stepped out of his car producing a big bunch of keys like a jailor. There were four or five locks on the door to the offices and as Luke fumbled with the various keys he turned to Paul and said: 'Hold on to this will you?'

Paul found himself holding a Magnum revolver. 'Is it loaded?' he inquired anxiously.

'Of course, it is. There's no point in carrying an empty revolver,' said cool hand Luke, who carried the gun everywhere after the riots.

'Is the safety catch on?' asked Jeffes.

'Revolvers don't have safety catches!' replied Luke.

'So there I was,' said Jeffes afterwards 'standing there in the midnight shadows holding a loaded revolver while this guy was picking locks. . . I was praying a police patrol wouldn't come around the corner.'

Dominic had a different problem. He had noticed after the first few days in Cape Town that when he met people and invited them to 'Call me Dom,' there was a suppressed smile.

A group of schoolgirls were touring *InterSpray* and asked his name. 'Just call me Dom,' he announced to fits of giggles.

Later he met a young Indian couple while staying up country in a wilderness cabin with his family: This time when they smiled at his suggestion to 'Just call me Dom', he plucked up courage to ask what was so funny. 'Dom', it turned out, is Afrikaans for idiot.

Leg Four

Completing the circle

Start Saturday, April 17,
Cape Town to Southampton 6,800 miles

'**D**on't get complacent.' cautioned Chay Blyth at the pre-race briefing in Cape Town. 'You can die just as easily offshore on this leg as you can in the Roaring Forties.'

Of the 12 crewmen who had gone overboard in the five Whitbread round-the-world races, nine have been victims of accidents when spinnakers were flying. Spinnakers would be flying for days on end on this final leg home.

On Cape Town's waterfront there was a carnival atmosphere with young girls handing out flags and scattering flowers and petals and the Good Hope Band playing a traditional send off. Overnight storms with heavy rain and high winds had left clear skies and light westerly winds for the race start, but towering swells were rolling into Table Bay and breaking over the harbour breakwater, discouraging some spectators from getting afloat.

As the fleet jostled for positions in the bay under the shadow of Table Mountain, a light plane flew overhead, trailing good luck messages, including one from the Sports Cafe. International Paint's

support vessel, a tugboat, was being tossed about like a toy.

When the start gun was fired at 1300 hours local time the ten yachts were starting with a clean sheet and an equal chance to revel in the welcome that awaited the first crew to sail up Southampton Water.

InterSpray crossed the line third in the middle of the fleet. Most yachts were hoisting spinnakers to run down to the next mark three miles away, but the big

Team talk before the gun goes for the start of the final run home to close the circle

swells were causing confusion for *InterSpray* and *Heath Insured*. The first turning buoy had been swept three-quarters of a mile out of position.

InterSpray, under full main, No 1 yankee and staysail, was upwind of all but *Heath Insured*, which now hoisted her spinnaker. Jeffes was about to go for the spinnaker when a shout came from the cockpit to gybe. Someone had noticed the buoy in the wrong place. The race committee were on the radio asking for a GPS fix on the buoy. They didn't know where it was either. *Heath* was forced to turn back to round the mark and both she and *InterSpray* sailed away with red protest flags streaming from their backstays. Lesson learned: 'look with eyes, not electronics,' said Julian.

Richard Tudor led the fleet round the elusive mark, but later slipped to eighth place after falling into an area of light winds with *InterSpray* and *Hofbrau*.

Nuclear Electric crossed the line in tenth position but climbed to second position overnight. Chittenden's crew were reported to have stripped their yacht

of excess weight by sharing seven sets of oilskins, boots and even toothpaste, between watches.

Chay's storm troopers were homeward bound at last, soon to swap the privations of the Southern Ocean for the tropical delights of steady trades, surfing downwind instead of beating into icy headwinds, with dolphins streaking in bow waves and shorts and T-shirts replacing Musto survival suits. Another dimension in sailing and seamanship to test their patience and skills.

This leg, above all else, promised to be a tactical battle. When yachts started to split away, which yachts did the skippers cover? With the South Atlantic high-pressure system, the doldrums and the Azores high to add to the equation, anything could happen over the next few thousand miles.

After 21,000 miles and 118 days and ten hours, *InterSpray* was in overall sixth position. The three race leaders on combined times were *Nuclear Electric* (115 days 10 hours) which held a 7 hour 56-minute lead on closest rival Mike

Golding in *Group 4*. *Hofbrau Lager* was 11 hours behind Golding. *InterSpray* had a lot of catching up to do.

By morning, *Group 4*, fastest across the Southern Ocean from Cape Horn to the Cape of Good Hope, were in the lead for the long run home. The fleet had split into two groups, with most 30 miles offshore. *InterSpray* was among the inshore group, lying in ninth place, but within sight of Richard Tudor, four miles ahead and *Hofbrau*, languishing in tenth place two miles astern. With a heavy swell and the south-east wind hardly more than a whisper, progress was frustrating.

It was going to be a psychological battle before the doldrums. Jeffes' tactics for next few days were to head as far north as possible following the coast and gybing west later in the week, when he was sure they had cleared the high pressure area.

Cape Town, like Rio and Hobart, was soon a happy memory as the crew got back into the watch system and sleep deprivation and long hours of studying weatherfax maps became the established pattern of life. *InterSpray*'s galley looked like a market stall with fruit, vegetables and large salamis taking up most of the room before new areas for stowage were found.

Depression could easily have set in as *InterSpray* found herself back in her customary ill-fated ninth position. But Julian telexed home: 'We're all fit and spirits are high.'

Something had to break their pattern of ill-luck.

According to an ill-informed *Times* report, published on the day the race re-started, the divide between racing and cruising in some yachts had 'not always been clear-cut.' The correspondent referred to *InterSpray*'s crew 'dogged by bad luck since Cape Horn . . . but only now has the reason emerged,' wrote Mr. Pickthall referring to the albatross fishing episode.

No one on *InterSpray* was cruising.

After the evening chat show, Richard Tudor gybed west and Jeffes decided to gybe at the watch change at 2200. The spinnaker pole topping lift chose that moment for the eye to break away from the pole. Without the downhaul well locked off, the heel flew up and broke through the stopper on the mast track, flailing around like a loose missile. They were lucky it didn't torpedo back through the mainsail

The end of the pole was eased down, the spinnaker tripped and dropped. It was only prompt action that prevented further damage. The thought of losing the heavyweight spinnaker at the start of this leg didn't bear thinking about. With the corporate kite up all day, crew were placing mental bets on how many days they would be flying a kite through the tropics.

The morning round up on day three showed *InterSpray* the furthest inshore to the coast of Namibia. It didn't help that many of the other yachts were sailing through the high with no apparent ill-effects, covering the same sort of distances as *InterSpray*, but on a shorter line to the equator. Only ten miles separated the first five yachts by the third afternoon – *Nuclear Electric*, *Group 4*, *Commercial Union*, *Pride of Teesside* and *Rhone-Poulenc*. They kept the breeze and were in front on paper because they were further west. The official results were based on the shortest distance between Southampton and Cape Town. It was a logical formula, but not always realistic.

Heath Insured, with a spinnaker wrap on the forestay, was sighted by *InterSpray* in the morning and overhauled to port.

One-legger Ruth Colenso soon found her sealegs after the first day's chop had reduced her to bucket watching, along with the rest of the afflicted. Of all *InterSpray*'s one-leggers, Ruth faced arguably the toughest social assignment – fitting in with a crew of 13 who had spent seven months evolving and perfecting their own private language, offbeat in-jokes, signals, and sundry rituals. In Southampton she had waved goodbye to a group, who for all their training together, still harboured individual uncertainties and inhibitions. In Cape Town she said hello to a close-knit crew that had faced so much together at close-quarters, that they had either lost, or vanquished, most, if not all, their inhibitions. Sea-manship was second nature to some and the yacht's systems were inbred. They could be discordant and quarrelsome with one another. They could be impatient to see jobs done their way. Ruth's initiation rites, as a 'foreigner' entering this seemingly aggressive tribe of native boat people, was a rite of passage within her passage home.

Alison had picked up a bug in Cape Town and had been confined to her bunk with gastro-enteritis but recovered within a week on various potions.

With the weather getting hotter by the day, there was no need for thermals any more and as the yachts tracked north layers were stripped away.

While *InterSpray* enjoyed one her best noon-to-noon runs of 226 miles on the third day out from Cape Town, French-man Bruno Peyron, aboard the catamaran *Commodore Explorer*, had broken the 80-day record set by Jules Verne's fictional hero. He had circled the globe in 79 days, six hours and sixteen minutes, at an average speed of 14 knots-plus, to win the Jules Verne Challenge trophy. So surprised were the organisers, the trophy hadn't even been made.

The early hours of day four brought their own drama for Julian's watch on *InterSpray* – emergencies always seemed to happen after midnight – Brian was on the helm and Carlton trimming when the lightweight kite split at the head and tore down both tapes to the clews. The situation was retrieved quickly and the heavy-weight kite hoisted, but there were over several hundred feet of seams to stitch. Patrick and Juliet spent two hours unrav-elling the mess and Patrick reckoned it would take at least three days to repair. The sewing party worked on deck, three from the standby watch and one from the deck watch.

With *Heath Insured* still in sight there was a four-hour match race in the morning, with intense concentration on both yachts.

As an incentive to sew faster each metre of stitching was rewarded with a bottle of Hofbrau lager. Work carried on during the night, rigging up the Aldis lamp as a spotlight suspended from the spinnaker pole, as the standby watch sewing circle stitched away.

As *InterSpray* sailed in light, fluctuating airs under her heavyweight spinnaker, Paul Buchanan became the first helms-man in history to heave-to under spin-naker, or so judged Dominic. Paul's sister, Ruth, meanwhile, was keeping the crew entertained by telexing from home a limerick a day on each crew member.

By mid-morning on day five, one side of the lightweight spinnaker was repaired and the tear near the head of the sail was also mended. There was also encouraging news on the radio chat show with *InterSpray* lying in fifth position. Over-night, *British Steel II* had gone from tenth to first place 100 miles west of the main fleet. As temperatures rose daily it was a joy to wear shorts and not have to climb into layers of sodden clothing. Swimwear was *de rigueur*. Jeff, Dominic and Ricky were attempting to supplement food supplies with some fishing, but with no luck so far and by evening, *InterSpray* was romping along at nine knots and the sewing party had moved to the galley. *Coopers & Lybrand* had blown out their heavyweight spinnaker and Richard Griffith estimated 30,000 stitches were needed – more than one for every mile of the Challenge. Stargazer Dominic watched a very bright Jupiter high in the

InterSpray powers through towering swells in Cape Town bay on her homeward run. Facing page: the spinnaker sewing circle work by night under the Aldis lamp

clear starry night sky. As she sunk to the west, Venus came up to the east with the sun.

InterSpray crossed the Tropic of Capricorn on day six and was now officially in the tropics. The sea temperature, which was 14°C in Cape Town was now 24°C and hot, arid winds off the African coast were a stark contrast to the bone-chilling winds off the Antarctic. Someone turned on the fan in the computer cupboard, but it seemed to suck air out of the saloon, instead of circulating cool air.

With all the fresh food some crew started to feel bloated, but although many spoke of diets, no one had started one.

The south-east trades were expected to carry the fleet through to approximately two degrees north of the equator and to the doldrums, the 200-300 mile wide belt of unpredictable winds. Opting for the shortest crossing route close to the African coast meant risking a wider belt of doldrums. The safer route, crossing somewhere between 26-30°W, carried the penalty of being considerably longer. As winds lightened on the approach to the doldrums, the yachts would need to tack downwind to maintain maximum speed.

Juliet, maintaining the yacht's Ocean Vigil log, was finding much to record after weeks spent in the desert of the Southern Ocean. Killer whales had been sighted chasing dolphins. At night in the tropics the sea was strangely illuminated by exploding blobs of blue-green phosphorescence – a bright pulse, or sparkle, which could last from a tenth of a second to two or three seconds. This bioluminescence could have been danger signals from jellyfish or squid as the yacht was viewed as an approaching predator.

On days eight and nine, *InterSpray* remained in fifth place and the crew had their first happy hour of the leg. Juliet, now assistant purser, was taking to her role as keeper of the ship's booze with more enthusiasm than she had found for the flags. Understandably, since she once ran a pub.

The spinnaker sewing went on around the clock. It took four crew one and a half

hours to do one metre. The lightweight kite would be operational by dawn, ready for when the lighter winds came.

Meanwhile, there was something of a sexist conspiracy among a section of male crew who were praising the cooking by Alison and Ruth so much that they hoped to create an artificial rivalry to raise standards to new heights of tastiness. Alison had come second to *British Steel II* in the McDougalls' cookery competition in Cape Town.

Coopers & Lybrand telexed the fleet inviting crew to take advantage of Prime Minister Major's new democratic honours selection method and nominate Chay Blyth for a knighthood. This prompted much late night discussion among *InterSpray*'s watches, as rebel crew drew up a phoney list, including nominations from Donald Duck and Stewart Alexander, *Independent* sailing correspondent.

During the early hours of day nine, Dominic was hit on the head by a flying fish. The note in the ship's log added: 'Paul Buchanan to eat for breakfast. . . the fish, not Dominic's head.' One fish the size of a sardine didn't go far between 14 people.

The spinnaker had been flying for seven days when *Coopers & Lybrand*'s stern light was seen soon after midnight ten miles away. By mid-afternoon, *InterSpray* had crossed the Greenwich meridian and was back in the western hemisphere, off the coast of Angola. The skipper commented that it would have been possible to read *War and Peace* in the time it took to gybe the spinnaker. The lights of *Coopers & Lybrand* were still on the starboard beam that night.

At noon on day ten, the ship's clock was altered to GMT, and with 1,673 miles covered since Cape Town there were 4,286 miles to Southampton. Brian, on chafe patrol, which had become more of a flying fish breakfast patrol, spotted *Coopers & Lybrand* crossing *InterSpray*'s track on opposite gybe that night. Vivien

was heading west. *Commercial Union Assurance* had caught a 12lb dorado, which may have explained why *British Steel II* again took the lead from them overnight – the sixth time the two yachts had changed position at the head of the fleet.

InterSpray had two flying fish for breakfast, cooked by Dominic. Also lying on the saloon table was an unusual catch for Julian – Paul Buchanan had suffered a knock in the teeth on the forehatch and Julian practised his dentistry skills for the first time since the Ushant-Fastnet Race, inserting a temporary filling on the saloon table operating theatre.

While *InterSpray* slipped back to seventh place on day 11, only 75 miles separated the first and tenth-placed yachts across a 350-mile wide front. The crew's sweepstake on finishing times varied from Carlton's optimistic May 16 to Dominic's accurate May 25 at 0800, which was to prove only hours short.

On day 13 the heavy kite was dropped for foot repair, where it had chafed on the forestay, and Paul Buchanan ascended the mast with assorted cameras to interview Duggie at work changing a spinnaker masthead block. He filmed him on video from the top spreader. Unfortunately, he followed this with an excursion to the end of the spinnaker pole, where the video camera detached itself from its cord around Paul's neck and fell into the sea.

The evening radio roundup included an unusual request, supposedly from Race HQ, suggesting that the fleet should go west of the Azores due to a submerged container. 'Is this a wind up?' someone wrote in *InterSpray*'s log. It was highly unlikely that RHQ could reach the yachts on 4146MHz. Spencer Drummond had a impersonator somewhere in the fleet.

Unknown to the rest of the fleet, who were enjoying the practical joke and eating alfresco dinners on deck, Adrian Donovan and his crew on *Heath Insured* were in the midst of a desperate life and death search for crewman Bill Vincent, who had dived off the stern of the dark blue yacht.

Adrian Rayson, on the helm of *Heath*, alerted by a female crew member's scream, yelled the words everyone had dreaded to hear for the last 24,000 miles – 'Man overboard!' – as other crew members pointed at Bill Vincent in the water.

Vincent turned to look at the yacht, but appeared to be making no effort to attract the attention of the crew. In fact, he appeared to be swimming away east from the yacht, observed Rayson.

The accident everyone feared happened when least expected and in a manner no one could have foreseen.

Vincent, a 47-year-old carpenter from Bath, had gone overboard at 1730, within feet of his crewmates – but he hadn't fallen. Minutes after easing the spinnaker pole forward from a starboard winch in the cockpit, he had stepped onto the top rail of the pushpit at the stern, wearing only swimming trunks.

As crewmate Samantha Brewster shouted 'Bill!', he made a perfectly executed dive. It was a premeditated, calculated act. 'He did not jump and nor was it an accident,' said Rayson. There was a moderate swell, a Force 3-4 wind and a warm sea. The water temperature was 82°F.

Skipper Adrian Donovan was on deck within 12 seconds and a danbuoy and lifebuoy were launched and the GPS man overboard 'panic button' activated. The yacht had been reaching under full mainsail and spinnaker at eight knots and other crew members hurried to drop the kite as the yacht turned back. But they lost sight of Vincent in the swell and the white horses.

The area was searched for two hours until dark, with two crew up the mast with binoculars, plus lookouts posted on bow and stern and amidships. The search continued after dark under spotlight.

The first *InterSpray* knew of the drama was five hours later, at 2240, when a telexed 'urgency message' concerning *Heath Insured* was received from Race HQ in Petersfield, asking the yacht to standby for more information and for skipper Jeffes to be alerted. *InterSpray* was asked to divert to *Heath* 124 miles away.

As they prepared to assess the course change Chay telexed the news that Vincent had gone overboard in 'an apparent suicide attempt.' Jeffes gave the call to drop the spinnaker and start the engine. *InterSpray* changed course and motor-sailed at nine knots under No 1 yankee to rendezvous with *Heath Insured* at 003° 06'S and 0007° 59'W.

'The problems of the race and circumnavigation are as nothing on receiving news like this and we are all devastated for Adrian and his crew,' wrote Julian in his log.

At 0105 Adrian Donovan radioed Jeffes to explain that there was no sign of Vincent and little hope of survival. Chay was on his way to inform the next of kin.

InterSpray was to spend three hours motoring towards *Heath Insured* before she received a message from Race HQ at 0130 to stand down. The crew were thanked for their prompt action and told that there was nothing more they could do. 'Please resume the race.' A fleet message also went out explaining that *Heath* had lost a man overboard.

Jeffes attempted to motor back to a restart point – a position estimated to be the yacht's comparative place in the fleet when they were diverted. He telexed Race HQ for advice and was told that continued motoring risked disqualification. He was advised to resume sailing and log all positions and details. He would be entitled to claim for redress.

InterSpray's crew couldn't help wondering why they had been chosen to divert to *Heath* when *Nuclear Electric* were just 50 miles away. Chittenden had

Dominic finally catches a fish, after 26,000 miles of the world's oceans

received no such request. The reason given was that *InterSpray* could motorsail, reaching across the wind, while *Nuclear Electric* would have to motor upwind. In the event Chittenden diverted anyway when he received the standard alert on the Inmarsat system, relayed by Falmouth Marine Rescue Control Centre.

The five hour delay in *InterSpray* being requested to go to *Heath's* assistance was attributable to the nature of the incident. Adrian Donovan conducted his own textbook search for Vincent until darkness fell. It was not until then that he relayed an urgent message to Race HQ back home. Understandably, given the sensitive circumstances of the incident, Donovan sent the message in code. Apart from the time taken to encode the message, he was not to know that when it arrived at Petersfield there would be no one on duty who could decipher it. By the time Race HQ had received the message, located somebody to break the code and relayed it to Falmouth MRCC, several hours had elapsed since Vincent dived overboard. Had it been a normal man overboard incident, a standard distress or urgency signal to all ships would have gone out straight away.

By 1000 that morning, *InterSpray* had re-hoisted her heavyweight spinnaker and an hour later *Heath Insured* were advised by survival experts that there was no chance of Bill Vincent being found alive. *Heath Insured* abandoned their search which had lasted for 18 hours.

Adrian Donovan held a brief service in memory of Vincent. As he finished, a rainbow appeared over the sky. Crew member Ken Pearson thought: 'It was the perfect epitaph for Bill, because that *was* him. . . he was all the colours of the rainbow.'

Chay Blyth had driven to Bath in the early hours of Friday morning to break the tragic news to Vincent's wife, Pauline, a schoolteacher, and his two sons Adam (17) and Daniel (15).

Adrian Donovan treated the bereavement as you would any death in the family. There was a period of mourning and then life had to go on. The complexities behind Bill Vincent's death could only be guessed at. His belongings were packed by his anguished crewmates in the two red boxes allotted to each crew member.

Heath Insured had taken part in the radio show the previous evening, 90 minutes after Vincent's mysterious death dive, and given nothing away about the dramatic search operation going on from their yacht.

Back home, anxious relatives and sponsors, shocked by Vincent's death, speculated on the supreme irony of a sailor's disappearance from a well-found yacht in calm conditions, after enduring and surviving the worst weather and sea conditions on the globe and being within days of completing his great adventure. It was a tragedy that deeply affected all involved in the Challenge and added a new dimension of camaraderie among the fleet.

The full circumstances of Vincent's death would be kept under wraps until the yacht arrived home to a Department of Transport Inquiry.

Adrian Donovan conducted his own inquiry aboard *Heath Insured* and compiled a written report with signed statements by the watch leader and all witnesses. The rest of the fleet were now sworn to silence, so that the official inquiry would not be prejudiced. The Southampton inquiry would rule a month later that Vincent had been lost at sea, presumed drowned.

There was a sad, melancholy mood on all the yachts as crew came to terms with Vincent's death. He had been one of the race's characters, turning into a salty seadog by Cape Town, with a bushy, grey beard. He had boasted that even his own family hadn't recognised him. The Challenge had become an intoxicating adventure which, according to some, he did not want to end.

Nicknamed 'Steps', after the boarding ladder he had built for his yacht, Vincent was also a loner who had seemed depressed and preoccupied with a personal problem on the final leg home.

For some there were feelings of anger and betrayal at the manner of Bill Vincent's death. Others closer to him felt guilt, no doubt, searching their memories to see if there had been some signal or cry for help that they had missed.

InterSpray's diversion to assist *Heath Insured* had put them 35 miles behind their last position. *Nuclear Electric* would also eventually seek an allowance for time lost going to aid *Heath* in their search for Vincent.

As the fleet approached the equator 100 miles away things were hotting up. Below decks it was like being in a pressure cooker. *InterSpray*'s crew were trying to sleep in the sail locker and Jeff was suffering from mild sunstroke, spending the night in the forepeak with a wet cloth on his forehead. Two sharks were spotted swimming 25ft from the yacht.

On May Day, Brian learned he had a job offer on a BP oil rig for 4 months – starting on May 28, a few days after the yacht was due back.

As fickle winds played with the yacht amidst tropical downpours and black thundery squalls, numerous sail changes were called for.

A new sailing term was coined by Duggie when the wind went from 00 to 35 knots true and the shout came down the boat: 'Are you ready in the cockpit?'

Duggie on the main sheet called back: 'Yoh!' in the manner of a US Marine.

'What the *** does that mean?' came the response from the foredeck, as *InterSpray* crashed through the night at 10 knots.

Thereafter cries of 'Yoh!' bounced around yacht above and below decks.

When the lightweight kite was hoisted for the first time since its repair the head looked like a toothy grin with all the stitching.

The continued strength of the southeast trades had pushed the doldrums some 200-300 miles further north. Paul Buchanan was carrying out scientific experiments to see if water went down the plug hole clockwise or anticlockwise in the southern and northern hemispheres. The results were inconclusive with the yacht's angle of heel.

InterSpray crossed the equator into the northern hemisphere at dawn on Day 16 at 013° 56'W. King Neptune, due on deck at midday to preside over the crossing the line ceremony, was late. Gladys had lost her clothes *en route*, explained Jeff. There was only one victim for Neptune this time – one-legger Ruth, plus a furry mascot, a dog otter glove puppet, which took up residence in the doghouse at Cape Town. The rest of the crew relished the prospect of Ruth's imminent indignity, but the yacht's two circumnavigating mascots, Gordon the Gopher and Hearty Bear, initiated on the outward passage, suffered again to keep her company. The crew took it in turns to daub Neptune's nasty brew over Ruth. A diversion in the afternoon was a passing school of 30-plus killer whales. Having lost three or four places after diverting to assist *Heath*, *InterSpray* achieved the fleet's best noon-to-noon run of 150 miles.

There was much discussion on the whereabouts of the ITCZ (Inter tropical convergence zone) plus a very bad smell on the boat with bilges full of black, sulphurous smelling liquid. Julian's standby watch spent two hours getting rid of it. It was now so hot on deck that bare feet burned.

By day 18 *InterSpray* had passed a notional half-way point, with less than 3,000 miles to go to the finish, and there was little doubt that they had arrived in the doldrums after eight sail changes during the morning, involving one of the three spinnakers. Calculations showed that they had made up most of the ground lost when they went to the aid of *Heath*.

Electrical storms surrounded the yacht with forked and sheet lightning as close as 300 metres. Some crew were careful to stand on the wooden slats in the cockpit, rather than the stainless steel deck. It was like being among mortar shells with blinding flashes of light and lightning bolts zig-zagging across the surface of the sea. During a lull, a swallow, blown off course, hitched a ride on the yacht for an hour.

Progress in the doldrums was a complete lottery. Hofbrau's Pete Goss said it 'was like sitting in a dentist's waiting room with an open appointment. One might waltz in and get away with a check-up, or endure hours of painful treatment.'

All ten yachts were convinced their brand of toothpaste was best.

No sooner had Julian telexed home that the hundreds of feet of stitching on the lightweight kite were holding than it was blown again on day 19.

The lightning that struck in a storm that followed was so close that John Davis claimed he could smell it. 'I looked up and expected the mast to look like a melted candle,' he said.

InterSpray had taken 100 miles from *Heath Insured* and *Hofbrau* in the last two days and the leader, *Group 4*, was now 81 miles ahead. All the yachts had broken free from the doldrums and were headed towards the Cape Verde Islands by day 20. A coating of fine red sand was blown on deck from the Sahara desert some 300 miles north-east and the sun set through a thick red dust haze. *InterSpray* was finding strange weather patterns for the area, with north-west winds, instead of the predicted north-east trades. The wind had died by mid-afternoon on day 21 and with the yacht virtually becalmed, Dominic decided to go for a 'last chance' swim. Patrick gave one of his looks of disbelief. 'You're kidding,' he said as Slick rigged up the scramble net over the side.

Dom dived over and eventually Patrick followed. . . and then Brian. Jeff dived off near the stern and Ruth was persuaded to join them. They felt acutely vulnerable with the nearest land miles away – underneath them. As the yacht picked up half-a-knot boat speed it was enough to make Jeff swim back double-quick. The swimmers had been back on board for half-an-hour, when a large fin circled the yacht. A shark of respectable size came idly by nosing the stern.

Later there was a spellbinding marine show as the sea came alive with some 30 dolphins, several Manta Rays, lazily sunbathing with one wing above the water, Portuguese Men of War (jelly fish with sails) and over 100 pilot whales, some making joyful leaps. The sea temperature, which had peaked at 30°C was now down to 24°C.

Fifty miles off the African coast, *Group 4* diverted to a fishing boat from Dakar with engine problems and a bedraggled crew of 15 who spoke in a French dialect. They gave them food (McDougalls and tinned sardines) and alerted rescue authorities. The stricken boat had been stranded for eight days without assistance.

Ten fishermen in an open boat approached *InterSpray* next day under engine. 'Pirates,' said the log book. Some thought it was a surfacing whale until they got closer.

Julian's watch was gaining something of a reputation when on day 22 they blew the asymmetric spinnaker in the early hours with Paul Buchanan on the helm. The sewing circle were back in action. But the day also proved a milestone for *InterSpray*'s fishing party which finally caught a fish, after 26,000 miles of ocean.

While the dorado was taken below, gutted, stuffed with sage, onion and sprinkled with lemon, two more were caught as Paul Buchanan prepared a fish starter for dinner. A fourth monster, 18ins long, was hauled aboard and the menu was amended so that fish became the

INTERSPRAY'S RACE AROUND THE WORLD

Above: intrepid lensman Paul Buchanan ascended the 86ft mast for this view from the spreaders – and then dropped the video camera overboard. Below: discussing the game plan and the Equator crossing point. Facing page: Ruth, with Hearty Bear and Dog Otter, fresh from her Crossing the Line ordeal at the merciless hands of King Plummer

main course, too. Shortly after this Carlton lost the last fishing hook and lure, together with 150 metres of nylon line, to one that got away.

As *InterSpray* tried to get round Dakar point, the navigator was plotting on a chart from the first leg. The rest of the fleet were on a similar track, though *Hofbrau* was 400 miles to the west, on a lone flyer heading through the Cape Verde Islands and still in light airs. *Heath Insured* was struggling 200 miles astern, also in light airs.

'They say it's not over till the fat lady sings,' reflected *Hofbrau*'s Andy Hindley. 'She's left home and is on her way to the theatre. If things keep going as they are, we are going to have to shoot her. . .'

After midnight on day 23, *InterSpray*, still ahead of *Hofbrau*, tacked onto starboard for what someone idly noted in the ship's log as her 'Day trip to Dakar'. It proved to be a singularly ill-fated trip. *Group 4* had gone in close and struck lucky. *InterSpray* got there and were faced with a choice: north-west, or north-east. *InterSpray* went north-east, 'around the town and almost on the beach.' During the night she got within 7½ miles of the coast of Senegal.

So far the north-east trades had not lived up to expectations, in either strength or direction, and the yachts made slow progress north, the pace-makers tacked away west, hoping for fresher winds out to sea. Their move paid off. *InterSpray* didn't get the lift she had hoped for. With headsails back up, the crew felt at home back at a 25 degree angle of heel again.

An apparent new weather routing rule created a storm of controversy which rocked the fleet on day 24. Richard Tudor had overheard *Rhone-Poulenc* and *Commercial Union* arranging and receiving weather information and yacht positions over the radio. Despite a clear understanding by other skippers that such practices constituted outside assistance (and this being confirmed at a skippers'

meeting after the Fastnet race by Chay Blyth), Spencer Drummond at Race HQ was now confirming that sponsors *could* send their yachts weather information and regular updates on the positions of close rivals, providing it was information publicly available. The difficulty was defining what was publicly available. For those prepared to pay, Bracknell could supply more sophisticated forecasts as part of its services. It was also significant that the two skippers concerned had not attended the post-Fastnet meeting, having been appointed in Rio.

Most skippers believed the new understanding created a substantial change in the rules less than two weeks before the finish. Such 'outside assistance' had been frowned on before. The goal posts were on the move again, it seemed.

Paul Jeffes faxed Race HQ to say that the contentious six-hourly positions analysis should be sent to all yachts, otherwise the big bucks sponsors, who could afford to pay extravagant telex bills, and employ someone to stay up all night, could buy an advantage within the rules. There was much heated discussion during an inter-yacht chat show. The problem for race organisers was that it proved virtually impossible to stop or monitor shore supporters from telexing information to yachts. The British Telecom Race Results were available to anyone back home with a fax machine.

Pete Goss tried to clarify things later on during a radio chat show by asking all skippers for an assurance that they were not, and would not, get outside information, other than what had been allowed during the race so far.

Race HQ attempted to stem the controversy by sending six-hourly positions and information on course, distance to go and speed to all yachts as soon as it was published on the BT results system. John became the latest number cruncher, fascinated by all the new information. Race HQ also reaffirmed that 'outside routing assistance' to individual yachts was not allowed. Any such routing and weather information had to be passed on to the rest of the fleet.

On day 25 *InterSpray* crossed her outward track at 0405 at position 018° 25'N and 019° 52'W. There was champagne at lunchtime to celebrate the unofficial circumnavigation. Next day, *British Steel II* were becalmed out to the west of the fleet and sailed 13 miles to *InterSpray*'s 53, while the leader, *Group 4*, covered 65 miles.

With expectations of a fast leg home being dashed, the food situation was now becoming desperate, with little in reserve and almost nothing other than McDougalls. The cooks' imaginations had virtually given up on methods of disguising the freeze-dried five flavours of porridge. Scone and bread mix remained a popular alternative. Carlton was bravely battling on in the galley creating stuffing mixed with instant mash, and cooked until it was crisp, with added McDougalls chicken and pasta.

There was a crew conspiracy to praise it, whatever it tasted like. Some of the crew dining on deck were throwing it overboard and coming back for seconds and in Duggie's case thirds. Their joke backfired as the mixture settled heavily on people's stomachs. John's insides were reported to be in turmoil and the heads were 'full of the disappointed. . .'

An uplifting piece of news came as *InterSpray* crept up to seventh on the leaderboard, ahead of *British Steel II*, in the radio round up.

It was Paul Buchanan's 31st birthday on day 28, as well as Chay Blyth's 53rd. Paul celebrated with a bottle of whisky and a cake decorated with a map of the world and the yacht's route. Written around the circumference was 'Go round the world the wrong way and you can count backwards. . . 29?' was the rhetorical question.

Ian MacGillivray on *Pride of Teesside*

sent a birthday rhyme to Blyth at Race HQ:
Those who go to sea for gain
are a little bit insane
but those who go to sea for pleasure
are certifiable by measure

The radio round-up reported a good run for *InterSpray,* whilst leading boats had fallen into a hole. *InterSpray* was listed in fifth place. The crew was elated and Paul Jeffes was like a dog with two tails. The yacht was now also receiving weatherfax maps from America and Spain – 'it's like having the telly back from the repairers,' said Julian.

There were now so many budding astro-navigators on board that some wondered whether *InterSpray*'s best chance of winning was to ask the American's to switch off the GPS satellites.

There was an extended happy hour that night as the crew looked forward to the westerlies that must come soon.

Nuclear Electric, still fighting her private duel with *Group 4*, for first place overall and line honours, had again stolen the lead from Mike Golding, with just 11 miles separating the two yachts.

Buried Hopes

The bubble burst for *InterSpray* next day when the 0200 watch found themselves staring at 0 boat speed 0 VMG on an ocean which was a mirror reflecting the moon and Venus. *InterSpray* lost 100 miles waiting south-west of the Canaries for the wind which drove other yachts, less than 20 miles away, further north.

As Jeffes later mused: 'This type of yacht race is like any other long, complex journey with numerous connections which depend on being in the right place at the right time.'

InterSpray was to miss every connection the rest of the way home to Southampton and dropped from 30 miles ahead of *Coopers & Lybrand* on day 28, with fourth position overall comfortably in

their pockets, to trail *Pride of Teesside*, in sixth position overall, in less than a week.

Soon Jeffes feared they would be looking over their shoulder to see if *Heath Insured* could close the gap less than 24 hours behind them and thereby push them down into seventh place overall.

The asymmetric spinnaker was flown for the first time since it had been repaired, but Julian had downgraded it to 10 knots apparent maximum. It held and filled well and everyone was pleased to see that the hours of sewing were worthwhile.

On day 30 the wind picked up to 15 knots and though it was a great relief to be sailing again, *InterSpray* had changed her fifth place with *British Steel II* and was back to ninth position.

On *Heath Insured*, Adrian Rayson reported: 'The day's since Bill's death have been fraught with frustration. Coming to terms with his loss we have become determinedly jocular and thrown ourselves back into the business of racing.'

With fickle winds and adverse currents and 200 miles behind *InterSpray* they must on occasions have felt they were taking part in a different race.

Just 1,500 miles from Southampton, *Commercial Union*, one of the first yachts to pick up overnight gale-force south-westerly winds, had recaptured the lead from *Group 4*. *British Steel II*, some 230 miles further out in the Atlantic, was also benefitting. At 1400 on day 30, nine miles was all that separated the top three yachts in distance to the finish and 120 miles separated ninth-placed *InterSpray* from the leader.

Watching the plots of other yachts stretching away it was hard to maintain morale as *InterSpray* slipped back, having closed up on the leaders so hopefully a few days before.

Previous pages: spot the champagne bottle! Jeffes and crew field bottles tossed over by International Paint's Peter Sims at the finish

On previous legs the pursers had over-stocked with food, but this time a weight and cost slashing exercise had efficiently reduced the surplus for the run home. Light winds now meant that *InterSpray* was running out of toilet paper as well as food. Pages from discarded novels were about to find new uses.

Madeira was sighted briefly on day 32, as the outline of a mountain was glimpsed under the cloud just before dusk.

During the night *Coopers & Lybrand* came across a dismasted and drifting 50ft catamaran. Radio contact with rescue authorities revealed that the yacht belonged to a singlehanded sailor who had been airlifted to hospital in Madeira.

InterSpray had 1,000 miles to go to the finish on day 33 and when the wind eventually came round to the south-west she was able to fly the heavyweight spinnaker and lay the course. But during a broach in a 35-knot gust across the deck at lunchtime two days later the spinnaker blew right down the luff tapes. Juliet was on the wheel applying full lock when the boom preventer snapped.

'What should I do now Carlton?' said the balloon in John's cartoon in the ship's log.

'Hang on a minute, I'll duck down and get our copy of *Heavy Weather Sailing*,' was Carlton's reply.

They were lucky to retrieve the pieces as the clew and luff tapes had separated from the body of the sail. Julian's watch were again to blame!

Down below, an entire tin of instant mashed potato powder spread itself over the galley and saloon. The broach also dislodged from the bilges two tubs of margarine and a can of butter from the previous leg. After two weeks of dried bread every cloud had a silver lining.

When the wind gods went to sleep at midnight the crew took it personally. Theirs was the only boat in the fleet to experience light winds.

As the leaders approached England,

requests for redress were being put forward. Paul Jeffes applied for three and a half hours for going to the aid of *Heath*, while *Nuclear Electric* asked for an hour. *Group 4* requested one hour and 40 minutes for going to the aid of the Senegalese fishing boat.

InterSpray found herself in another private wind system on day 36, 300 miles behind the pack of eight and making five knots to most others yachts' 10 knots. Tensions were not far below the surface banter as the crew saw that other yachts would finish next day in front of crowds of spectators and in the glare of the media.

News filtered through that *Group 4* had won line honours at 0733 on day 37. Within 70 minutes *Commercial Union* and *British Steel II* had also finished second and third. *Nuclear Electric* sailed across the line shortly after 1300 in a nerve-wracking finish, holding her lead over Mike Golding by just 70 minutes after 151 days' racing (and after allowances had been made for both crews going to the aid of boats).

John Chittenden and his Chittendales had won the toughest yacht race around the world on combined times in the closest finish yet in any global voyage. John had become the first sailor to race both ways around the world. The best man had won. Jeffes sent 'Chit' a telex of congratulations and everyone on *InterSpray* was delighted for him.

Before the day was ended, *Rhone-Poulenc*, *Coopers & Lybrand*, *Hofbrau Lager* and *Pride of Teesside* had all finished.

The atmosphere on board *InterSpray*, with some 250 miles still to go, was difficult to describe. The word funereal kept cropping up in Paul Jeffes' mind.

'We have buried so many hopes and dreams out here in the Bay of Biscay. The only thing to look forward to is the wake. Everyone is being very polite and helpful – just as they are at a family funeral. Lots of black humour, much of it

at the expense of Chay and the event, because there is still a surprising amount of bitterness at our Hobart penalty.

Having worked their way halfway up the fleet after lying ninth, Jeffes felt 'comprehensively shafted by the wind gods again!'

'From a position 20 miles from *Commercial Union*, I managed to snatch defeat from the jaws of victory,' he lamented. 'I don't believe anyone except Richard Tudor created their own luck. He did and deserved better. Everyone else just took what came along. Regrettably it did not come to us until 12 hours later.'

Julian and Jeffes had both become manic depressives. 'We are like a couple of yo-yos alternating violently from bitter sarcasm to black rages and to hugely laborious efforts to be positive and forward looking. So far we have avoided declining simultaneously into a black rage of despair and frustration. God help everyone aboard if we do,' said Jeffes.

The reactions of the crew, as always, were interesting. John Davis was holding things together with the wisdom of his years. 'But you can see it still hurts,' said Jeffes. 'It's the helplessness that is so awful.'

Jeffes was now dreading the arrival in Southampton. The prospect of being the object of everyone's sympathy quite simply filled him with dread.

'I suppose, like everyone else, I will put a brave face on it and smile, but inside I hate it like hell. It's a shame how destructive competition can be. It's a tremendous achievement to get round, even more so to skipper the boat with so many novices, and yet I can take no pleasure or pride in that at all.'

Right now to Jeffes it was all a wasted effort and a failure. He hoped it didn't come across too clearly to the crew, but living so closely to people for so long he admitted it was very hard to avoid.

InterSpray received a telex from Race HQ commiserating and informing them

Above: we finally made it! The crew wave to their families on the supporters' ferry as they head for the finish line. Facing page: as we tied up for the last time, the yacht was engulfed in a wave of families and supporters

that the wind would fill from the south-west at 15-20 knots. Their word came true at about 1400 when the spinnaker came down and the genoa went up as they laid a course home. By 2100 they had 130 miles to go to Ushant.

England, the promised land, was sighted for the first time in eight months when the silhouette of Start Point came into view just before dawn on day 38. As the Monday morning sun cast its long rays on the dark, featureless landscape, the outline of hills edged with cliffs emerged from the shadows into a three-dimensional patchwork of green fields

'The best looking land of all our landfalls,' thought Paul Buchanan.

Three hours later, and still off Start Point, the log entry cautioned: 'Do not expect anything from the wind gods.'

The gods continued to taunt *InterSpray* that day as she covered 17 miles in one five-hour period. The sea off Portland Bill, normally a maelstrom, was glassy smooth. The yacht had never experienced a true

InterSpray's terrible trio: Dominic, Patrick and Jeff

flat calm during the entire race until this point, when they had to drop the mainsail.

'We were going home and we were in sight of home, but we couldn't do anything to hasten our arrival. We felt we'd let everyone down,' said Alison.

Jeffes, in one of his lowest moments of despair, had been ready to put the engine on and retire from leg 4, or the entire race.

That evening Portland Coastguard broadcast a warning to *InterSpray* that the Navy would be firing live ammunition from 1900 to 2300 in sea area Romeo. Jeffes called Portland Naval Base Ops room to find out where sea areaRomeo was. When he gave them his co-ordinates he discovered he was slap (bang?) in the middle of their firing range. A frosty-voiced young lady told him: 'I strongly recommend you vacate the area immediately.'

'You don't seem to understand the situation madam,' said Jeffes. 'We are a sail-powered vessel and there is no wind. We will either need a tow from one of your firing range safety boats, or a direct hit would put us out of our misery...'

Jeffes added, for good measure: 'How good a shot are you?' The frosty voice subsided into chuckles.

As the anchor was being prepared, in case the tide started to take the yacht backwards, Paul sent a telex to International Paint in Southampton:

'I have just heard from Portland Naval Operations that our present position is bang (literally) in the midst of their firing range and that they will be firing live rounds into it from 1900 to 2300. Tonight, frankly, a direct hit would come as a welcome relief, so I've told them just to carry on. We are fully occupied hanging on to the last few shreds of sanity.'

The crew could see red tracer fire and flashes of artillery from the practice firing range.

By late morning on day 39, seven miles from the Needles and with the tide soon to turn, the possibility loomed of being stuck outside the Solent for another six hours. Sailing can be the cruellest sport. But the wind held and by 1300 *InterSpray* was through the Needles Channel and doing 9 knots. The moment the crew and their families and friends had all waited for was closer.

As *InterSpray* came up the Solent, Alison was posted on the bow to look for the supporters' ferry. Families had gathered in Ocean Village for several days on tenterhooks. Their waiting game had gone on for too long as well and they wore custom printed T-shirts emblazoned with the legend: 'Still waiting for *InterSpray*' alongside the figure of a skeleton.

The crew must have heard us before they saw our ferry through the grey afternoon mist, as a barrage of multiple foghorns and cheers sounded, with waving balloons and banners.

As *InterSpray* rounded Calshot Spit buoy, a glorious sight running at nine knots under full main and genoa, the ecstatic cheers went up. The end of an epic nine month battle was in sight. The crew's nightmare of the last few days was over. It had been the worst week in the entire 28,000 mile race around the world, they said. And given the hardships they had endured the comment was a graphic measure of the depth of their frustrations. The wide smiles of relief said it all from the crew. Dominic danced a jig on deck. Julian beamed. Tears of relief and pride were wept openly.

As *InterSpray* surged alongside the ferry, champagne bottles were deftly tossed across by International Paint's Peter Sims and fielded by Jeffes and his crew. Six catches and two misses.

Jeff disappeared offstage, returning from below decks to an ovation as he held aloft *InterSpray's* 15th passenger – Gladys, who was spanked and lashed to the pulpit. Quite what the troop of Hertfordshire schoolchildren aboard the ferry, who had followed *InterSpray* around the world, made of Gladys, their teachers did not say.

The yacht powered up Southampton Water, saluted by passing ferries and small boats and gathering a flotilla of support vessels. She finally crossed the finish line by Dock Head, where the gun fired with a puff of smoke and a flare ignited.

It was all over.

InterSpray had held onto her sixth place overall, with a combined time around the world of 156 days 14 hours and nine minutes. She had sailed a total of 27,634 miles.

The race was over, but the welcome had only just begun.

As the genoa was dropped, Peter Sims thoughtfully arranged for a fast inflatable to take Barry, Roger and myself, the one-leggers, to join our crew mates as Customs boarded *InterSpray* by Town Quay.

It was a special moment for the crew of 17, reunited together for the first time since our stirring dawn departure from these waters 241 days and several lifetimes ago. We had never been apart in spirit. We had each shared in triumph and misfortune on Mr. Blyth's brave odyssey. It was a voyage that had encompassed heights and depths of personal emotion as well as circling the globe.

If accomplishment had to be measured in victory, *InterSpray* had won two of the four fleet starts, in Rio and Hobart.

And she made the fastest passage from Cape Horn to Hobart, despite suffering a broken bottlescrew. Her 269 mile noon-to-run down the coast of South America, to Le Maire Strait, was one of the fastest in the race, putting her in the running for a special RORC trophy, to be awarded at the Challenge prizegiving in September.

We motored into Ocean Village on a wave of emotion, sharing a curious, detached sense of achievement. Duggie bravely struck up a final tune on his bagpipes for this last stretch of the long homecoming, but it was all but drowned out by an incredible cacophony of ship's sirens, blaring horns, cheers, whistles and applause resounding across the water. Crowds lined the dockside and the balconies of Canute's Pavilion. There were more banners and balloons. The transoms of the other eight Challenge yachts, which had waited for us for two days, were thronged with fellow crewmates and skippers. As we came alongside the pontoon, the Australian national anthem was playing over the PA system in John's honour. Chay Blyth was there, as he had been for each yacht at every stopover, spraying the crew with a magnum of champagne. Suddenly the yacht was engulfed in a wave of family and supporters. It was a sensational welcome for all of us.

If you hadn't known we were ninth, you would have thought we had won the race.

INTERSPRAY'S RACE AROUND THE WORLD

Above left: InterSpray's supporters' ferry. Above: the 28,000 mile kiss between Julian and Trisha. Facing page: homecoming hug for Hannah from dad Dominic

Race Leg 4 Cape Town to Southampton

Placing	Yacht Name	Arrival	GMT	Days	Hrs	Mins	Secs
					Leg Time		
1st	Group 4	23 May	06:33:58	035	19	33	58
2nd	Commercial Union	23 May	07:27:27	035	20	27	27
3rd	British Steel II	23 May	07:43:32	035	20	43	32
4th	Nuclear Electric	23 May	12:19:40	036	01	19	40
5th	Rhone-Poulenc	23 May	12:41:51	036	01	41	51
6th	Coopers & Lybrand	23 May	21:08:44	036	10	08	44
7th	Hofbrau Lager	23 May	21:17:08	036	10	17	08
8th	Pride of Teesside	23 May	23:13:30	036	12	13	30
9th	InterSpray	25 May	14:48:03	038	03	48	03
10th	Heath Insured	27 May	10:49:12	039	23	49	12

Final Race Results: Combined Times (Legs 1 to 4)

Placing	Yacht Name	Days	Hrs	Mins	Secs
		Combined Time			
1st	Nuclear Electric	151	11	49	11
2nd	Group 4	151	13	59	36 *
3rd	Hofbrau Lager	152	15	45	56
4th	Coopers & Lybrand	154	17	59	56
5th	Pride of Teesside	155	16	06	48 *
6th	InterSpray	156	14	09	10
7th	Heath Insured	157	10	29	18 *
8th	Rhone-Poulenc	159	04	07	22
9th	Commercial Union	159	17	26	13 *
10th	British Steel II	163	00	25	07

* Combined time modified by protest committee

Postscript

Unlike any other round the world yacht race, the crews in the British Steel Challenge all trained together before being assigned to the ten yachts. They were one big, happy family and the race wasn't over until the last boat came home. In Rio, yachts had sailed out at midnight to meet tail-end Charlie *Commercial Union*. In Hobart, the unmasted fleet motored out to greet the dismasted *British Steel II*.

In Southampton, it was the turn of *Heath Insured* to be in the spotlight as the fleet declared its unique solidarity.

Two days after *InterSpray's* arrival home, her crew sailed on their last mission, with the rest of the Challenge yachts, to salute Adrian Donovan's crew as they finally crossed the finish line. Donovan's yacht had been delayed by her 18-hour search for crewman Bill Vincent, tragically lost overboard near the Equator. A few days later, *Heath Insured* and the Southampton Harbourmaster's launch had sailed into the Solent in a Force 7 for a memorial service, with Vincent's widow and Chay Blyth, and dropped two wreaths in the water.

At a welcome home party for *InterSpray*, hosted by International Paint at the Royal Southampton Yacht Club, David Hodgson paid his tribute to the crew. We hadn't won the race or won a leg, but he presented inscribed medals to each crew member.

The 12 amateur circumnavigators had all made personal sacrifices. Each had overcome the limitations of inexperience, the constraints of careers, and the burden of finance − with £14,850 to be found before the race began.

This had been a race in which there were no losers. To get to the starting line was an act of courage. To cross the finishing line, an act of heroism. In between there was endurance, frustration and disappointment. Failure didn't get a look in.

Commitment came, too, from wives, husbands, children, parents, girlfriends, boyfriends, and bosses. The race had taken over the lives of those at home who watched and waited as surely as it dominated the lives of crew. Supporters faced their own withdrawal symptoms from the addictive daily dialling for the race results by phone, fax and Ceefax.

POSTSCRIPT

For skipper Paul Jeffes it had been a formidable balancing act to sail the yacht at her best and to satisfy the aspirations of his crew. On some yachts the unskilled were excluded from playing a full part. But Paul's style of leadership was democratic, not autocratic. He gave a free rein to his senior watchleaders. Jeffes' rationale was that a crew contributing equally to the running of the yacht would be a happier team, sharing higher morale and performing more effectively as a unit.

For most of us, this had been a one-off adventure and everyone on board *InterSpray* shared in the equal distribution of tasks, from galley duties, to sail repair, helming and sail trimming. Only in extreme weather did the strongest and most experienced take the major roles. Some racing potential may have been surrendered by allowing newcomers to the sport to develop their skills. But John Davis spoke for the crew when he said that the experience had been an overwhelming one and everyone had appreciated the opportunity to develop new strengths and experiences.

John presented Paul with a laminated half-model of *InterSpray*, made from timber taken out of the yacht. 'It's done a circumnavigation and a bit more,' he explained, since he had taken it home to Australia from Cape Town to make it in his workshop. A brass plaque listed the names of the crew.

Paul, astonished at the well kept secret, replied: 'I've been thanked by so many people for bringing their husbands, boyfriends and daughters back in one piece. My reply has always been the same. To thank the crew for bringing *me* back in one piece. It's been a case of interdependency. . . it's "inter" everything on *InterSpray.*'

The crew had sailed together for a trophy, but came home with a much greater prize – friendship and self-fulfillment. Between Southampton on September 26, 1992, and Southampton on May 25, 1993, there had been Arctic icebergs, tropical flying fish, whales, dolphins torpedoing through luminous seas, albatrosses, the aurora australis, shooting stars and the green flash.

As Jonathan Raban wrote in *Sea Room*: 'The sea adventure is more than an adventure. It is a rite of passage, as decisive as a wedding. It marks the end of the old self and the birth of the new. It is a great purifying ordeal. Storms and salt water cleanse the ne'er-do-well and turn him into a hero. . .'

'Am I glad you're back. You've been made redundant, the bank has foreclosed, the eldest wrote the car off and is in intensive care, and the youngest has shacked up with a . . .'

191

Appendix

Liquid speed

Interspray was the only yacht in the British Steel Challenge sponsored by a marine product company – International Paint, a subsidiary of Courtaulds Coatings and a leader in paint development and technology.

All ten Challenge yachts were painted with International Paint products above the waterline (Superyacht 800 System) and below (the first of a new generation of Micron CSC antifoulings).

Courtaulds, the international chemicals, coatings, packaging and fibres group, has sales of some £2 billion per annum and employs 21,000 people in 41 countries across the world.

The International Paint division coats some fifty per cent of all sailing boats world-wide, as well as a third of the world's shipping. Everything, in fact from an 8ft pram dinghy to the *Queen Elizabeth 2*.

The company has been involved with Chay Blyth since his historic circumnavigation 'the wrong way' 22 years ago. The original 59ft *British Steel* ketch was painted with International products, and all Blyth's subsequent yachts have been protected by International. But paint technology has advanced dramatically since 1971, when *British Steel* returned to port in excellent condition after a more

severe battering than most yachts encounter in ten years hard sailing. The InterSpray technique was developed as a new concept in spray application for yachts in controlled conditions.

Another Courtaulds Coatings subsidiary, VC Systems, has the ultimate in low-drag for record-breaking yachtsmen and women competing in major sailing events, including the America's Cup, the Whitbread Round the World Race, the BOC Challenge, the Admiral's Cup and the Route du Rhum.

VC Systems' high-tech Teflon-based antifoulings were used by Florence Arthaud to win the 1990 Route du Rhum, in her trimaran *Pierre 1er,* and Peter Blake and Robin Knox-Johnston on their 85ft catamaran *ENZA New Zealand*, in their bid for the Jules Verne Round the World in 80 Days Challenge. Courtaulds' VC Systems are also sponsoring Titouan Lamazou's 145ft ketch *Tag Heuer,* bidding to break the 79 day 6 hour record set by Bruno Peyron and *Commodore Explorer* in April, 1993.

The 1990 Whitbread winner *Steinlager 2* used coatings supplied by Courtaulds' New Zealand marine company, Epiglass.

Courtaulds also sponsor Formula One motor racing, supporting the highly successful Marlboro McLaren team.